ENGLISH DEFENDERS OF AMERICAN FREEDOMS 1774-1778

ENGLISH

DEFENDERS

of American Freedoms

1774-1778

Six Pamphlets Attacking British Policy

Compiled by PAUL H. SMITH

American Revolution Bicentennial Office

Library of Congress   Washington   1972

Library of Congress Cataloging in Publication Data
Smith, Paul Hubert, 1931–   comp.
    English defenders of American freedoms, 1774–1778.
    Includes bibliographical references.
    CONTENTS: A sermon preached before the Incorporated Society for
the Propagation of the Gospel in Foreign Parts. A speech intended to have
been spoken by the Bishop of St. Asaph, on the bill for altering the charters
of the Colony of Massachusetts Bay. By J. Shipley.—Considerations on the
measures carrying on with respect to the British colonies in North America,
by M. Robinson-Morris, Baron Rokeby. [etc.]
    1. U.S.—History—Revolution—Foreign public opinion—Collections. I.
U.S. Library of Congress. American Revolution Bicentennial Office. II. Title.
E249.3.S55   301.15'43'9733   78–37002
ISBN 0–8444–0009–2

For sale by the Superintendent of Documents, U.S. Government Printing Office,
Washington, D.C. 20402. Price $5.95. Stock Number 030–001–00047–8
Catalog Number LC 1.2 : EN 3/774–78

THE texts of the pamphlets included here were taken from the original American editions in the collections of the Library of Congress or, in the case of Mrs. Macaulay's *Address*, at the Library Company of Philadelphia.

Only minimal changes have been made in the original 18th-century pamphlets. Terminal punctuation has been standardized, and typographical errors have been silently corrected in cases where it was felt that they would lead to confusion. Otherwise, the original publications have been followed throughout, with no effort to amend archaic spellings, style, or grammar.

Footnotes which appeared in the pamphlets themselves are printed at the appropriate locations within the text. Compiler's notes are included at the end of each section.

CONTENTS

ENGLISH DEFENDERS
OF AMERICAN FREEDOMS
1774-1778

Introduction

ALTHOUGH few large bodies of primary material related to the American Revolution remain unused, the English political pamphlets which formed a vital part of the pre-Revolutionary debate and were reprinted and circulated freely on both sides of the Atlantic have continued to be ignored. This neglect may be attributed to various factors: the forbidding quantity of the literature, the inaccessibility of many rare works, nationalistic preoccupations, and a historical tradition that long subordinated intellectual to political, economic, and social issues. Thus, despite even the remarkable influence of the "imperial" school of historians in the 20th century, the political literature which accompanied the coming of the Revolution has not been studied as the product of a genuinely Anglo-American debate.

This omission is all the more surprising in view of the fact that during the past two decades scholars have focused greater attention on the intellectual qualities of the American Revolution than ever before. As Gordon Wood so aptly noted in 1966, "we now seem to be fully involved in a phase of writing about the Revolution in which the thought of the Revolutionaries, rather than their social and economic interests, has become the major focus of research and analysis." One need only mention a few historians in this connection to confirm Professor Wood's observation, and the quality of their work fully justifies the conclusion that this "renewed insistence on the importance of ideas in explaining the Revolution has now attained a level of fullness and sophistication never before achieved. . . ."[1] But notwithstanding the often brilliant achievements of such scholars as Caroline Robbins, Clinton Rossiter, Edmund Morgan, Bernard Bailyn, Gordon Wood, Trevor Colbourn, Alan Heimert, Adrienne Koch, and Cecelia Kenyon, significant gaps remain in our understanding of the intellectual world of the American revolutionists.

[1]

Interestingly enough, historians have recently devoted more attention to the earlier origins—the 17th- and early 18th-century background—of American political culture than to the English intellectual
ferment that accompanied the American Revolution. Thanks to the
achievements of Professor Robbins, for example, we now know a
great deal about the transmission of the ideology of the 18th-century
"commonwealthman" from the overthrow of Stuart absolutism to the
reign of George III.[2] And we have been supplied a provocative
hypothesis for analyzing the 18th-century American political system
in Professor Bailyn's studies of the sources of American political
culture.[3] The outline that has already become familiar is one of a
fundamentally British political ideology rooted in the 17th-century
experience that saw the triumph of "balanced" government as the
product of the desperate struggle with the Stuart monarchs. Thus
Britons believed that to preserve liberty it was necessary to maintain
harmony between the three elements of government, but political
stability was thought to be perpetually threatened by the encroachments of "power" against "liberty." In the transitional age between
monarchical control of government and the triumph of the House of
Commons, a system of "influence" had emerged to ensure the year-
to-year operation of government, but that same system—which elevated the manipulation of "factions" and "connexions" to the level of
statecraft—was judged to be a seedbed for corruption.

The fear of corruption, which was conceived as the forerunner of
moral and social dissolution, was heightened in America because of
the dependent nature of colonial institutions and their vulnerability to
manipulation by venal officials whose acquisition and use of power
posed the gravest threats to liberty in the Colonies. This condition
gave all the more force, therefore, to the writings of purveyors of the
radical political tradition, who schooled Americans in the consequences of corruption and the omnivorous appetites of power, as well
as to the work of the most popular historians, who gave such a
Whiggish cast to Anglo-American history in the 18th century. It was
but a small step for Americans to reach the conclusion that their ills
could be traced to the venality of England's political life and the
corruption of her society. Political liberty in England—witness John
Wilkes and the Middlesex elections—had already fallen prey to
Crown-controlled Ministers whose pursuit of power had destroyed the
traditional balance between the Crown and Parliament. American
liberty was sure to be the next victim of a ministerial conspiracy that

[2]

threatened to impose upon the Colonies an unlimited parliamentary supremacy even more absolute than any authority formerly exercised by the Crown.

Although this background has been analyzed in detail up to the beginning of the American crisis, historians have generally veered from the study of English radical influence on America after 1774. Once the point is reached at which the Americans denied the authority of Parliament over the Colonies, the historical focus in America is almost exclusively on events leading to war and independence and that in England, on ministerial policy and preparations to subdue the rebellion. After the Boston Tea Party, the momentum of the events themselves is accepted as the controlling factor. Taking an implicitly deterministic view, historians have shown less interest in what Americans continued to read from England after 1774. The possibility that the revolutionary upheaval was accompanied by a truly Anglo-American debate which continued well into the war for independence, or that each side continued to be significantly influenced by essays and reports written by the citizens of the opposing state and which historians might analyze with profit, has been ignored.

The present volume deals with but a single class of English pamplets—those written in defense of America after the North Ministry turned to coercion. This material has been rarely noted even by specialists and remains largely unknown to most students of the period. The omission is all the more notable because abundant evidence survives to testify to the influence which these works had. That influence is recorded in the numerous American editions in which many of the English pamphlets appeared, in the references to them by many American political writers, and in the explicit statements of leading contemporaries like the patriot-historian David Ramsay.

It came as a surprise in 1965 to learn from Thomas R. Adams' bibliographical study of American political pamphlets to 1776 that four of the 11 works most frequently reprinted before the publication of *Common Sense* came from the hands of English critics of the North Ministry.[5] The most popular of these, second only in circulation to Paine's phenomenal classic, was written by a Lord Bishop of the Church of England, Jonathan Shipley, Bishop of St. Asaph. Bishop Shipley's work appeared not only in a dozen American editions but also in newspaper, magazine, almanac, and broadside form. The influence of English writers can also be seen in American pamphlets published immediately before the Revolution. Works written in England after the coercive legislation was introduced in Parliament could have left their mark on only those few American writers who continued to publish tracts up to the eve of independence. A notable example of that influence can be found in Alexander Hamilton's *The Farmer Refuted,* which drew directly from Shipley, Robinson-Morris, and Cartwright—three of the authors represented in this volume.[6] And in the foremost contemporary history of the Revolution, David Ramsay noted explicitly the important uses the Patriots made of favorable English opinion in the final phases of the struggle to forge American unity after 1774:

> In order to awaken the attention of the people, a series of letters was published, well calculated to rouse them to a sense of their danger, and point out the fatal consequences of the late acts of Parliament. Every newspaper teemed with dissertations in favour of liberty—with debates of the members of Parliament, especially with the speeches of the favourers of America, and the protests of the dissenting Lords. The latter had a particular effect on the Colonists, and were considered by them as irrefragable proofs that the late acts against Massachusetts were unconstitutional and arbitrary.[7]

A reading of these works readily confirms Ramsay's evaluation of the impact in America of the literature of English dissent. Indeed, it is difficult today to understand how any American who had read tracts such as Bishop Shipley's *Speech Intended To Have Been Spoken* could have remained unconvinced that the King's Ministers were guilty of the most arbitrary assault on colonial liberties, that the Colonies were fully justified in issuing a call for a Continental Congress, and that Americans were forced by necessity to armed resistance against the tyranny of the mother country.

Such works obviously gave renewed respectability to dissent in America and deprived those favoring passive resistance of any real authority in the Colonies. Tories who denounced the patriot tactics and urged obedience to established authority, professing confidence that American grievances would be redressed and scoffing at exaggerated fears that their liberties were imperiled by the King's Ministers, were at a marked disadvantage when forced to contend with arguments that came from the pens of English bishops, deans, and lords. Thus American leaders, armed with the knowledge that some of the

[4]

most independent and respected men in England were alarmed at the very same "ministerial conspiracy" that they denounced, were able to attain a sense of confidence and conviction in their cause that would have been difficult to acquire had they stood alone. One can only conjecture the ultimate consequences, but the apparent avidity of Americans for English radical tracts invites speculation. Such support from abroad was an antidote to be administered to waverers and fainthearts who might otherwise have been unable to persevere in the face of adversity. Surely Americans thereby gained a heightened sense of rectitude and a more intensely felt belief in their cause. Moreover, before the Franco-American alliance the example of English radicals was employed to hinder the development of sentiment for negotiating a premature peace. Finally, Americans learned from English writers that their tactics of resistance were destined to succeed, that Parliament's attempts to coerce the Colonies were bound to end in the ruin of Britain, and that the American crisis might topple the North Ministry and bring to power a more responsible government.[8]

Although no attempt has been made to propound new interpretations of the American Revolution, preliminary analysis of English pamphlet sources raises useful questions. A comparison of American and English pamphlets may tell us whether American works were, after all, marked by a distinctively inflated or hysterical rhetoric. If remarkable similarities are detected between the English and American pamphlet literature, can the colonial response be attributed to American anxieties over deviations and retrogressions from the European norms which had characterized provincial American life? Can such comparisons provide further insights into the nature of the mimetic impulse in the colonies? Have modern historians overemphasized the breadth of the English consensus concerning parliamentary supremacy and the indivisibility of sovereignty? Did English radicals contribute to the erosion of common ground once shared by Americans and opposition Whigs by insisting that parliamentary authority must be made responsible to the people? Has our traditional focus on Pitt and Burke as American champions been overstated, so that the real defenders of the American cause have been overshadowed? Has the English radical impulse between 1774 and 1783 been slighted because the movement eventually fell victim to the reactionary wave that swept across England in the French Revolutionary era?

This volume was designed to promote a fuller understanding of the American Revolution, to rescue some important contemporaries of

that era from obscurity, and to call attention to a few of the neglected treasures of the Library of Congress. A fuller understanding of
the popularity of these works will be useful in evaluating the American susceptibility to radical arguments. In the absence of detailed
studies, some historians may find in the American use of English
radical pamphlets evidence that Americans were deeply divided on
the eve of the Revolution, while others may attribute the popularity
of these writers to the solidarity that Americans achieved in 1776. In
any event, it seems unwise to affix labels to the American Revolution
by employing such oft-used terms as radical, moderate, or conserva-
tive until we more fully understand the Americans' perception of
contemporary political radicalism in the mother country.

NOTES

[1] Gordon S. Wood, "Rhetoric and Reality in the American Revolution,"
William and Mary Quarterly, 3d series, 23:3–4 (January 1966).

[2] Caroline Robbins, *The Eighteenth-Century Commonwealthman: Studies
in the Transmission, Development, and Circumstances of English Liberal
Thought from the Restoration of Charles II until the War with the Thirteen
Colonies* (Cambridge, Mass., 1959).

[3] Bernard Bailyn, *Ideological Origins of the American Revolution* (Cambridge, Mass., 1967), and *The Origins of American Politics* (New York,
1968).

[4] This is not to imply that students of English history have entirely ignored
the impact of the American crisis, but such interest has been primarily confined to abortive domestic reform. See, for example, Eugene C. Black's recent
study, *The Association: British Extraparliamentary Political Organization,*

1769–1793 (Cambridge, Mass., 1963). "Sustained American agitation probably contributed as much as any single factor to the direction of radical activity in Great Britain. Englishmen learned from the American example. There was a bond of personal friendship and sympathy between American thinkers and politicians and the radical dissenters in Britain." But the significant qualification is that "intellectual speculation and sympathy for the colonial cause did nothing to unsettle the political situation in Great Britain. The domestic implications of the imperial dispute only became inescapable after the outbreak of fighting. North's inability to win, the entry of France and Spain, and the bleak prospects in foreign affairs contributed directly to the sudden development of extraparliamentary organizations in 1779." ibid., p. 28–30. For other studies which indicate the renewed interest in domestic reform in the age of the American Revolution, see Ian R. Christie's *Wilkes, Wyvill and Reform; the Parliamentary Reform Movement in British Politics, 1760–1785* (London, 1962); and Carl B. Cone's *The English Jacobins: Reformers in Late 18th Century England* (New York, 1968).

⁵ Thomas R. Adams, *American Independence: The Growth of an Idea* (Providence, 1965). Adams is now preparing a study of the English pamphlet literature of the American Revolution, a work which will undoubtedly again place the historian in his debt.

⁶ Harold C. Syrett, ed., *The Papers of Alexander Hamilton* (New York, 1961), vol. 1. See p. 145–146 and 161 for direct quotations from Robinson-Morris and Shipley, and p. 122 for extensive paraphrasing of Cartwright.

⁷ David Ramsay, *History of the American Revolution* (London, 1793; reprinted New York, 1968), vol. 1, p. 115–116. For evidence of the even more explicit and extensive use made of the Earl of Abingdon's pamphlet by American leaders, see *infra,* p. 193.

⁸ The Speaker of the Pennsylvania Assembly, describing radical tactics for defeating Tory attempts to reject proposals of the Continental Congress, explained to a friend in February 1775 that "Ld North is staggering And a little Firmness will tumble him down." Edward Biddle to Jonathan Potts [February 25, 1775], Jonathan Potts Papers, Manuscript Division, Library of Congress.

Jonathan Shipley

BISHOP OF ST. ASAPH

JONATHAN Shipley is known to Americans primarily because of his long and close friendship with Benjamin Franklin, who was acquainted with Shipley and his family and was a frequent visitor at their Hampshire estate, Twyford. Franklin wrote the first part of his famous autobiography at Twyford in August 1771, and it was with the Shipleys, who traveled the few miles from Twyford to South-ampton to greet him, that he spent much of his time during his last brief visit to England, en route to America from France, in 1785.

Shipley and Franklin shared many interests and held remarkably similar views on Anglo-American relations during the early 1770's. They had many friends in common, and Franklin was elected to the Society of Arts which had been organized by Shipley's brother William. The similarity of their style, which paralleled similarities in their temperament and beliefs, even led many to suspect when the bishop's celebrated *Speech Intended To Have Been Spoken* first appeared in 1774 that it had been written by Franklin.

Shipley (1714-88) was educated at Oxford and began his clerical career in 1743 under the wing of the controversial Benjamin Hoadly, then Bishop of Winchester. He proceeded normally up the ladder of clerical preferment until he was consecrated Bishop of Llandaff in February 1769. Although the inner history of his appointment is obscure, it is significant that in 1769 clerical nominations emanated from the unconventional young Duke of Grafton, who also nominated John Hinchcliffe as Bishop of Peterborough the same year. In the 1770's Shipley and Hinchliffe were the only Lords Spiritual who publicly opposed the ministry on American policy. Shipley's prompt translation to the more lucrative see of St. Asaph barely five months later is unmistakable proof that he then enjoyed political favor, but his remarkably long tenure of 28 years at St. Asaph, where he re-mained until his death, is equally unmistakable evidence that even a

[9]

gifted bishop could not oppose the policies of his government and continue to advance in the 18th-century church.

Although Franklin's influence on Shipley's American views cannot be established precisely, it is clear that he made an important contribution to the publicizing of Shipley's work in England and was largely responsible for its success in America.[1] The Bishop of St. Asaph had been selected for the honor of delivering the sermon at the annual meeting of the Society for the Propagation of the Gospel in February 1773, and he used this occasion to focus attention on the distressing state of American affairs. Certainly his friendship with Franklin provided much of the information which led him to express his concern. The sermon, which was routinely published by the society, was a pointed commentary on England's policies in America after 1763 but was nevertheless innocuous enough to have escaped special notice had not the alert Franklin recognized the appeal of Shipley's statement and the impact his calm and reasoned comments would have in America. In April 1773 Franklin dispatched copies to Boston and Philadelphia, and by June the *Sermon* was attracting comment in the American newspapers.[2] At least five American pamphlet editions appeared in 1773, and notices continued to appear in the papers as late as February 17, 1774, when the entire second half of the *Sermon* was reprinted in Purdie & Dixon's *Virginia Gazette*.

To his Boston correspondents, to his friend Joseph Galloway in Pennsylvania, and to his son William, the Governor of New Jersey, Franklin praised the *Sermon* for its "favourable Sentiments relating to the Colonies." To Shipley he wryly added, "I think even the New Englanders will for once have a good opinion of a Bishop." [3] A few months later, after he had received responses from America on the reception accorded the *Sermon,* Franklin sent the following report to his friend:

Inclosed I send a Boston newspaper in which the sermon is advertised. The speaker of the Assembly of the Massachusetts, in his letter to me says, "The Bishop's sermon is much liked, as it discovers a catholick spirit, and sentiments very favorable with regard to America." Dr. Chauncey an ancient dissenting Minister of Boston writes, "The Bishop of St. Asaph's sermon I got reprinted in 24 hours after it came to hand. 'Tis universally received here with approbation and wonder, and has done much good. It sold amazingly. A second impression was called for in two days."

I daily expect to hear more of it from the other colonies.[4]

By 1773 Franklin's press-agent activities in England had assumed broader dimensions and occupied an increasing proportion of his time. As agent for the Colonies of Massachusetts, Pennsylvania, Connecticut, and Georgia, he had long been concerned with keeping a favorable view of American affairs before English readers, but he was now also deeply involved in the further work of shaping the American image of British opinion. The purpose behind the publicizing of Shipley's *Sermon* must have been to stiffen the Americans' resolve and to strengthen their sense of purpose by demonstrating that sensible English leaders perceived the justice of American demands. Similarly, Franklin's concern with public opinion in Massachusetts had led him to send to Boston the famous Hutchinson-Oliver letters. These sensational documents were published almost simultaneously with Shipley's *Sermon* and triggered a controversy that soon overshadowed the bishop's work.

Shipley next took up his pen in defense of America by opposing British ministerial proposals for changing the government of Massachusetts. The Ministers hoped to stifle the radical opposition which had recently resulted in the destruction of British tea in Boston harbor. By the spring of 1774, the reasoned discourse and calm analysis which so appealed to men of Shipley's and Franklin's stamp had nearly disappeared from discussions of American problems in Parliament, and Shipley sought to attract favorable notice by the tone as well as by the substance of his argument. Now that the situation was more urgent, the bishop's remarks struck with even greater force, and conditions in America, where he was already known as a friend of the Colonies, ensured his work an enthusiastic reception. Franklin, of course, was not alone in the effort to put the pamphlet before the largest audience possible, for many Americans recognized that the open opposition of dissenting Lords in Britain was a powerful stimulant to the American protest movement, encouraging the meek or wavering and arousing the insensitive to the threat to American liberties posed by the Coercive Acts. As part of the opposition campaign against the coercive legislation, the *Speech* went quickly through four London editions, the last of which, Franklin reported, consisted of 5,000 copies.[5] Probably the most successful pro-American piece to appear in England, it "had an extraordinary Effect, in changing the Sentiments of the Multitudes with regard to America." [6]

In the Colonies the reception of the *Speech* was truly remarkable. A brief and succinct appeal, it was widely reprinted in the American newspapers in September and October 1774, coinciding with the deliberations of the First Continental Congress. Often covering the entire front page or issued as a special supplement—and brief enough to be printed on a single large sheet—it was placed within the reach of the great majority of politically active Americans. At least 12 pamphlet editions appeared in eight American cities and towns, making it by far the most frequently printed political pamphlet in America before the publication of Paine's *Common Sense* in 1776. The *Speech* was also circulated as a broadside and reprinted in its entirety in both *Daboll's New England Almanack for 1775*—an uncommonly large printing by pamphlet standards—and *The Royal American Magazine.*[7]

The appeal of Shipley's work is no mystery. Openly critical of the Ministry but moderate in tone and generous in spirit, Shipley explained the deterioration of Anglo-American relations in terms that most Americans had already come to accept. Couching his *Sermon* in the language of the Golden Rule and enjoining British leaders to heed Christ's injunction to bear good will toward all men, the bishop issued a plea for a return to a happier past. "May the wise and good on both sides, *without enquiring too curiously* into the grounds of past animosities, endeavor by all prudent means to restore that old publick friendship and confidence, which made us great, happy and victorious." Nearly every American must have approved his observation that "the true art of government consists in *not governing too much,*" and many had already come to believe that their difficulties could be traced "to the artifices of *factious men, who wish to grow eminent by the misfortunes of their country.*"

Shipley's *Speech,* written a year later in opposition to the immediate threat of the Massachusetts Government Bill, had a sharper focus. Ostensibly intended for delivery before the House of Lords, it mixed flattery with gentle criticism, history with ominous predictions, and sharp barbs with commonsense observations. Little wonder that many thought it came from the hand of Franklin. To Shipley the American Colonies were one of England's chief glories, and he felt that no rash measures should be adopted which threatened their continued loyalty. Arbitrary taxation—"plunder authorized by law"—had been responsible for the mischief already done, but it was not too late to recover the good will of the Colonies. "It was a happy idea, that made us first consider them rather as instruments of commerce than as objects of government." Until recently, "the idea of taxing them never entered our heads." In return, England had received the gratitude and fidelity of the Colonies, which had "looked upon England with reverence and affection." And why had this mutually beneficial relationship been placed in jeopardy? "To save the credit of one imprudent measure of administration? I have known friendship preserved and affection gained, but I never knew dignity lost, by the candid acknowledgement of error."

The Massachusetts bill, of course, was far more dangerous than previous measures. To change the government of a Colony without the consent of its citizens "implies a most total abject and slavish dependency" which no free people can accept. Should the attempt succeed, England would acquire the power of governing America "by influence and corruption" and would finally achieve the ruin of both countries. "My Lords," he warned, striking an ominous note, "I look upon North America as the only great nursery of freemen now left upon the face of the earth." As this bill "tends to debase their spirits and corrupt their manners, and destroy all that is great and respectable in so considerable a part of the human species," it is the duty of every Englishman to oppose it. Shipley's militant posture, all the more remarkable because he was a bishop, clearly shows that there were in England articulate writers whose consciences carried them beyond partisan politics.

NOTES

[1] For Franklin's publicity activities in England at this time, see *Benjamin Franklin's Letters to the Press, 1758–1775*, edited by Verner W. Crane (Chapel Hill, 1950). For references to Shipley's pamphlets, see *The Writings of Benjamin Franklin*, edited by Albert H. Smyth (New York, 1906), vol. 6, p. 30–31, 52, 245–246, 250.

[2] Thomas R. Adams, *American Independence: The Growth of an Idea* (Providence, 1965), p. 77–79.

[3] Franklin to Shipley [ca. June 1773], in John L. Peyton, *Rambling Reminiscences of a Residence Abroad* (Staunton, Va., 1888), p. 280.

[4] Franklin to Shipley, August 21, 1773, ibid., p. 277.

[5] Franklin to Thomas Cushing, September 15, 1774, Smyth, *Writings of Franklin*, vol. 6, p. 246.

[6] Franklin to Thomas Cushing, October 6, 1774, ibid., p. 250. Catharine Macaulay asserted in a letter of September 11, 1774, to John Adams: "I have just read the Bishop of St. Asaph's speech on the affairs of America and think it one of the most capital performances I have seen of modern times." Adams Family Papers, reel 344.

[7] It has not previously been noted by historians that *Daboll's Almanac* was a vehicle for publicizing Shipley's essay. Shipley's portrait is engraved on the cover of the *Almanac* with the inscription: "The Patriotic Bishop, Dr. Jonathan Shipley." The *Speech* appeared in the August and September 1774 issues of the *Royal American Magazine*, at the request of "Massachusettensis," who submitted it to the printer in the hope that it would be published so "that the disinterested and benevolent author may receive that tribute of thanks from the people of this province and continent that is justly due to him for this token of his *Philanthropy*." For the broadside copy, which carried the title "The Whole Speech of the Right Reverend Doctor Jonathan Shipley, Lord Bishop of St. Asaph, In Favour of the Boston Charter," see Charles Evans' *American Bibliography*, No. 13625.

A

SERMON

Preached before the

Incorporated Society

FOR THE

*Propagation of the Gospel in
Foreign Parts;*

AT THEIR

ANNIVERSARY MEETING

IN THE

Parish Church of St. Mary-le-Bow,

On FRIDAY *February* 19, 1773.

By the Right Reverend

JONATHAN Lord Bishop of St. ASAPH.

LONDON Printed:

BOSTON, New-England, Re-Printed:

And to be Sold by THOMAS and JOHN FLEET,
at the *Heart* and *Crown* in Cornhill, 1773.

27

ADVERTISEMENTS

THE following SERMON, printed in *London,* and re-printed in *Boston,* is admirably well adapted to lead those, who may think proper to read it, into just Sentiments of the *impolicy* of the British Ministry in their conduct towards the Colonies, and of the only effectual method they can take to promote that love, harmony, peace, and mutual confidence, without which neither *England,* nor *America,* can be truly happy. It has been highly spoken of, by the best writers on the side of Liberty, in the public Papers at home, and recommended to the perusal of all, who have at heart the real welfare of the *whole* British Empire, and not a detached part of it only. As it was preached by a Lord Bishop, and before so great and respectable a Body as the honorable Society for propagating the Gospel, it will, doubtless, be thought eminently worthy of the attention of *Episcopalians* in this part of the world; especially, as it may reasonably be supposed to contain the real sentiments of that Society, who have given their thanks to the preacher of this Sermon, and desired its publication for the common good. Some parts of this Sermon relate peculiarly to the affairs of the Society before whom it was preached; for which reason, those parts of the Sermon might have been omitted: but it was judged expedient to reprint the *whole,* lest it should be said, detached passages only were selected, and others suppressed, with a view to serve a turn.

The EDITOR.

A SERMON

Before the Society for the Propagation
of the Gospel.

LUKE Chap. ii. VER. 14.
Glory be to God in the highest, and on Earth
Peace, good will towards Men.

I KNOW no passage in the holy scriptures, that may be adapted with more propriety to our present meeting, than this declaration from the angel of the gracious purposes of Heaven in publishing the Gospel. That which was the design of the gospel itself must necessarily be the chief object of a Society instituted to propagate it. The generous office, we have undertaken, is by instructing distant countries in religious truths to promote the peace and happiness of mankind. It is by such actions that the holy scriptures allow the sons of men to consider themselves as glorifying God; and such, we are assured, are the most likely to obtain his favour and good will to men. Without entering into a farther explication of the words, suffer me to desire that you will keep in your minds the general principle contained in them; and you will find it easily applicable to the facts, the circumstances, and the different situations of things, which I shall take leave to mention, as being more or less connected with the credit and influence of this Society.

The first object of our zeal was the conversion of the Indians; and it should seem no difficult task to influence the minds of men, who have few religious notions of their own growth, and appear to have no strong prejudices in favour of them. Such minds one would think might easily be led to receive a religion of the most simple form, consisting of a few great luminous principles, and inculcating plain rules of life and conduct, which must approve their usefulness in desarts, as well as in cities. Such doctrines, founded on Divine authority, would, in all appearance, be particularly welcome, where the restraints of law and government have but little force. Yet it has happened contrary to our hopes, that the preaching of the gospel has been of small efficacy amongst the Indians. The sagacity for which they are remarkable seems to be of a partial kind, and to partake

[17]

more of instinct than of reason. They can employ great art to obtain their ends; to procure what they desire; or to gain a superiority over an enemy: but their passions and habits proceeding always in one narrow track, they have neither relish nor discernment for the clearest truths, to which they have not been accustomed. After shewing the greatest address and courage in subduing or surprising an enemy, they cannot comprehend that it would be generous not to torture him; and that it would be wise to give such treatment as they would wish to receive. They have besides an untameable savage spirit, which has refused to hear the voice of instruction; which has obstinately rejected the arts and improvements of the Europeans, and has hitherto only adopted the most beastly of their vices.

For these reasons, though we ought not to remit our endeavours, yet I fear we have little reason to hope for their conversion, till some great change in their manners has made them abandon their savage vagrant life, and prepared them for the discipline of law and religion.

But a more promising field is opened to our hopes, in the populous provinces of our own colonies. The rapid increase of their numbers on every side, in a country where the means of subsistence are easy and open, together with the perpetual accession of inhabitants from Europe, are continually forming new congregations. Now knowledge of all kinds will probably be rare amongst men who are entering into the first rudiments of society; and while their attention is bent on procuring the necessaries of life, it is not to be expected that they should be either diligent or successful in the improvement of religious knowledge. Here therefore the instructions that are conveyed to them by the liberality of this Society, may be of essential and durable service. This is sowing the good seed in a fruitful soil; and what is so planted may produce returns of an hundred fold, and afford fruit and nourishment to future generations. Allow me to indulge a little the pleasure of contemplating in prospect the good that may result in after times from this our labour of love.

Perhaps the annals of history have never afforded a more grateful spectacle to a benevolent and philosophick mind, than the growth and progress of the British colonies in North America. We see a number of scattered settlements, formed at first for the purposes of trade, or from a spirit of enterprize; to procure a maintenance, or to enjoy the exercise of their religion, *which in those unhappy days was refused them at home*, growing by degrees, under the protection of their mother-country, who treated them with the indulgence due to their weakness and infancy, into little seperate common-wealths. Placed in a climate, that soon became fruitful and healthy by their industry; possessing that liberty which was the *natural growth of their own country,* and secured by her power against foreign enemies, they seem to have been intended, as a solitary experiment, to instruct the world to what improvements and happiness mankind will naturally attain, when they are suffered to use their own prudence, in search of their own interest. I must repeat it again as an observation not unworthy of this audience and this occasion, that there is no instance in the records of time, where infant colonies have been treated with such a just and liberal indulgence.

Had these settlements been left to shift for themselves, they would have perished and been swept away by the rough course of accidents, like seeds that are scattered by the winds, of which not one in a thousand take root and come to maturity. Had they been planted by any kingdom but our own, the inhabitants would have carried with them the chains and oppression, to which they had been inured at home: they would have been subject to the schemes of ministers and favourites, and have suffered more from their ignorance than from their rapine. At best they could only have hoped to be considered as the live stock upon a lucrative farm, which might sometimes be suffered to thrive for the sake of its produce.

But Britain from the beginning has treated her colonies in a very different manner. She has not sold them her protection at the price of their liberty; she has always been ready to encourage their industry, to relieve their wants, and to revenge their injuries; and has sought no other advantage from so generous a conduct, but the mutual benefit arising to distant countries from the supply of each other's wants. Adhering to these maxims, she has continued to reap the fruits of her own wisdom and moderation in a surprising encrease of national greatness; while her prosperous colonies are spreading without interruption over a vast continent, that may in a few centuries rival the commerce, the arts and the power of Europe.

It is difficult for man to look into the destiny of future ages, the designs of Providence are too vast and complicated, and our own powers are too narrow, to admit of much satisfaction to our curiosity. But when we see many great and powerful causes constantly at work, we cannot doubt of their producing proportionable effects. The colonies in North America have not only taken root and acquired strength; but seem hastening with an accelerated progress to such a powerful state, as may introduce a new and important change in human affairs. Descended from ancestors of the most improved and enlightened part of the old world, they receive as it were by inheritance all the improvements and discoveries of their mother-country. And it happens fortunately for them to commence their flourishing state at a time when the human understanding has attained to the free use of its powers, and has learned to act with vigour and certainty. They may avail themselves not only of the experience and industry, but even of the errors and mistakes of former days. Let it be considered for how many ages [a] great part of the world appears not to have thought at all; how many more they have been busied in forming systems and conjectures; while reason has been lost in a labyrinth of words, and they never seem to have suspected, on what frivolous matters their minds were employed. And let it be well understood, what rapid improvements, what important discoveries have been made in a few years, by a few countries, with our own at their head, which have at last discovered the right method of using their faculties. May we not reasonably expect that a number of provinces, possessed of these advantages, and quickened by mutual emulation, with only the common progress of the human mind, should very considerably enlarge the boundaries of science. The vast continent itself, over which they are gradually spreading, may be considered as a treasure, yet untouched, of natural productions, that shall hereafter afford ample matter for commerce and contemplation. And if we reflect what a stock of knowledge may be accumulated by the constant progress of industry and observation, fed with fresh supplies from the stores of nature, assisted sometimes by those happy strokes of chance, which mock all the powers of invention, and sometimes by those superior characters which arise occasionally to instruct and enlighten the world; it is difficult even to imagine to what heighth of improvement their discoveries may extend.

And perhaps they may make as considerable advances in the arts of civil government and the conduct of life.

We have reason to be proud, and even jealous, of our excellent constitution. But those equitable principles on which it was formed, an equal representation, (the best discovery of political wisdom) and a just and commodious distribution of power, which with us were the price of civil wars, and the reward of the virtues and sufferings of our ancestors, descend to them as a natural inheritance, without toil or pain. But must they rest here as in the utmost effort of human genius? Can chance and time, the wisdom and the experience of publick men, suggest no new remedy against the evils, their vices and ambition are perpetually apt to cause? May they not hope, without presumption, to preserve a greater zeal for piety and publick devotion than we have done? For sure it can hardly happen to them, as it has to us, that when religion is best understood and rendered most pure and reasonable, that then should be the precise time, when many cease to believe and practise it, and all in general become most indifferent to it. May they not possibly be more successful than their mother-country has been, in preserving that reverence and authority, which is due to the laws? to those who make? and to those who execute them? May not a method be invented of procuring some tolerable share of the comforts of life to those inferior useful ranks of men, to whose industry we are indebted for the whole? Time and discipline may discover some means to correct the extreme inequalities of condition between the rich and the poor, so dangerous to the innocence and the happiness of both. They may fortunately be led by habit and choice to despise that luxury, which is considered with us as the true enjoyment of wealth. They may have little relish for that ceaseless hurry of amusements, which is pursued in this country without pleasure, exercise, or employment. And perhaps after trying some of our follies and caprices, and rejecting the rest, they may be led by reason and experiment to that old simplicity, which was first pointed out by nature, and has produced those models which we still admire in arts, eloquence and manners. The diversity of new scenes and situations, which so many growing states must necessarily pass through, may introduce changes in the fluctuating opinions and manners of men, which we can form no conception of. And not only the gracious disposition of Providence, but the visible preparation of causes, seems to indicate strong tendencies towards a general improvement.

And I hope that these matters, which I have presumed to dwell upon, perhaps a little too minutely, will not appear totally foreign to the present occasion, if we reflect that to whatever limits the population of our colonies may extend, whatever states and kingdoms they may form; through all the progress of their fortunes and prosperity; the labours of this Society will probably continue to operate with an increasing influence. That sober and reasonable sense of duty, which has been taught under our direction to a few scattered villages, may give its character hereafter to the religion and morals of a powerful state. The weak and imperfect fruits we reap at present may bear no higher proportion to the future benefits that may arise, than that of a few scattered seeds to the fulness of the harvest.

And perhaps the disinterested zeal of this Society for the instruction of our brethren in North America, may tend to REVIVE that union and cordiality between the mother-country and its colonies, which for the common utility ought never to have been interrupted. It is by no means decent from this place to censure the conduct of our superiors, or even to suppose it blameable; but surely as good subjects we may wish and endeavour to heal the wounds of our country, without enquiring by what hand they were inflicted. We may, and I think we ought to wish, that the true interest of the whole extensive community may govern our future contests, and regulate all our claims. Our mutual relation was formed, and has hitherto subsisted, by a perpetual communication of benefits. We want the produce of soils and climates, that differ so much from our own; and they will long have occasion for the fruits of our arts, our industry and our experience. And should they ever cease to want our protection, which as long as we render it beneficial to them they never will; yet we may still continue united in interest, in commerce and the grateful remembrance of old services. May the wise and good on both sides, *without enquiring too curiously* into the grounds of past animosities, endeavour by all prudent means to restore that old publick friendship and confidence, which made us great, happy and victorious. To countries so closely united it is needless, and even dangerous, to have recourse to the interpretation of charters and written laws. Such discussions excite jealousy, and intimate an unfriendly disposition. It is common utility, mutual wants and mutual services, that should point out the true line of submission and authority. Let them respect the power that saved them; and let us always love the companions of our dangers and our glories. If we consider their prosperity as making part of our own, we shall feel no jealousy at their improvements: and they will always chearfully submit to an authority, which they find is exercised invariably to the common advantage. During all our happy days of concord, partly from our national moderation, and partly from the wisdom, and sometimes perhaps from the carelessness of our ministers, they have been trusted in a good measure with the entire management of their affairs: and the success they have met with ought to be to us an ever memorable proof, that the true art of government consists in *not governing too much*. And why should friendship and gratitude, and long attachments, which inspire all the relish and sweetness of private life, be supposed to be of no weight in the intercourse between great communities? These are principles of human nature, which act with much greater certainty on numbers than on individuals. If properly cultivated they may to us be productive of the noblest benefits; and at all events, will neither lessen the extent of our power, nor shorten the duration of it.

When things are on so reasonable a footing, if there should happen to be any errors in government, they will soon be corrected by the friendly disposition of the people and the endeavours to separate the interest of the colonies from that of Great Britain will be received with the indignation, that is due to the artifices of *factious men, who wish to grow eminent by the misfortunes of their country.*

Even in that future state of independency, which some amongst them ignorantly wish for, but which for their true interest can never be too long delayed; the old and prudent will often look back on their present happiness with regret; and consider the peace and security, the state of visible improvement, and brotherly equality, which they enjoyed under the protection of their mother country, as the true golden age of America.

I need not suggest how favourable those dispositions must prove to the reception of the religious and benevolent doctrines, which it is the business of this Society to propagate. Under a mutual inclination to peace and good will, the lessons of piety we teach will be heard with that fair attention which always turns to the advantage of truth; and the claims we will make will be estimated (which is all we ought to desire) by the reasonableness of them.

I own I feel upon my mind a strong impression of the publick advantages that would result from this benevolent and christian policy; and I could wish for the interest of mankind, and of our country in particular, that it may not be thought wholly of a visionary nature. I think I can see a strong and immediate demand upon us for such a conduct, from the situation we are in, and the unusual occurrences that have passed before us within *a few years.* There seems at present to be a great and general commotion, and tendency to change, in the minds of men. Animated by the gradual improvement of knowledge, and the fortunate example of this country, our neighbours have had the courage to think with greater freedom on the most important subjects, and to look for something better in religion and government, than they find established among themselves. And even in this land of liberty, where we have been long in possession of the most solid and valuable truths, the spirit of enquiry is still at work, and urging its pursuits with a dangerous freedom, that risks more than it can hope to gain. At the same time not only discontent and faction, but the real difficulties of things, the extent, the fluctuation and the intricacies of commerce afford sufficient exercise for political wisdom. Add to this a vast accession of distant territory, the art of governing which we are *yet to learn*. Our colonies are rising into states and nations. The extreme boundaries of the world are opening to our view; and regions, unknown to our fathers, may soon become the objects of contention. In this great shifting scene of human affairs, the concerns of this extensive empire are growing every year into more importance and dignity. It behoves us to adopt some plan of conduct, that shall be suitable to our situation and the high character we sustain. The interest of Britain, considered singly by itself, ought not at present to be the sole; and in a few ages may not be the most considerable object of attention. *We have already tried what advantage is to be found in governing by force, and have no reason to be proud of the experiment.* What benefit has accrued to the publick from the plunder and desolation of an industrious helpless people? The whole profit, we have reaped from so much injustice and dishonour, has ended in fraudulent schemes, vain and extravagant expectations, ruinous expence and luxury; attended with a general loss of credit and confidence, a sudden suspension of commerce and industry, and an almost total stoppage of the main springs and vital motions of society. It requires no common degree of wisdom to deliver our country from such gains and such prosperity as this!

A great liberal commanding spirit is wanting; such as has appeared but rarely in modern times, but was better known to the ancients; which, without computing and calculating what is strictly due, can extort affection and gratitude by publick services; which can sacrifice little and even great interests to the establishment of a solid permanent authority, founded on justice and moderation: which permitting its subjects to enjoy and improve all their natural advantages, can always avail itself of their wealth and numbers for the defence or the glory of the empire; *and is sure to find the most powerful resources of government in their friendship and love.*

We presume not to instruct our rulers in the measures of government: but it is the proper office of a preacher of the gospel of peace, to point out the laws of justice and equity which must ultimately regulate the happiness of states as well as of individuals: and which are no other in effect than those benevolent christian morals which it is the province of this Society to teach, transferred from the duties of private life to the administration of publick affairs. In fact, by what bond of union shall be hold together the members of this great empire, dispersed and scattered as they lie over the face of the earth? No *power* can be swift or extensive enough to answer the purpose. Some art must be employed to interest all the distant parts in the preservation of the whole; which can only be effected by serving, obliging and protecting them. It ought not to be the first object in contemplation, what we are to get by them; but how we can best improve, assist and reward them; by what benefits we may procure their happiness and win their affection. But is government then intitled to no emoluments in recompence for all its cares? I answer, that they who have the heart to do good to those who depend upon them, will always meet with an ample return. None are so sure to reap the benefits of the soil, as they who have spared no expence in the cultivation. And it is universally true, that the more we exact from our subjects, the less we shall gain from them. "BOUNTIFULNESS IS A PLENTIFUL GARDEN, AND MERCIFULNESS ENDURETH FOR EVER." Let the distant nations, that depend upon us, be made to know and feel that they owe their peace and happiness to our protection. Let them be encouraged to consider themselves not as our slaves, but as our friends and brethren. And let us endeavour to wipe away the tears from the poor oppressed natives of India; and suffer them, if possible, to enjoy some taste of the legal security and civil liberty, which renders life dear to ourselves; which are blessings hitherto unknown to those climates, but more grateful to the heart of man, than all the fruits and odours which nature has lavished upon them.

This righteousness and mercy, which is due to all men, but especially to those who are under our protection, is the law of nature, the command of religion, and it ought to be the first and leading maxim of civil policy. But it is amazing how slowly in all countries the principles of natural justice, which are so evidently necessary in private life, have been admitted into the administration of publick affairs. Not many ages ago, it was customary to engage in war without a reasonable cause or provocation, and to carry it on without humanity or mercy. Since then, it is happily become necessary for states to explain their motives, and justify their conduct, before they begin to destroy their fellow-creatures. And blessed be his memory who first taught the soldier to spare the useful husband-man, and to feel a horror at the shedding of innocent blood.

It has been the policy of government, such as it is, from the earliest times, to keep distant provinces and colonies under the most severe restraints and subjection. Yet when those restraints have been removed, the mother-country has always been a great gainer by the advantages she has communicated to her subjects. Indeed it is a truth, not more important than it is evident and obvious, that the most sure and effectual method of receiving good from men is to do good to them; or, as St. Paul beautifully expresses it, "TO PROVOKE ONE ANOTHER TO GOOD WORKS." But the minds of men are not sufficiently prepared and enlightened by experience to adopt it in practice. *A time, I doubt not, will come,* in the progressive improvement of human affairs, when the checks and restraints we lay on the industry of our fellow-subjects, and the jealousies we conceive at their prosperity, will be considered as the effects of a mistaken policy, prejudicial to all parties, but chiefly to ourselves. It would be a noble effort of virtuous ambition to anticipate this discovery; to break through the prejudices and selfish spirit of the age; to find a better path to our true interest; and to make our country great, and powerful, and rich, not by force or fraud, but by justice, friendship and humanity.

I should not have dwelt so long on so unusual a subject, had it not been for the great and almost infinite importance of it. The virtue of a private man assists and supports a few individuals; but this publick virtue does good to thousands and tens of thousands. The former relieves the distress of a friend, or of a family: the latter acts in a higher sphere; it founds states and kingdoms, or makes them prosperous and happy. Yet all this merit, which a nation can never sufficiently acknowledge, at least all that we presume to describe, consists in the right application of the plain good rules, which are so often repeated to us in scripture; "WHATSOEVER YE WOULD THAT MEN SHOULD DO UNTO YOU, DO YE EVEN SO UNTO THEM. FOLLOW THAT WHICH IS GOOD TO ALL MEN. LOOK NOT EVERY MAN ON HIS OWN THINGS, BUT EVERY MAN ALSO ON THE THINGS OF OTHERS. BEAR YE ONE ANOTHER'S BURTHENS, AND SO FULFIL THE LAW OF CHRIST." But these truths lie before the eyes of men, like medicinal herbs in the open field; and for want of applying them to their proper objects, they remain ignorant of their virtues. Yet we may say, with a pious confidence, that this has not been our own case. This Society has thought that we could not obey these divine precepts in a manner more agreeable to the true spirit of them, than by teaching to distant nations the truths that are best calculated to make them happy. Could we teach them to the great and the wise of this world, that would be happiness indeed; that would be the most effectual and the most beneficial Propagation of the Gospel, that the world has yet seen. Mankind would then have an experimental proof of the salvation offered to us from above; and would acknowledge with gratitude the propriety of that message from Heaven, "GLORY BE TO GOD IN THE HIGHEST, ON EARTH PEACE, GOOD WILL TOWARDS MEN."

At the Anniversary Meeting of the Society for the Propagation of the Gospel in Foreign Parts, *in the* Vestry-Room *of St.* Mary-le-Bow, *on* Friday *the* 19*th Day of* February, 1773;

AGREED, That the Thanks of the SOCIETY be given to the Right Reverend the Lord Bishop of St. Asaph, for his Sermon preached this Day by his Lordship before the SOCIETY and that his Lordship be desired to deliver a Copy of the same to the SOCIETY to be Printed.

Richard Hind, Secretary.

A

S P E E C H

INTENDED TO HAVE BEEN SPOKEN

By the Bishop of St. Asaph,

ON THE

B I L L

FOR

ALTERING THE CHARTERS

OF THE

Colony of Massachusetts Bay,

L O N D O N, PRINTED:

PHILADELPHIA, Reprinted and Sold by
BENJAMIN TOWNE, in *Front-Street*, near the
. *Coffee-House.*

1774

ADVERTISEMENT.

THE Author of the following Speech might justify his manner of publishing it by very great authorities. Some of the noblest pieces of eloquence, the world is in possession of, were not spoke on the great occasions they were intended to serve, and seem to have been preserved merely from the high sense that was entertained of their merit.

The present performance appears in public from humbler but juster motives; from the great national importance of the subject; from a very warm desire and some faint hope of serving our country, by suggesting a few of the useful truths which great men are apt to overlook.

The Author has abstained most religiously from personal reflections. He has censured no man, and therefore hopes he has offended no man. He feels most sensibly the misfortune of differing from many of those whom he wishes to live and act with; and from some of as much virtue and ability as this kingdom affords. But there are also great authorities on the other side; and the greatest authoritity can never persuade him, that it is better to extort by force, what he thinks may be gained more surely by gentle means.

He looks upon power as a coarse and mechanical instrument of government, and holds the use of it to be particularly dangerous to the relation that subsists between a mother country and her colonies. In such a case he doubts whether any point ought to be pursued, which cannot be carried by persuasion, by the sense of a common interest, and the exercise of a moderate authority. He thinks it unnecessary to lay down the limits of sovereignty and obedience, and more unnecessary to fight for them. If we can but restore that mutual regard and confidence, which formerly governed our whole intercourse with our colonies, particular cases will easily provide for themselves. He acts the part of the truest patriot in this dangerous crisis, whether he lives at London or at Boston, who pursues sincerely the most lenient and conciliating measures; and wishes to restore the public peace by some better method than the slaughter of our fellow citizens.

A
SPEECH, &c.

IT is of such great importance to compose or even to moderate the dissentions, which subsist at present between our unhappy country and her colonies, that I cannot help endeavouring, from the faint prospect I have of contributing something to so good an end, to overcome the inexpressible reluctance I feel at uttering my thoughts before the most respectable of all audiences.

The true object of all our deliberations on this occasion, which I hope we shall never lose sight of, is a full and cordial reconciliation with North America. Now I own, my Lords, I have many doubts whether the terrors and punishments, we·hang out to them at present, are the surest means of producing this reconciliation. Let us at least do this justice to the people of North America to own, that we can all remember a time when they were much better friends than at present to their mother country. They are neither our natural nor our determined enemies. Before the Stamp Act, we considered them in the light of as good subjects as the natives of any county in England.

It is worth while to inquire by what steps we first gained their affection, and preserved it so long; and by what conduct we have lately lost it. Such an inquiry may point out the means of restoring peace, and make the use of force unnecessary against a people, whom I cannot yet forbear to consider as our brethren.

It has always been a most arduous task to govern distant provinces, with even a tolerable appearance of justice. The viceroys and governors of other nations are usually temporary tyrants, who think themselves obliged to make the most of their time; who not only plunder the people, but carry away their spoils, and dry up all the sources of commerce and industry. Taxation, in their hands, is an unlimited power of oppression; but in whatever hands the power of taxation is lodged, it implies and includes all other powers. Arbitrary taxation is plunder authorized by law. It is the support and the essence of tyranny; and has done more mischief to mankind, than those other three scourges from heaven, famine, pestilence and the sword. I need not carry your Lordships out of your own knowledge, or out of your own dominions, to make you conceive what misery this right of

[31]

taxation is capable of producing in a provincial government. We need only recollect that our countrymen in India, have in the space of five or six years, in virtue of this right, destroyed, starved and driven away more inhabitants from Bengal, than are to be found at present in all our American Colonies! more than all those formidable numbers which we have been nursing up for the space of 200 years, with so much care and success, to the astonishment of all Europe. This is no exaggeration, my Lords, but plain matter of fact collected from the accounts sent over by Mr. Hastings, whose name I mention with honour and veneration.[1] And I must own, such accounts have very much lessened the pleasure I used to feel in thinking myself an Englishman. We ought surely not to hold our colonies totally inexcusable for wishing to exempt themselves from a grievance, which has caused such unexampled devastation; and, my Lords, it would be too disgraceful to ourselves, to try so cruel an experiment more than once. Let us reflect, that before these innovations were thought of, by following the line of good conduct which had been marked out by our ancestors, we governed North America with mutual benefit to them and ourselves. It was a happy idea, that made us first consider them rather as instruments of commerce than as objects of government. It was wise and generous to give them the form and the spirit of our own constitution; an assembly in which a greater equality of representation has been preserved than at home; and councils and governors, such as were adapted to their situation, though they must be acknowledged to be very inferior copies of the dignity of this House, and the Majesty of the Crown.

But what is far more valuable than all the rest, we gave them liberty. We allowed them to use their own judgment in the management of their own interest. The idea of taxing them never entered our heads. On the contrary they have experienced our liberality on many public occasions; we have given them bounties to encourage their industry, and have demanded no return but what every state exacts from its colonies, the advantages of an exclusive commerce, and the regulations that are necessary to secure it. We made requisitions to them on great occasions, in the same manner as our princes formerly asked benevolences of their subjects; and as nothing was asked but what was visibly for the public good, it was always granted; and they sometimes did more than we expected. The matter of right was neither disputed nor even considered. And let us not forget that the people of New England were themselves, during the last war, the most forward of all in the national cause; that every year we voted them a considerable sum, in acknowledgement of their zeal and their services; that in the preceding war, they alone enabled us to make the treaty of Aix la Chapelle, by furnishing us with the only equivalent for the towns that were taken from our allies in Flanders;[2] and that in times of peace, they alone have taken from us six times as much of our woolen manufactures as the whole kingdom of Ireland. Such a colony, my Lords, not only from the justice, but from the gratitude we owe them, have a right to be heard in their defence; and if their crimes are not of the most inexpiable kind, I could almost say, they have a right to be forgiven.

But in the times we speak of, our public intercourse was carried on with ease and satisfaction. We regarded them as our friends and fellow citizens, and relied as much upon their fidelity as on the inhabitants of our own country. They saw our power with pleasure; for they considered it only as their protection. They inherited our laws, our language, and our customs; they preferred our manufactures, and followed our fashions with a partiality that secured our exclusive trade with them more effectually than all the regulations and vigilance of the custom house. Had we suffered them to enrich us a little longer, and to grow a little richer themselves, their men of fortune, like the West Indians, would undoubtedly have made this country their place of education and resort. For they looked up to England with reverence and affection, as to the country of their friends and ancestors. They esteemed and they called it their home, and thought of it as the Jews once thought of the land of Canaan.

Now, my Lords, consider with yourselves what were the chains and ties that united this people to their mother country, with so much warmth and affection, at so amazing a distance. The colonies of other nations have been discontented with their treatment, and not without sufficient cause; always murmuring at their grievances, and sometimes breaking out into acts of rebellion. Our subjects at home, with all their reasons for satisfaction, have never been entirely satisfied. Since the beginning of this century we have had two rebellions, several plots and conspiracies; and we ourselves have been witnesses to the most dangerous excesses of sedition. But the provinces in North America have engaged in no party, have excited no opposition; they have been utter strangers even to the name of Whig and Tory. In all changes, in all revolutions, they have quietly followed the fortunes, and submitted to the government of England.

Now let me appeal to your Lordships as to men of enlarged and liberal minds, who have been led by your office and rank to the study of history. Can you find in the long succession of ages, in the whole extent of human affairs, a single instance where distant provinces have been preserved in so flourishing a state, and kept at the same time in such due subjection to their mother country? My Lords, there is no instance, the case never existed before. It is perhaps the most singular phoenomenon in all civil history; and the cause of it well deserves your serious consideration. The true cause is, that a mother country never existed before, who placed her natives and her colonies on the same equal footing; and joined with them in fairly carrying on one common interest.

You ought to consider this, my Lords, not as a mere historical fact, but as a most important and invaluable discovery. It enlarges our ideas of the power and energy of good government beyond all former examples; and shews that it can act like gravitation at the greatest distances. It proves to a demonstration, that you may have good subjects in the remotest corners of the earth, if you will but treat them with kindness and equity. If you have any doubts of the truth of this kind of reasoning, the experience we have had of a different kind will entirely remove them.

The good genius of our country had led us to the simple and happy method of governing freemen, which I have endeavoured to describe. Our ministers received it from their predecessors, and for some time continued to observe it, but without knowing its value. At length, presuming on their own wisdom, and the quiet disposition of the Americans, they flattered themselves that we might reap great advantages from their prosperity by destroying the cause of it. They chose in an unlucky hour to treat them as other nations have thought fit to treat their colonies; they threatened, and they taxed them.

I do not now enquire whether taxation is matter of right; I only consider it as matter of experiment; for surely the art of government itself is founded on experience. I need not suggest what were the consequences of this change of measures. The evils produced by it were such as we still remember, and still feel. We suffered more by our loss of trade with them than the wealth flowing in from India was able to recompence. The bankruptcy of the East India Company may be sufficiently accounted for by the rapine abroad, and knavery at home; but it certainly would have been delayed some years, had we continued our commerce with them in THE SINGLE ARTICLE OF TEA.

But that and many other branches of trade have been diverted into other channels, and may probably never return intire to their old course. But what is worst of all, we have lost their confidence and friendship; we have ignorantly undermined the most solid foundation of our own power.

In order to observe the strictest impartiality, it is but just for us to inquire what we have gained by these taxes as well as what we have lost. I am assured, that out of all the sums raised in America the last year but one, if the expences are deducted, which the natives would else have discharged themselves, the net revenue paid into the Treasury to go in aid of the Sinking Fund, or to be employed in whatever public services Parliament shall think fit, is eighty five pounds. Eighty five pounds, my Lords, is the whole equivalent we have received for all the hatred and mischief, and all the infinite losses this kingdom has suffered during that year in her disputes with North America. Money, that is earned so dearly as this, ought to be expended with great wisdom and œconomy. My Lords, were you to take up but one thousand pounds more from North America upon the same terms, the nation itself would be a bankrupt. But the most amazing, and the most alarming, circumstance is still behind. It is that our case is so incurable, that all this experience has made no impression upon us. And yet, my Lords, if you could but keep these facts, which I have ventured to lay before you for a few moments in your minds (supposing your right of taxation to be never so clear) yet I think you must necessarily perceive that it cannot be exercised in any manner that can be advantageous to ourselves or them. We have not always the wisdom to tax ourselves with propriety; and I am confident we could never tax a people at that distance, without infinite blunders, and infinite oppression. And to own the truth, my Lords, we are not honest enough to trust ourselves with the power of shifting our own burthens upon them. Allow me, therefore, to conclude, I think unanswerably, that the inconvenience and distress we have felt in this change of our conduct, no less than the ease and tranquillity we formerly found in the pursuit of it, will force us, if we have any sense left, to return to the good old path we trod in so long, and found it the way of pleasantness.

I desire to have it understood, that I am opposing no rights that our legislature may think proper to claim: I am only comparing two different methods of government. By your old rational and generous administration, by treating the Americans as your friends and fellow-citizens, you made them the happiest of human kind; and at the same time drew from them, by commerce, more clear profit than Spain has drawn from all its mines; and their growing numbers were a daily increasing addition to your strength. There was no room for improvement or alteration in so noble a system of policy as this. It was sanctified by time, by experience, by public utility. I will venture to use a bold language, my Lords; I will assert, that if we had uniformly adopted this equitable administration in all our distant provinces, as far as circumstances would admit, it would have placed this country, for ages, at the head of human affairs in every quarter of the world. My Lords, this is no visionary or chimerical doctrine. The idea of governing provinces and colonies by force is visionary and chimerical. The experiment has often been tried, and it has never succeeded. It ends infallibly in the ruin of the one country or the other, or in the last degree of wretchedness.

If there is any truth, my Lords, in what I have said, and I most firmly believe it all to be true; let me recommend it to you to resume that generous and benevolent spirit in the discussion of our differences, which used to be the source of our union. We certainly did wrong in taxing them: When the Stamp Act was repealed, we did wrong in laying on other taxes, which tended only to keep alive a claim that was mischievous, impracticable and useless. We acted contrary to our own principles of liberty, and to the generous sentiments of our sovereign, when we desired to have their judges dependent on the crown for their stipends as well as their continuance. It was equally unwise to wish to make the governors independent of the people for their salaries. We ought to consider the governors, not as spies intrusted with the mangement of our interest, but as the servants of the people recommended to them by us. Our ears ought to be open to every complaint against the governors; but we ought not to suffer the governors to complain of the people. We have taken a different method, to which no small part of our difficulties are owing. Our ears have been open to the governors, and shut to the people. This must necessarily lead us to countenance the jobs of interested men, under the pretence of defending the rights of the crown. But the people are certainly the best judges whether they are well governed; and the crown can have no rights inconsistent with the happiness of the people.

Now, my Lords, we ought to do what I have suggested, and many things more, out of prudence and justice, to win their affection, and to do them public service. If we have a right to govern them, let us exert it for the true ends of government. But, my Lords, what we ought to do, from motives of reason and justice, is much more than is sufficient to bring them to a reasonable accommodation. For thus, as I apprehend, stands the case. They petition for the repeal of an act of parliament, which they complain of as unjust and oppressive. And there is not a man amongst us, not the warmest friend of administration, who does not sincerely wish that act had never been made. In fact, they only ask for what we wish to be rid of. Under such a disposition of mind, one would imagine there could be no occasion for fleets and armies to bring men to a good understanding.

But, my Lords, our difficulty lies in the point of honour. We must not let down the dignity of the mother country, but preserve her sovereignty over all the parts of the British Empire. This language has something in it that sounds pleasant to the ears of Englishmen, but is otherwise of little weight. For sure, my Lords, there are methods of making reasonable concessions, and yet without injuring our dignity. Ministers are generally fruitful in expedients to reconcile difficulties of this kind, to escape the embarrassments of forms, the competitions of dignity and precedency, and to let clashing rights sleep while they transact their business. Now, my Lords, on this occasion can they find no excuse, no pretense, no invention, no happy turn of language, not one colourable argument for doing the greatest service, they can ever render to their country? It must be something more than incapacity that makes men barren of expedients at such a season as this. Do, but for once, remove this impracticable stateliness and dignity, and treat the matter with a little common sense and a little good humour, and our reconciliation would not be the work of an hour. But after all, my Lords, if there is any thing mortifying in undoing the errors of our ministers, it is a mortification we ought to submit to. If it was unjust to tax them, we ought to repeal it for their sakes; if it was unwise to tax them, we ought to repeal it for our own. A matter so trivial in itself as the three-penny duty upon tea, but which has given cause to so much national hatred and reproach, ought not to be suffered to subsist an unnecessary day. Must the interest, the commerce and the union of this country and her colonies be all of them sacrificed to save the credit of one imprudent measure of administration? I own I cannot comprehend that there is any dignity either in being in the wrong or in persisting in it. I have known friendship preserved and affection gained, but I never knew dignity lost, by the candid acknowledgment of an error. And, my Lords, let me appeal to your own experience of a few years backward (I will not mention particulars, because I would pass no censures, and revive no unpleasant reflections) but I think every candid minister must own that administration has suffered in more instances than one, both in interest and credit, by not chusing to give up points that could not be defended.

With regard to the people of Boston, I am free to own that I neither approve of their riots nor their punishment. And yet if we inflict it as we ought, with a consciousness that we were ourselves the aggressors, that we gave the provocation, and that their disobedience is the fruit of our own imprudent and imperious conduct, I think the punishment cannot rise to any great degree of severity.

I own, my Lords, I have read the report of the Lords Committees of this house, with very different sentiments from those with which it was drawn up. It seems to be designed, that we should consider their violent measures and speeches, as so many determined acts of opposition to the sovereignty of England, arising from the malignity of their own hearts. One would think the mother country had been totally silent and passive in the progress of the whole affair. I on the contrary consider these violences as the natural effects of such measures as ours on the minds of freemen. And this is the most useful point of view, in which government can consider them. In their situation, a wise man would expect to meet with the strongest marks of passion and imprudence, and be prepared to forgive them. The first and easiest thing to be done is to correct our own errors; and I am confident we should find it the most effectual method to correct theirs. At any rate let us put ourselves in the right; and then if we must contend with North America, we shall be unanimous at home, and the wise and the moderate there will be our friends. At present we force every North American to be our enemy; and the wise and moderate at home, and those immense multitudes, which must soon begin to suffer by the madness of our rulers, will unite to oppose them. It is a strange idea we have taken up, to cure their resentments by increasing their provocations; to remove the effects of our own ill conduct, by multiplying the instances of it. But the spirit of blindness and infatuation is gone forth. We are hurrying wildly on without any fixed design, without any important object. We pursue a vain phantom of unlimited sovereignty, which was not made for man; and reject the solid advantages of a moderate, useful and intelligible authority. That just God, whom we have all so deeply offended, can hardly inflict a severer national punishment, than by committing us to the natural consequences of own own conduct. Indeed, in my opinion, a blacker cloud never hung over this island.

To reason consistently with the principles of justice and national friendship, which I have endeavoured to establish, or rather to revive what was established by our ancestors, as our wisest rule of conduct for the government of America, I must necessarily disapprove of the Bill before us, for it contradicts every one of them. In our present situation every act of the legislature, even our acts of severity ought to be so many steps towards the reconciliation we wish for. But to change the government of a people, without their consent, is the highest and most arbitrary act of sovereignty that one nation can exercise over another. The Romans hardly ever proceeded to this extremity even over a conquered nation, till its frequent revolts and insurrections had made them deem it incorrigible. The very idea of it implies a most total abject and slavish dependency in the inferior state. Recollect that the Americans are men of like passions with ourselves, and think how deeply this treatment must affect them. They have the same veneration for their charters that we have for our Magna Charta, and they ought in reason to have greater. They are the title deeds to all their rights both public and private. What? my Lords, must these rights never acquire any legal assurance and stability? Can they derive no force from the peaceable possession of near two hundred years? And must the fundamental constitution of a powerful state be for ever subject to as capricious alterations as you may think fit to make in the charters of a little mercantile company, or the corporation of a borough? This will undoubtedly furnish matter for a more pernicious debate than has yet been moved. Every other colony will make the case its own. They will complain that their rights can never be ascertained; that every thing belonging to them depends upon our arbitrary will; and may think it better to run any hazard than to submit to the violence of their mother country, in a matter in which they can see neither moderation nor end.

But let us coolly inquire, what is the reason of this unheard of innovation. Is it to make them peaceable? My Lords, it will make them mad. Will they be better governed if we introduce this change? Will they be more our friends? The least that such a measure can do, is to make them hate us. And would to God, my Lords, we had governed ourselves with as much œconomy, integrity and prudence as they have done. Let them continue to enjoy the liberty our fathers gave them. Gave them, did I say? They are coheirs of liberty with ourselves; and their portion of the inheritance has been much better looked after than ours. Suffer them to enjoy a little longer that short period of public integrity and domestic happiness, which seems to be the portion allotted by Providence to young rising states. Instead of hoping that their constitution may receive improvement from our skill in government, the most useful wish I can form in their favour is, that heaven may long preserve them from our vices and our politicks.

Let me add farther, that to make any changes in their government, without their consent, would be to transgress the wisest rules of policy, and to wound our most important interests. As they increase in numbers and in riches, our comparative strength must lessen. In another age, when our power has begun to lose something of its superiority, we should be happy if we could support our authority by mutual good will and the habit of commanding; but chiefly by those original establishments, which time and public honour might have rendered inviolable. Our posterity will then have reason to lament that they cannot avail themselves of those treasures of publick friendship and confidence which our fathers had wisely hoarded up, and we are throwing away. 'Tis hard, 'tis cruel, besides all our debts and taxes, and those enormous expences which are multiplying upon us every year, to load our unhappy sons with the hatred and curses of North America. Indeed, my Lords, we are treating posterity very scurvily. We have mortgaged all the lands; we have cut down all the oaks; we are now trampling down the fences, rooting up the seedlings and samplers, and ruining all the resources of another age. We shall send the next generation into the world like the wretched heir of a worthless father, without money, credit or friends; with a stripped, incumbered, and perhaps untenated estate.

Having spoke so largely against the principle of the bill, it is hardly necessary to enter into the merits of it. I shall only observe, that even if we had the consent of the people to alter their government, it would be unwise to make such alterations as these. To give the appointment of the governor and council to the crown, and the disposal of all places, even of the judges, and with a power of removing them, to the governor, is evidently calculated with a view to form a strong party in our favour. This I know has been done in other colonies; but still this is opening a source of perpetual discord, where it is our interest always to agree. If we mean any thing by this establishment, it is to support the governor and the council against the people, i.e. to quarrel with our friends, that we may please their servants. This scheme of governing them by a party is not wisely imagined, it is much too premature, and, at all events, must turn to our disadvantage. If it fails, it will only make us contemptible; if it succeeds, it will make us odious. It is our interest to take very little part in their domestic administration of government, but purely to watch over them for their good. We never gained so much by North America as when we let them govern themselves, and were content to trade with them and to protect them. One would think, my Lords, there was some statute law prohibiting us, under the severest penalties, to profit by experience.

My Lords, I have ventured to lay my thoughts before you, on the greatest national concern that ever came under your deliberation, with as much honesty as you will meet with from abler men, and with a melancholy assurance that not a word of it will be regarded. And yet, my Lords, with your permission, I will waste one short argument more on the same cause, one that I own I am fond of, and which contains in it, what, I think, must affect every generous mind. My Lords, I look upon North America as the only great nursery of freemen now left upon the face of the earth. We have seen the liberties of Poland and Sweden swept away, in the course of one year, by treachery and usurpation. The free towns in Germany are like so many dying sparks, that go out one after another; and which must all be soon extinguished under the destructive greatness of their neighbours. Holland is little more than a great trading company, with luxurious manners, and an exhausted revenue; with little strength and with less spirit. Switzerland alone is free and happy within the narrow inclosure of its rocks and vallies. As for the state of this country, my Lords, I can only refer myself to your own secret thoughts. I am disposed to think and hope the best of Public Liberty. Were I to describe her according to my own ideas at present, I should say that she has a sickly countenance, but I trust she has a strong constitution.

But whatever may be our future fate, the greatest glory that attends this country, a greater than any other nation ever acquired is to have formed and nursed up to such a state of happiness, those colonies whom we are now so eager to butcher. We ought to cherish them as the immortal monuments of our public justice and wisdom; as the heirs of our better days, of our old arts and manners, and of our expiring national virtues. What work of art, or power, or public utility has ever equalled the glory of having peopled a continent without guilt or bloodshed, with a multitude of free and happy commonwealths; to have given them the best arts of life and government; and to have suffered them under the shelter of our authority, to acquire in peace the skill to use them. In comparison of this, the policy of governing by influence, and even the pride of war and victory are dishonest tricks and poor contemptible pageantry.

We seem not to be sensible of the high and important trust which providence has committed to our charge. The most precious remains of civil liberty, that the world can now boast of, are lodged in our hands; and God forbid that we should violate so sacred a deposit. By enslaving your colonies, you not only ruin the peace, the commerce, and the fortunes of both countries; but you extinguish the fairest hopes, shut up the last asylum of mankind. I think, my Lords, without being weakly superstitious, that a good man may hope that heaven will take part against the execution of a plan which seems big not only with mischief, but impiety.

Let us be content with the spoils and the destruction of the east. If your Lordships can see no impropriety in it, let the plunderer and the oppressor still go free. But let not the love of liberty be the only crime you think worthy of punishment. I fear we shall soon make it a part of our natural character, to ruin every thing that has the misfortune to depend upon us.

No nation has ever before contrived, in so short a space of time, without any war or public calamity (unless unwise measures may be so called) to destroy such ample resources of commerce, wealth and power, as of late were ours, and which, if they had been rightly improved, might have raised us to a state of more honourable and more permanent greatness than the world has yet seen.

Let me remind the noble Lords in Administration, that before the stamp act they had power sufficient to answer all the just ends of government, and they were all completely answered. If that is the power they want, though we have lost much of it at present, a few kind words would recover it all.

But if the tendency of this bill is, as I own it appears to me, to acquire a power of governing them by influence and corruption; in the first place, my Lords, this is not true government, but a sophisticated kind, which counterfeits the appearance, but without the spirit or virtue of the true; and then, as it tends to debase their spirits and corrupt their manners, and destroy all that is great and respectable in so considerable a part of the human species, and by degrees to gather them together with the rest of the world, under the yoke of universal slavery; I think, for these reasons, it is the duty of every wise man, of every honest man, and of every Englishman, by all lawful means to oppose it.

FINIS

NOTES

[1] Warren Hastings (1732–1818), Governor-General of Bengal, who was then implementing broad administrative reforms in India which were of great interest to Parliament.

[2] The treaty of Aix-la-Chapelle of 1748, which brought an end to the War of the Austrian Succession, was essentially a return to the status quo ante bellum. Fort Louisbourg, which the Americans had captured in 1745, had been returned to France at the peace table to balance losses suffered elsewhere.

Matthew Robinson-Morris

BARON ROKEBY

T HOSE Englishmen who wrote pamphlets in defense of America on the eve of the American Revolution were moved to take up their pens against the policies of the North Ministry from a variety of motives. But despite the influence of personal and party considerations, one cannot fail to be impressed that many did so solely out of their strong desire to preserve traditional English liberties, to promote the well-being of their country, and to secure justice for America. Of these, no concerned citizen was more distressed at the policies of his Government or more fearful for the survival of a venerable libertarian heritage than Matthew Robinson-Morris, the second Baron Rokeby (1713-1800). An independent old Whig without ambition for place, who sought neither fortune nor favor, he was moved upon the occasion of the American crisis of the 1770's to speak forcefully against the coercive program of the Government of George III. The four essays which he wrote between April 1774 and December 1776,[1] all on the subject of America, are his sole published works and, in fact, nearly the only reminders of his long life.

Born into an old Kent family, he was christened Matthew Robinson but accepted the additional name Morris in 1746 to secure an inheritance from his mother's estate. In 1794 he became Baron Rokeby in the Irish peerage.[2] A Fellow of Trinity Hall, Cambridge, possessed of ample fortune, a good library, and a bent for seclusion, Robinson-Morris was known to be a knowledgeable observer but an infrequent participant in active political affairs. He sat in the House of Commons for Canterbury between 1747 and 1761 but did not stand for reelection at the expiration of his second term. Devoted to habitual exercise and the practical arts of the husbandman, noted for his eccentric eating habits and odd personal appearance, he lamented the increasing materialism of British society and the intense ambition of certain political figures and pointedly shunned the lures of the city of London. He could have been driven to voice his political opinions in the public forum only upon what he perceived to be great provocation.

The appearance of his *Considerations on the Measures Carrying on With Respect to the British Colonies in North America*, the first and most significant of his works, was immediately applauded in the Colonies. It quickly appeared in seven American editions, making it second only to Shipley's *Speech* among political tracts written before *Common Sense*. Three English editions testified to the interest that the work aroused in Britain.

Although Robinson-Morris' immediate concern was the North Ministry's proposed legislation for altering the Government of Massachusetts, he did not confine himself merely to the problem of dealing with elements in the Colonies resisting British control. His discussion covers a broad range of American affairs. Underlying his entire argument was the assumption that the American discontent was of recent origin, arising from unjustified British attempts to tax the colonists. Such taxation violated the English Constitution and clearly marked Britain as the aggressor in the crisis. His survey of the origins and nature of colonial rights, which revealed a considerable grasp of both colonial history and recent American affairs, could easily have been written by an American. His rejection of the argument that there was no middle ground between American independence and rigorously enforced obedience was aimed at leaders on both sides of the Atlantic who refused to accept compromises that Robinson-Morris considered to be in the best interests of all English-speaking peoples.

By far the greater part of the essay is taken up by a discussion not of political theory but rather of practical problems. On the matter of taxation, he asserts, it is vain to tax the Colonies because England already obtains maximum profit through her monopoly and regulation of American commerce. The advantages derived from the American trade are often unappreciated in England because the profits and revenue from that source are constantly drained away to Europe to service the enormous charges on the national debt. These advantages are no less real, however, merely because the Ministry seems blind to the true condition of the economy. And since it is impossible to obtain "more than all" from the Colonies, Britain is risking a ruinous war without any prospect for tangible gain.

An important part of the essay, and to American readers perhaps the most interesting, is devoted to a discussion not of Britain's right but of her inability to coerce the American Colonies. Robinson-Morris' argument, often cast in quaint language but compelling even to a modern reader, must have been read eagerly in the Colonies, since he reviews in detail the strength of American resistance should the home Government persist on its present course and fail to avert war. The Americans can put 300,000 to 400,000 fighting men in the field, men not less capable than those who tasted victory over the French at Louisbourg. England must expect that the Colonies will be united, for they have already erected a system of Committees of Correspondence, and as no fleet can capture a continent even the vaunted British Navy will not be able to surmount the handicaps England will face in a land war. The English economy will founder on the rocks of another commercial crisis, which will be more severe than the disastrous slumps suffered during previous colonial boycotts. The present tax structure and load of debt already threaten the nation's solvency. Arguing a more original line, he declares that a social upheaval would face Britain, since warfare against the colonists would constitute a civil war, and the oppressed classes in England—particularly the exploited common soldier and seaman—would likely choose the side of America. And with some prospect of gaining new advantage at Britain's expense, what course would the West Indies—or even Ireland—take once war erupted? Finally, in addition to all of these problems, Britain would be assailed by foreign enemies, who undoubtedly already delight at the very policies now being pursued by the Ministers of George III.

Having considered "the rectitude, the practicability and the profit to be expected from our present measures," and confessing that he could do little more by way of reasoned argument, Robinson-Morris turns in his concluding paragraphs to evoking sympathy for America. Let us put ourselves in the place of the Americans, he appeals, and not that of the Governors upon whom we have so exclusively depended for information and advice. He had no doubt of the result if he could get Englishmen to listen. "Were my countrymen now in England dipped once in the River Delaware, I dare say, that it would make an almost miraculous change in their opinions." The basic problem was the perversity of those now in power: "there would be hurt not the hair of the head of an American, were it to be voted by all our country." "Americans should consider that two different parts of a country may be oppressed by one and the same hand." The

Ministry could not escape responsibility, despite recent efforts to place the blame for the current crisis on the head of Dr. Franklin. "It is idle and childish to be crying out against this or that private person. The truth is, that whenever governments heap up combustibles, there will always be found a hand to put the match to them."

A work of insight and influence, of impressive knowledge and temperate tone, of timely appeal and wide distribution, Matthew Robinson-Morris' *Considerations* should not remain in obscurity.

NOTES

[1] *Considerations on the Measures Carrying on with Respect to the British Colonies in North America* (1774); *Appendix to the Considerations on the Measures Carrying on . . .* (1774); *A Further Examination of our Present American Measures . . .* (1776); and *Peace the Best Policy . . .* (1777). The last two works can only be judged as weak performances. The *Further Examination* alone ran to the excessive length of 256 pages, for which the author publicly apologized in his prefatory remarks, and it added little of substance to his first essay.

[2] Information on Robinson-Morris' life can be obtained from *A Brief Character of Matthew Lord Rokeby* (Kent, 1817) by Samuel Egerton Brydges; *The House of Commons, 1754–1790* by Lewis B. Namier and John Brooke (New York, 1964), vol. 3, p. 367–368; and the *Dictionary of National Biography*.

CONSIDERATIONS

ON THE

MEASURES CARRYING ON

WITH RESPECT TO THE

BRITISH COLONIES

IN

NORTH AMERICA.

By Lord Cambden.

*There is neither King or Sovereign Lord on
Earth, who has, beyond his own Domain,
Power to lay one Farthing on his Subjects,
without the Grant and Consent of those who
pay it ; unless he does it by Tyranny and
Violence.*

Philippe de Commines, Ch. 108.

LONDON: PRINTED,

AND

NEW-YORK: RE-PRINTED,

By JOHN HOLT, in DOCK-STREET, near the

COFFEE-HOUSE. 1774.

CONSIDERATIONS, &c.

NO one knows, how far every person in Britain may be interested in the event of the measures now carrying on with respect to our colonies in North America. This seems to entitle any man, on account of his own stake therein, to speak his sentiments on the subject. The concern of the community gives to them likewise for their better security a claim, that every opinion may be offered for consideration. These things result from the nature of a free society and particularly from the constitution of Great Britain, where the people choose one part of the legislature and where every man is supposed to have ultimately a share in the government of his country.

One point in dispute between us and the Americans is the right of taxing them here at home. This may be said to concern the power of our parliament. But so does every general proposition of right and wrong. When any thing is affirmed to be unjust, does not it conclude and is it not almost synonimous to the saying, that a law made to enforce it would be so too, and beyond the proper power of a legislature? Vengeance and punishment do in the course of things, assuredly pursue states and nations for their oppression and injustice; against the commission of which it is beyond question the right of every member of the community to warn the rest.

I say it with submission, but the power of the Parliament is the right of the public. The particular members of that most respectable body are in the statutes enacted by them no more personally interested, than the rest of their countrymen. These pass through their hands, but being so passed, they are themselves bound to obey them in common with others. They are indeed our trustees and guardians in that high office, but they will, on that account be the more inclined, that every step taken or to be taken by them should be fully and carefully examined, like all other honest men, earnest for the interest of those, whose concerns are committed to their care.

[51]

A consideration of the measures now proposed may likewise possibly lead to some nice and delicate conjectures or circumstances, whether of the present time or of that to come. But it need not be said, that the writer only finds the one, and guesses at the other; they depend on an author much higher than Princes or their ministers, but who is pleased to suffer the actions of those to have most essential effects in the producing them. What can then be a more fit means to induce a due reflection on our proceedings and to insure from them a desireable success, than to lay before the public or the governors of it, some possible consequences of their conduct?

We have not far to seek for the cause of the present situation of things between the mother-country and our colonies of North America; of the opposition and disturbances on the one hand, and of the violent laws, motions and preparations on the other. These all undoubtedly proceed from our having taxed those colonies without their consent. Affection and union obtained between us before; there succeeded instead animosity and opposition, as soon as that was attempted; however peace and satisfaction were on our staying our hands again restored. We are now once more come back to the charge, and the spirit of discord seems likewise returned seven times stronger, than it was before. Other broils and contests may, and many no doubt will arise from this cause, should it proceed; but this is the origin, the spring and the source. The right itself of this measure is in question, as well as the expediency of it; I will therefore presume to say something to that proposition.

The inhabitants of our colonies in North America are supposed to consist of about two millions of persons; they occupy and possess a very extensive territory, much larger than Great Britain; they are not themselves the original people of the country, but they now stand in their place; and they have in general been born and bred there, however they receive likewise yearly from other places many, who mix themselves with them; they have divided themselves into several different governments; they have according to certain rules or laws agreed upon among them allotted every man his own; they have felled the forests; they have cleared and tilled the land, they have planted it, they have sown it, they have stocked it with cattle; they have built themselves houses; they have entered into exchange and commerce; they have spared and saved for a future day or for their families; they have by many and various means acquired many and various sorts of property; they are by nature entitled to welfare and happiness, and to seek and pursue those blessings, by all the methods not attended with fraud or violence towards others, which they shall conceive and believe the most probable to procure or ensure them; they have for that end a right to freedom in their governments and to security in their persons and properties; none are warranted to deprive or dispossess them of these things; should on the contrary one man or a body of men advance any claim, which tended to enslave all the persons or to unsettle all the property of this great community, to divest them of every thing, which they possess and to leave them nothing, which they could call their own, of all that they have thus inherited earned or acquired; the very enormity, the evil and unnatural consequences of such a proposition would of themselves sufficiently shew its absurdity, weakness and unreasonableness.

These are all either primarily, essential, inherent rights of human nature, or such as do with respect to persons in the situation before described, necessarily flow and follow from them. Those were conferred upon them by the great Author of their being when he was pleased to endow them with the faculties of men, with the perception of good and evil, with the means of self-preservation and self-defence, with the organs of reason and of speech, and with a capacity to associate themselves for their mutual protection and support. They are common to all mankind; they subsist at all times, in all regions and all climates; in Turkey, in Spain, in France, in Old England and in New, in Europe and America; whenever and wherever a number of men are found to be the objects of them. I don't mean that they are in all these places always, or at this time possessed and enjoyed as they ought to be. But they are to answer for that, who do so commonly employ to the enslaving and oppressing of mankind the powers, which these entrust only for their protection and defence. However this is only abuse, violence and injustice; the right nevertheless subsists and remains.

It is not on this subject necesary to enter into a long and minute detail of reasoning. These principles are with us common and public; they are founded on the good, the welfare and the happiness of mankind. They were the principles of our ancestors, of our grandfathers and of our fathers; they may perhaps not be at present in their full vigour; however, I trust, that they are not yet so worn out or lost from among us, but that they still remain the principles of the nation. They are to describe them by a word well known in our language the principles of Whigs; whereby I don't however mean of certain modern Whigs, who seem more fond of the word, than of any thing belonging to the character; who have perhaps at one time or other of their lives counter-acted all the measures and contradicted all the principles that ever did honour to the name; but I mean of Whigs before the Revolution and at the time of it; I mean the principles which such men as Mr. Locke, Lord Molesworth and Mr. Trenchard maintained with their pens, Mr. Hampden and Lord John Russel with their blood and Mr. Algernon Sydney with both; names, which must surely by all Englishmen ever be revered, as those of some of the first among men. But let me add, that they are not only the principles of speculative students in their closets, or of great but unfortunate men, whom their zeal and virtue have led to martyrdom for the liberties of their country and the welfare of mankind; but that they are likewise the real principles of our present actual government, the principles of the revolution, and those on which are established the throne of the King and the settlement of the illustrious family now reigning over us.

On the same principles rest, both in general many rights of the Americans, and in particular the right now before us. These are hereby involved and interwoven with our highest and most sacred concerns; we cannot lift up our hands to take them away without forfeiting our national character, without renouncing the tenets and maxims whereon we have, on our most important and critical occasions, ever acted as a people, and without declaring that we claim a right to resist and oppose all those who oppress us ourselves, and at the same time to trample upon and tyrannize over all others, where we hope that we have the power to do it with impunity.

But it may be said, that these are indeed in themselves very true and commendable opinions, but that they are here introduced on subjects not worthy of them, a duty of a few shillings upon some sorts of paper or parchment, and of a few pence upon a pound of tea. Let us therefore more particularly consider the nature of the claim and pretention in question. Suppose then, one person to have in his pocket an hundred pounds, but another to have the right to take it from him, or to put it into his own pocket, or to do with it what he pleases; to whom does that money belong? This needs no answer. Suppose the sum to be a thousand or ten thousand pounds? That makes no difference. Suppose one person to have a right to demand of another not only one certain sum or what he has about him, but as much as he pleases, and as often? This goes to the all of that other. But suppose not one single person only to be subject to such demands from one other, but a number of men, a colony, or any other community, to be so subject to the demands of some other society. What then? Why then that will go in like manner to their all. This seems to be so evident, that whoever shall multiply words on the subject will hardly do it for the sake of being convinced.

But is this case that of the Americans; for it is said that the money raised on them is to be employed for their own benefit, in their civil service or military defence? Let me ask then, who are in their case to determine, whether any money is at all wanted for such purposes; they who pay it, or they who take it? They who take it. Who are to determine the quantity wanted? They who take it. Who are to determine how often it is wanted? They who take it. Who are to determine whether it is really laid out in the purposes pretended? They who take it. Suppose the Americans should be of opinion, or declare that the money so raised is used not for their advantage, but the contrary; is that a bar to the raising? No. Suppose them to complain that the money pretended to be laid out in their civil service is given to corrupt their Governors or Judges; is that a bar to the raising? No. Suppose them to signify that the money alledged to be used in their military defence is employed in paying troops to enslave them, and which they had rather be without; is that a bar to the raising? No. Wherein then does this differ from will and pleasure in the most absolute sense?

This claim affects therefore most clearly the all of the Americans. Two millions of people, subject to no less than twelve different governments, and inhabiting, possessing, and being masters of a country exceedingly larger than that of those who make the claim, or in whose name it is made, have on this ground, no property at all, nothing which they can truly call their own, nothing but what may at any time be demanded of them, but what they may be deprived of without and against their will and consent. It cannot therefore surely be a question whether or no, this is a matter of such a magnitude as to deserve the most serious discussion. But it might here be without further words, left to every man's determination, whether this is on the one hand a reasonable ground, whereon to put into confusion all the parts of the British empire, to throw the mother country and her North American colonies into the most deadly feuds and in all appearance a civil war with one another, or whether it is not on the other hand a proposition inconsistent with the essential laws of nature, subversive of the first and inherent rights of humanity, and contrary to the principles whereon our forefathers defended and under the sanction of which they have through so many civil wars and with the deposition, banishment and change of so many Princes, delivered down to us the rights and properties, which Englishmen now enjoy.

But it is in this dispute very often represented; that a total and absolute dependance on the British Parliament without any exception whatsoever either with regard to taxes or any other, is liberty itself; it is British liberty, which is the best of liberty. I answer, who says otherwise in the case of us, who choose that Parliament; but that in some other cases, this position may perhaps be more liable to question. Our North American colonies are as to their internal constitution a very free people, as free as the Venetians, the Dutch or the Swiss, or perhaps more so than any of them. This proceeds from their Assemblies being not only the nominal but the real representatives, of those whom they govern. These are elected fairly, fully, and often. In these Assemblies their liberty consists, and it is certainly true and genuine. But change the scene a little; let any one colony be taxed and governed not by their own, but by the Assembly of another; what is then become of this their genuine liberty? It is gone and lost with their own Assembly. Let all the colonies be so subjected to the Assembly of some one among them. That won't mend the matter. Let us take a larger scale. Suppose this power over them be lodged in the Parliament of Ireland. We are never the nearer. Let us come towards home. Were the kingdom of Ireland under the taxation and direction of the British Parliament would they then think themselves to be very free? For an answer to this question enquire of one of that country. Place then the Irish under one of the Assemblies before mentioned. They would be yet further from home and it might not be better with them. Let us take our own turn. Suppose Great Britain on the like conditions under the Parliament of Ireland. God forbid. I think that I have but one more point, before that I am at an end of my combination. Place over our heads with all these powers in their full force, the Assembly of Massachusetts Bay, what then? I fancy that we should soon change a certain tune and sing another song, than what we do now. Let me then most seriously question any man, from whose breast all candour and justice are not totally banished, where is, as to liberty or property, the difference between any of the cases now supposed and that original one which has given occasion to them. I speak this no otherwise than with the utmost reverence and respect towards our own legislature; but are we to conceive, or would it be a compliment to them or does any one mean to say, that they are not men or that they are to be excepted and exempted from the reasons and the rules, which obtain and take place in the case of all the rest of mankind?

One of the long robe may perhaps demand the exact time when these rights begin in rising and growing states to take place, and how many years, months and days a colony must first be settled. I may venture to promise to resolve such an one, when he shall tell me in how many years, months and days an oaken plant grows to be an oaken tree, or a boy becomes a man; which seem to be two much easier questions. The boundaries are seldom nicely distinguishable, where nature proceeds with an even and constant hand. But it is not difficult to answer that the event has already taken place, when near two millions of people are in full and peaceable possession of such a country as is occupied by our North-American colonies.

It may likewise be asked, whether these laws are applicable to all cases of private property between man and man. But the full resolution of this question might demand a Spanish casuist or a book as big as a volume of our statutes at large. Any man may for me, amuse himself with trying the titles of nations to the territories and possessions, which they fill, enjoy and inhabit, as he would do those between man and man, about a house and garden, and should the process in the first case last as long in proportion, as one does in the latter before some Courts of Justice in Europe, the defendants need not perhaps desire a longer or surer possession.

But may not these principles go too far, if carried to the extent? That is indeed a very serious question and perhaps well worthy of consideration. Our colonies are content that we should at our pleasure regulate their trade, provided that what we do is bona fide, really, truly and sincerely for that purpose and that only; but they deny that we shall tax them. They assent and agree to the first; but they absolutely refuse the last. These two different points do likewise not stand on the same foundation; they have to the one, submitted ever since their origin; it has been corroborated by their perpetual and constant consent and acquiescence; the other is a novelty, against which they have from its first attempt, most strongly protested and acted. Why cannot we therefore content us with the line drawn by themselves and with the present establishment, from which we receive such prodigious benefit and advantage, now arising, and yearly increasing? But may not they in time extend their objections to this also? The course of things and the flux of years will certainly produce very many things more extraordinary than that. All the whole of our colonies must no doubt one day without force or violence fall off from the parent state, like ripe fruit in the maturity of time. The earth itself having had a beginning, cannot but decay likewise, pass away and have an end. But why should we be over curious about objects perhaps very far remote, and disturb ourselves about a futurity which does not affect us, and the distance of which we don't know. Why should we shake the fruit unripe from the tree, because it will of course drop off, when it shall be ripe. Every time has its own circumstances, according to which the events of it must be provided for, when they happen. That cannot now be done. New and unreasonable demands, injustice, oppression, violence on our parts, will forward and hasten these events even before their time; let us withhold our hands from these things; we have never yet had reason to boast ourselves of such expedients, nor, let me add, ever to repent us of the contrary conduct.

There are no doubt in all governments many, most important points unsettled and undetermined; such in particular as relate to the limits between the power of the Sovereign and the obedience of the subject. This must always be the case between Kings and their People, principal States and their dependencies, Mother Countries and their Colonies. It is very much the part of every prudent ruler, whether the First Minister of a Prince or any other, to avoid with the utmost care and solicitude all measures, which may possibly bring any such critical circumstances into public debate and dispute. It is always a bad sign when such contests arise; they cannot do so without the disorder of the whole, but they are to the Sovereign in particular, ever dangerous and often fatal. They may perhaps be compared to gunpowder, than whose grain nothing is more harmless, while it is at rest; but let it be put into action and it will make the wildest ravages all around, or overthrow the strongest bulwarks and fortifications.

To how many of these questions did our Charles the First give in his time rise or occasion, and how dearly did he abide it! How many points of this sort are undetermined between Great-Britain and Ireland, which are now to our mutual happiness, intirely dormant, but which started and pursued with obstinacy and eagerness, might make one or both of the islands run with blood. They need perhaps be no

[58]

further looked for, than certain doctrines formerly advanced by Mr. Molyneux on the one hand, and the law of Poinings on the other.[1] But it has pleased Providence to shelter us hitherto from this mischief. It is not now perhaps many months, since we did not want an opportunity to have engaged in one such. The alterations of a late bill from that country were only accidental. But does any one doubt, whether some forward man might not have been found, who would on occasion have furnished reasons better or worse to maintain the right of making them. But how much more prudent was our conduct? If peace and harmony are then so beneficial and desirable between Great-Britain and Ireland, and the measures producing or insuring them good, upright and wise; why do these things so alter their nature, when they are applied to America?

The present accursed question between us and our colonies, how long was it unknown or unthought of! Who heard of it from the first rise of these settlements, until a few years ago; that a fatal attempt forced it into notice and importance? But it is now already setting at work fleets and armies; it threatens the confusion and perhaps the destructon of both countries and but too probable of one of them; although God only knows whether the calamity will fall on that of the two, which many men may now imagine and believe to be the most in danger.

This point is not alone; there are other questions of the same sort, concerning which no man now disturbs himself; but which stirred and started by new demands or any other means, might in like manner band against one another Great Britain and its colonies. Princes and states never do better, than when their claims are not fathomed, nor if I may use the expression, the bottom of them not over curiously founded and examined. The terms of municipal laws usually favour the Sovereign, they are often framed or drawn by his creatures and dependents; the law of nature is more commonly in support of the people and the public; it is the production of him who sees with an equal eye, Prince and subject, high and low, European and American. God forbid, that two such parts of the British empire, as the mother country and her colonies should in our times divide and contend against another on the sanction of these two different laws, which ought in every state to be constantly blended and united, and which can never without its utter disorder and confusion be made to strike and clash against each other. Whenever that shall happen, let us be assured, that we are running upon a rock, whereon we cannot but make shipwreck.

I have hitherto on the law of nature and the common rights of humanity considered the claim of the Americans, not to be here in England taxed by us, against their own will and consent. It rests firmly on that foundation; but I don't mean to say that it rests on that only. Could this be removed, there would yet remain another on which it would nevertheless stand sure and unshaken; I mean that of the special constitution of Great Britain, which does herein most justly and wisely coincide with the general constitution of humanity, and require that the property of no man living under its protection, should without his consent by himself or representative, be taken from him, or according to the language of the times, that representation should go along with taxation.

But this argument has particularly been in the hands of the first men of our times. They have set it in its full light, and their authority has recommended it to the attention of their country. It is well known and well understood, and I am persuaded that it is unanswerable. But I bear more respect to both these persons and to the public, than to go over it again so much to its disadvantage. I will therefore beg leave only to assume this reason, and to join it to my former; when the right of the Americans will stand on this double foundation, of the general law of nature and of the particular constitution of Great Britain.

However it has been said, that the Americans are in our Parliaments virtually represented. How that should be when they are not really so, I shall leave to be explained by those who advance it. But God forbid, that the condition of British subjects should ever be such, as for a whole people of them to be in danger of being stripped of all their properties, only by the logick of such an unmeaning word or distinction, as that is.

But what are the exact bounds and limits of real representation? I will excuse myself from entering into that question. But will an American scruple to say; that if in any future time things should here at home be from their present state so far changed, and the constitution of Great Britain so lost, that a great majority of its representatives shall be named by a handful of needy men; that they shall most evidently and most notoriously be both chosen by a corrupt and undue influence, and be afterwards guided and governed by the same; will he not say, that it may at that distant day better become such a mock representative to prove their own right of taxing Britain, than to pretend to tax America?

So much for consent and representation. But there is another ground, whereon the Americans likewise rely, which is that of their own provincial charters. I shall leave the particulars of this subject to themselves, who are best acquainted with them. However, I will in general say, that their charters are no doubt in aid and assistance of the two sanctions before mentioned, very properly brought for the shortening and silencing of disputes and debates, by the producing the special authority of government. But they must be interpreted by those before mentioned, and consistently with them. They cannot be construed so as to overturn the others. It would be the most down-right absurdity and the most direct contradiction in itself, to talk of a Grant, or Patent, or Charter of rights given to any one, to take away all the rights he had in the world, to confer on him the privilege of having nothing of his own now, nor of being able to acquire any such thing in time to come, neither he himself or his descendants after him. Every thing of this kind must be understood so as to coincide with the original, inherent rights of any single person or community, whether as men or as Britons.

Charters would without doubt be for some purposes very effectual, if every thing would take place as it is written on a paper or parchment. Suppose a parcel of miserable people starved out of their native country, or persecuted and prosecuted there, because they don't believe just what some other men do or pretend to do; that they cannot leave their homes without the consent of their persecutors; that they must take with them a piece of parchment, did their tyrants write thereon, that their descendants shall go upon all fours, shall be born with hoofs instead of hands, and with instinct instead of reason and the faculty of speech, and that these things would so happen; this might, to be sure, give very notable powers over them; they might then be yoked as horned cattle, saddled and bridled as horses or fleeced and sheared as sheep; the difference in the species would naturally and necessarily effect this; but nothing of all this will come to pass. This future offspring will notwithstanding be born with the nature, the qualities and the talents, and consequently with the claims, the rights and privileges of men. But suppose these strange terms to be on account of the absurdity of them dropped, but that there are instead, really entered on the parchment or charter such an arbitrary superiority, such despotic and uncontrolable powers and perogatives over these poor people and their posterity, as are only fitting, suitable and analogous to the former circumstances, will this in right or in reason be a whit more valid than the other, or where is the sense or justice in demanding such enormous consequences, when we are forbidden the natural premises, from which alone they can follow? Suppose that it was on a paper or parchment written in fair characters; that the horses and other cattle of the New Forest in Hampshire, should have to them and their heirs for ever, the said Forest, and it might be added, to hold in free soccage of the manor of East-Greenwich; suppose that dents were made, in the paper or parchment, and a stamp put upon it, and that it was signed, sealed and delivered, as an act and deed; what would be the effect? It will be answered that it would be a thing to laugh at; for how should brute beasts take property, who have neither understanding or capacity, or any means for that purpose; that it would be contrary to nature for them so to do. But let me demand in my turn, where is the difference in the effect, whether it is written that beasts shall become men, or that men shall become beasts; that a number of beasts shall be able to take and hold property, or that a community of men shall not? The one is just as contrary to nature as the other. It might indeed be a happy day for despotism, could such things be done; but they are beyond its strength. The great author of the world has for transcendent purposes of his unfathomable wisdom placed in the hearts of men, pride, ambition, avarice and self-interest; but he has at the same time been pleased with his most benevolent hand, and by the laws of nature and the course of things, to set bounds to the power of these passions, which they can pass no more, than the sea can exceed its shores.

So much for charters in general. However I will likewise say something concerning one particular charter, before I leave the subject. When the havock among charters happened in England a short time before the revolution, and which contributed not a little to produce that event, America was not spared. About the year sixteen hundred eighty four a quo warranto was on that head issued against Massachusetts Bay. Some of the colonies did on the like occasion give way and throw themselves on the pleasure of the King. Massachusetts Bay refused to do this. They were ex parte, and for non appearance, condemned and their charter shared the same fate as that of the city of London and so many others. Four years afterwards the revolution happened. As soon as ever the news of it arrived at Boston the colony declared in favour of it. They took possession of King James's Governor and of the rest of his creatures and sent them all home to England. But then it will perhaps be said, they recovered in return their charter. Is there almost faith in man to believe otherwise? Other colonies fared well enough, who had not withstood the will of the King, and whose charters had not been vacated in the court of justice. They did themselves put them again in execution and no words were made. Our own charters here at home were likewise returned. The colony of Massachusetts Bay went on that account first into the convention Parliament; but there they could not get through. It is well known that our Parliaments are not usually dissolved or prorogued, while any business is depending, which there is an inclination to pass. They had then nothing left but to beg and pray of the King's ministers. But is it credible that they could not procure the restoration of their charter, of these revolution ministers, of these makers and unmakers of Kings, who had so lately been on the same bottom with them, and in whose cause the colony had so readily declared itself, but who had now obtained their own ends? Tired out therefore with delays and not being sure of the worst that might happen, they were obliged in the end to accept of a new charter, mutilated and castrated of many of the most important and essential privileges of the old. I shall take notice of no other particulars, than that, before they chose annually their own Governor, Deputy Governor, and Secretary. These were from this time to be appointed during pleasure, by the King. Of what extreme consequence the change in the nomination of these their three chief officers has proved to them, no man at all acquainted with the name of Massachusetts Bay can be so ignorant of their history, as not to be informed and sensible. Hence their differences with their own Governors there, and with our ministers at home. Hence their present military Governor and the armies and fleets now gone, or going against them. Hence the strange provision, said to be in agitation, that their blood may not be liable to be answered for there. They would otherwise, in all appearance, be at this moment on these subjects in the same situation, as their neighbours of Connecticut and Rhode Island, with whose charters their own agreed, until they lost it by their resistance and opposition to the will of the two last Stuarts; when the others saved theirs by giving way. I shall leave my readers to judge, whether it was the good or the evil contained in this poor piece of parchment, which thus united against it, *Stuart* Kings and *revolution* ministers. But this charter must certainly have been granted under an evil planet, if what some people say be true; that it is now again under displeasure at home, and on the brink of being once more reversed and altered. But that event has not, at the writing of this, happened. I am therefore perfectly persuaded, that should any thing of that kind take place, it will on the contrary be the restoration of those its former privileges and powers, which was so unreasonably and so unjustly denied at the revolution. But let any one consider this history of a charter, and then reflect, whether mankind have not reason to bless themselves, that they have some rights of a higher nature than charters, superior to them and independent of them.

But are not we the parent country? That is a very respectable word, but so likewise is the relation of it mutual. It has always hitherto had its full weight with our colonies of North America, and will probably continue to have, if we can content ourselves with any tolerably reasonable sense and use of it. But was every master and mistress of a family resident there, the immediate son and daughter of a father and mother living now at this time in England; yet they being gone from us and having established themselves, and got families of their own, and having acquired a large territory, we could by no means even as true and real parents, make out any claim having such consequences, as that which we advance. However the fact is very different; they left us in former times a part of the public, as well as others; they are since become hardly our cousin's cousins, and no man knows how far we might mount towards Adam or Noah to settle the real relation between us. But was their history told, as it deserves: How they have made these their great establishments at their own charge, and with almost no expence of ours: How we have ever had the total command of the produce of that immense country, so as to regulate the commerce and exportation of it merely according to our own advantage and convenience; that this is grown to be an object of perhaps no less than four millions sterling a year, all turned towards our profit; could the extreme benefits be all set forth, which we have by these means received, from the first foundation of these colonies to this time, and the cheerfulness, fidelity and loyalty wherewith they have submitted to this; and sincere and warm friendship and affection, which they have ever born us, while we kept ourselves within these bounds; the assistance which we have received from them in war, as well as the profits in peace; could all these circumstances be, with very many others favourable to them, told and represented together, and in their full light, the story itself would bid fair to make these harsh and unmerited acts of Parliament drop out of our hands, if we held them at the time. However at least don't let us extend a figurative and metaphorical saying, to the divesting of all their properties, near upon two millions of people, and make it at the same time a warrant for ourselves to hold towards them an unjust, rapacious and unnatural conduct, directly contrary to that of real parents towards their children, and totally inconsistent with the expression, whereon we would ground our pretensions.

But how do these projectors and promotors of taxes and taxing, hold concerning Ireland? Do they reckon *that* to be likewise within the jurisdiction of their ways and means, and in the same predicament with America? Adventurers went formerly from hence, others succeeded, more followed, until they were masters of the island. It might be added, that this was done with a much greater expence of the blood and the treasure of this country, than our settlements in America ever cost us. The Representative Body of Ireland is called a Parliament; that of America, an Assembly. The term of kingdom obtains in one country, and that of colony in other. Is there any charm in the sound of these words, which makes a difference? or would the author of the Stamp Act have gone thither also, had the people of America shewn a facility to his first attempts with them, and if the Parliament of Ireland had ever made difficulties to his future demands there? Does any one imagine that learned, or other arguments would have been wanting to maintain the rectitude of the one measure, any more than of the other?

But is there any medium? Must not we either rigorously enforce obedience from our colonies, or at once generously declare them free and independent of all allegiance to the crown of Great-Britain? To which I answer, if there is a medium between Great-Britain and Ireland, why may there not be also between Great-Britain and North America. The claims of the colonies are not higher than those of Ireland. Certain rules of mutual respect preserved between us and that neighbouring part of the King's dominions, keep us on the best and happiest terms together, terms of perpetual and almost unspeakable profit and advantage to England. Does this overturn the constitution of Great Britain, or weaken the dependency on its crown, as some language has been? Why should not then forbearance, moderation and regard towards that, a little more distant portion of our country, produce in one case effects consonant and answerable to what the like causes do in the other. It is most evident and may in general be depended on, that no evil consequences can happen from any condition or situation between Great Britain and her colonies, which does actually and advantageously obtain between Great Britain and Ireland. How was it there twenty years ago, before the first or the last of these taxes were either of them thought of? All was then peace, calm and content. The repealing the first of them, the Stamp Act, did that do any mischief? Not unless the reconciling, uniting and connecting again all the parts of our government be such. There was hardly any where to be found a man, but who was pleased and happy in the measure; except a minister or two at home, who lost their power and their places on the occasion, and except a few sycophants abroad, who hoped to recommend themselves, by traducing and disturbing those, to whom they owed assistance and protection, and who desired to fish in troubles, which they themselves contributed greatly to create. What evil star reigns then at this period, that these blessings cannot now take place, as they formerly did?

I have on this subject no mind to play with the name of Ireland. I presume to introduce on the scene, and to couple, as it were, with America, that country only, in order to expose the more plainly, by the instance of the one, some notions advanced concerning the other, and at the same time to the utmost of my small power, to recommend, inculcate, and enforce that cautious, considerate, brotherly and affectionate conduct towards each, which I am sure that they both of them most exceedingly well deserve, whether of the government, or of the people of England.

It is sometimes made a claim on the Americans, that we incurred on their account a great expence in the late war. On whose account have we not since the Revolution incurred a great expence? Our whole history from that time to this, is little else, but a scene of prodigality in the service of different People, or Princes, for which no man can give any good reason. However, I answer on this occasion with the fact. We did not engage in the late war at the request of the Americans, nor upon any desire or inclination of theirs. The language, at the same time was on the contrary, that the less concerned the inhabitants of our colonies appeared to be about the incroachments of the French, the more reason we had to be jealous on the subject. I believe, that I may, in support of what I am saying, venture to appeal to those, who are the best acquainted with that period. Had it been otherwise, we should no doubt have heard enough of it. Substantial reasons might be given, that the Americans judged better in the case, than we. There may be ground for us to condemn ourselves, for not having consulted them more on the subject, than we did, before that we were so hasty to take up the hatchet. However, there is not the least pretence for charging to their account the consequences of a war, which we undertook without any instance and application from them, and entirely of our own motion.

But the honour of Government is concerned. That is certainly an unaccountable reasoning, though not perhaps very uncommon; that if government or in plain English, the minister and those about him, do a thing which shall be wished to be undone, they are therefore to proceed in the same road and do many more such, until at length the case may perhaps be beyond redress. Surely the more credit is lost the deeper that people are plunged into mischief. The welfare and happiness of five or six millions of mankind, or more, is a prodigious object. Whoever puts himself at the helm of our state, undertakes in a manner for that. We are all mortal and fallible. One in such a situation had need to march with the unmost caution, circumspection and foresight; should he make an unlucky step, it is his highest duty to endeavour instantly to retreat and retrieve it. A late minister repealed an act similar to the one in question, and that statesman well knew what to do and what to avoid. In the present case a gulph is before us, which will not admit many steps forward, but that the government and the public will both go headlong.

But their outrages. I presume these to be an object of discourse, as well as any other subject; how can they otherwise be discussed and considered? However I shall without declaring any opinion of my own take them up only in the light, as they may appear to an American. He will certainly say, that these receive their complexion from the claim of the colonies not to be taxed by us, and accordingly as that shall be grounded or not. If that is not well founded, that then their opposition is unlawful, whether only concert and combination or force and violence. That the latter indeed may be productive of more mischief than the former, but that they are on such a supposition both of them entirely unwarrantable. I would in this case willingly speak freely but without offence; he would therefore certainly add, that should the Americans on the other hand have a real right not to be so taxed, they are undoubtedly intitled likewise to the necessary means of using and enjoying that right. That this is a rule of the law of nature as well as of the law of the land, or rather that the latter has only borrowed it from the former. I speak with great submission; but he would without doubt proceed, that the means used on this occasion were absolutely those necessary ones and no other; that an object was artfully or judiciously chosen for this tax, which is so constant a part of diet or luxury, that it was totally impossible to prevent the tax from taking place, without hindering the commodity itself from being introduced; that therefore the Americans must absolutely do that, or lose their right; that the endeavouring to do it by a general concert and agreement would have been no better than building a city out of the sands of the sea; that thereupon the town of Boston did at a sort of public meeting, use every instance and application possible, both with the Captains of the tea ships and with the Governor, that the tea might be returned, untouched and undamaged as it came; that this would secure their right, and they desired no more; that this was absolutely refused; that there was thereupon no expedient left for the preserving their right but destroying the tea; that this was without any express authority of the town, done by private people, but in all appearance with the general inclination and with the least mischief and damage done possible; that there was some tea spilt, but no blood; that this refers the whole to the first and original question of the right; that the Americans make thereon the same claim, as the people of Scotland would have in an essential circumstance of the union; or those of Ireland, should the line observed between them and Great Britain be passed in any point, which would affect their whole interest and welfare, as a nation; that in the other colonies the Governors and Captains consented to the sending back the tea or shutting it up in such a manner as never to be sold or dispersed; that these did not therefore in their cases make immediate force necessary, but that their act was in effect the same and stands on the same ground. That there is nothing malignant in the whole matter, nothing but a determined desire to support this their great and necessary right. This is no doubt the American idea, as appears by many proofs and papers from that side of the water. I shall myself presume to speak no opinion in the case, much less will I call again on the names of our ancestors, in support of this pretension. But should it be observed, that it ends in a question, which concerns the bounds and limits of government; I cannot on the occasion but repeat and enforce, by this example, the remark before made, of how dangerous and deadly a nature the disputes and contests are, which lead thither.

So much for the rectitude of taxing the Americans! But I may be told that I have not yet touched the true point, that I have been doing little more, than a man who rides post out of his road. That statesmen and politicians do indeed sometimes talk of the right and the wrong, of the justice and injustice of measures; but that this is all only ostensible reasoning, while there may be at the bottom, nothing which they care less about. That the great do every where bear hard on the little, the strong on the weak. That the hawk hunts the partridge, the lion the wolf, and the wolf the lamb; that powerful princes and states oppress the helpless, and the high and the rich those beneath them; that this is the course of the world, and the chapter of the law of nature, which we intend to consult and to follow; that we want money at home; that our debts are very heavy, and our resources but too near an end; that we have yet fleets and armies, and are determined to bend to our will our colonies of America, and to make them subservient to our wants and occasions; that this is at the bottom, and that all my casuistry may in the mean time serve the purposes of grocers and pastry cooks; that if people must write about matters of state, they ought to do it like men. Very well; I join issue hereon, don't let us go too fast; one thing at a time.

I answer that you cannot force them, nor is there any appearance that you can. The number of free people in these colonies is reckoned at towards two millions. The common calculation is of one sensible or fighting man in five persons, and this is supposed to be rather under than over the truth. This will give us at least between three and four hundred thousand fighting men on the number before mentioned. Mr. *Rome* tells us indeed, in some letters, &c. lately published in opposition to the colonies; "that there is hardly any thing more common, than to hear them boast of particular colonies that can raise on a short notice a hundred thousand fighting men."[2] However to have nothing to do with these exaggerations, and to take only the number before mentioned; what expectation can there be of sending from hence an army fit to subdue that continent? A country not defended indeed on the side of the sea, with forts and castles built by men, but extremely strong within, by the natural fortifications of forests and of rivers.

But can they arm so many? In any country very greatly taxed, and much more so than its inhabitants would willingly bear with, it is not impossible, consistently with such a state of things, to arm the whole body of the people. These might be apt to count noses and to consider, who were the stronger, they themselves, or the tax gatherers, and the Red-coats, or White-coats, or Black coats, or any other, who support them. The difficulty would be yet greater, were there any further dissatisfaction. But these are all democratical governments, where the power is in the hands of the people, and where there is not the least difficulty, or jealousy about putting arms into the hands of every man in the country.

But are they united among themselves? In the cause of not being taxed by us, it is well understood, how much they are so. All accounts and reports from thence, of all men, and of all parties, run in that stile, and concur in that circumstance. It was so experienced, to a very great degree, concerning the Stamps, and has now been found the same, on the occasion of the Tea. Their conduct has, in the case, been every where alike, and correspondent. The Tea, is either returned, without being landed, or received, without being suffered to be sold, at New-York, at Pennsylvania, at Carolina, at all the places to which it was sent. We reckon entirely without our host, if we don't expect to have to do with a union of that continent, or depend on any measures insufficient to subdue the whole.

But, let me ask; how can we expect otherwise? They are not unacquainted with the history of the mother-country. They know the weight of the taxing hand here. They have heard of our debt, of one hundred and forty millions of pounds sterling, incurred since the Revolution, besides other hundreds of millions spent currently within the same period. The time to come is to be judged of by the time past. Will our brethren of America expect, that this hand should be lighter on them, at a distance, or that our breasts will feel more for them than for ourselves? Let an Englishman make the case his own, and question himself; what he should think, were he of that country, and his whole fortune and concerns there. Would not he believe his all, to be at stake upon the cast? Does any one in America, or in England, imagine, that all these disputes and feuds are only at the bottom, about a duty of three pence upon a pound of tea? How can then any candid man doubt, whether there will be a general union and concurrence on the subject, or wonder if there is so?

They are said to have already Committees of Correspondence, and no doubt necessity will teach them other means of moving and acting together. Every thing is done there by choice and election; they will probably have at their head, as capable and as wise men, as are to be found among them. The power and influence of Governors, and other civil officers appointed from hence, must on an open rupture have an end. Our authority would perhaps then extend little further, than where it was enforced by our own troops.

But what are an untrained and undisciplined multitude? Could not an experienced officer, with a few regular regiments, do what he would in America? I answer, that a different story may be told. In the war before the last, our measures directed at home, were every where unsuccessful. The plains of Flanders were fatten'd with some of the best blood of Britain, and of Ireland. Our Government was shaken almost to the foundation, by a rebellion contemptible in its beginning. Were we more fortunate in our attempt by sea against Pondicherry, or that afterwards against Port l'Orient? But the people of New England, maintained at that time, the honour of our arms. It is well known, that they carried on, with their own counsels, and with their own soldiery, and under the command of one of their own planters, against Cape Breton and Louisbourg, an expedition, the event of which need not now be told. We did not begin in a much better manner the last war. I am unwilling to call to mind our first campaigns in Germany, our situation and treaty of Closter Seven, the fate of Minorca, or the histories of Bradock, and Abercrombie. But who were at that time the first to stem the tide of our ill fortune? Was not it an American militia, who, commanded by Sir William Johnson, a gentleman at that time of the country, met, fought, and beat the French and Indians, under Monsieur Dieskau, and made prisoner their commander? But what wonders were afterwards done by our people properly conducted and directed? It is very true, and I am sure, that I have no inclination to depreciate them. But neither did those of America, want their share therein. However, the courage of our countrymen was never yet questioned; but may they always unite, and employ it against our common enemies, and never be encamped, or embattled against one another, either in America, or any where else.

But we are masters at sea, and where ever our ships can come, we may do, whatever a fleet can. Very true; but it cannot sail all over North America. It is said, that Marshal Saxe had, before the declaraton of the last war but one, and at the time of our army being in Germany, conceived a design to have landed on our coast, with ten thousand men, and to have tried the fortune of a brisk march to London. He did not find this so easy to execute, as he thought for. He was most happily disappointed. But there was an object. No one can tell the consequence, had he succeeded. The present is a very different matter. No immediate impression upon the town of Boston, nor possession taken of it, by means of a fleet, nor the same circumstance

[71]

with regard to any other towns of America, liable thereto, by their situation, will carry the command of that whole continent, or force it to submit to measures so universally against their bent and inclination.

It may, however, be said, that this is not the plan. The charter of the town of Boston is to be changed, and their trade suspended, and other measures of the very strongest sort to be enforced against them. The moving mountain is, according to the imagination of Dr. Swift, to hang over them, and the sun not to shine, nor the rain, or the dew to fall on them, until they are brought to submission, and made, to the rest of America, an example, of the danger of refractoriness and disobedience, to the mother country; all which we think may, and will, with time be compassed and accomplished.

This is indeed, as to the question of force, the true point of the matter; I mean, *which* will at last, and at the end of a long trial, get the better; but I add, that this will probably not be Great Britain. Here I must again crave leave to write with freedom. If it is the first wisdom of a private man, to know himself; so must it likewise be that of a State, to consider in all its measures its own condition and situation. The searching into our circumstances neither makes or mars them. But what must be our case, should we have any wound or mischief, and that it might not be probed or examined? We must ever suppose our adversaries to be informed, and not by shutting our own eyes, pretend to blind other people. I shall therefore, without scruple inquire into the state of the public, as far as it concerns my subject.

The condition of the great staple manufactures of our country is well known. Those of the linen and the silk are in the greatest distress, and the woollen and linen are now publickly banded and contending against one another. One part of our people is starving at home on the alms of their parishes, and another running abroad to this very country, that we are contending with. The produce of North America, used to be sent yearly to Britain, is reckoned at about four millions sterling; the manufactures of Britain and other commodities returned from hence, at nearly the same sum; the debts due from people in America to the British merchants here, at about six millions, or a year and a half of that commerce. I say, the time past must be our guide with respect to that to come. Supposing therefore the Americans to act in this case, as they did in that of the stamp act; we shall then have yearly until the final settlement of this affair, manufactures to the value of four millions sterling, left and heaped on the hands of our merchants and master manufacturers, or we shall have workmen and poor people put out of employ, and turned adrift in that proportion. There will likewise be drawn from our home consumption and out of our general trade and traffick, North American commodities to the same value, and debts will, to the immense sum above mentioned, be with-held from private people here. This was the train of things begun before, and we must look for the like again. What effects these things will produce, considering the present state of our trade, manufactures, and manufacturers, the condition of our poor at home, and the numbers of our people running abroad, it don't want many words to explain and set forth. They were before very severely felt, for the time that they lasted, and it is apprehended, that the present situation of the public is yet more liable to the impression. These are some of the difficulties and distresses which we are, for the sake of a trial of skill with our colonies, going to bring on ourselves, and which must be perpetually magnifying and increasing, as long as the unnatural contest shall continue.

To these a former administration gave way; but it is to be supposed, that the present has, by returning to the shock, resolved to be more callous on the occasion, and to leave the Americans, the merchants, and the manufacturers to settle among themselves their matters, as they may. Our people will indeed be less clamorous about the ears of their betters, if they shall all run and emigrate out of the kingdom. But there is a circumstance not yet mentioned, which will bid fair to go further, and which may but too probably involve in one common confusion, the nation, the government, and the administration itself. I mean the danger of a disorder or failure of the public revenue, the difficulty or impossibility to pay the interest of the debt, the navy, the army, the civil list, and our other expences; if the present contention shall proceed, and continue.

I desire in explanation of this, to consider our present income, our out goings and our resources. I will not enter into any detail thereon; the particulars in gross, will be sufficient for the purpose before us. I will however, in order to be the better understood, premise something about the revenue in general. It may be divided into two parts, the one of taxes laid in perpetuity, the other of such as are granted by the year and for the year. The first part consists of all our taxes in general whatsoever, except the land-tax, and the annual malt tax; the latter consists of these two only. Perpetual taxes are now, in the language of Europe, often expressed by the name of funds, as affording a fixed and settled foundation for any special use, and particularly for that of borrowing money. It was to answer the interest of our debts, that our own funds were established, and they are now pledged for that purpose. These of ours have been chiefly thrown into three great common ones, called the general, the aggregate, and the South Sea funds. These are sometimes, with all other funds or perpetual taxes whatsoever, destined and settled for the discharge of the interest of our debt, comprehended and united together in discourse, and called the Sinking Fund; although there is in reality no one particular Fund of that name, any more than there is such a piece of money as a pound sterling, or a French livre. The Civil List is placed on the same Funds, as the interest of the Public Debt. What remains annually of the whole collection of those Funds, after the satisfying these two incumbrances is, what is meant by the surplus of the Sinking Fund. I have thought proper to preface these few things, that my own language may, at least, be understood, in what little I shall say on the subject.

The interest of our debt amounts to near upon five millions a year; all annuities for lives or years, every thing redeemable or irredeemable included. The civil list is eight hundred thousand pounds a year. The surplus of the sinking fund is changing and uncertain, that being composed of very many variable parts. It is impossible to fix it, but I will at an average, for the sake of round numbers, suppose it to be two millions and more—about as much more as will answer to what the interest of the debt may want of five millions. We shall then have about seven millions three quarters, for the produce of our perpetual taxes and funds. Our annual taxes remain then only to be considered, which are easily reckoned; the land tax granted for a million and an half at three shillings in the pound, as it now is; the malt tax always granted at three quarters of a million. These sums put together give us about ten millions of pounds sterling, being our present annual national income, and likewise our present annual national expence; including what may at times be paid towards the discharge of the public debt, and besides the collection, which is not to my present purpose. Should any one be of opinion, that the surplus of the sinking fund is either over charged or undercharged, he has my consent to make such addition to it, or subtraction from it, as he shall please. Neither the one or the other will affect the argument I am upon. Our receipts and disbursements will in either case go hand in hand. I shall therefore without any more nice disquisition, take these at the medium of about ten millions sterling each.

[74]

So much for our income and our expences. Let us next consider our resources; I mean what resources we may be supposed to have in our power, without creating any new debt. The first to occur will be the surplus of the sinking fund. We apply of course to this, on almost all occasions. We are by law obliged to discharge regularly the interest of our debt; but whatever we may be in prudence and a proper care of ourselves and of those after us, we are by no contract or engagement, bound to do more, or to pay off any part of the principal of it. This surplus is therefore one resource; but it is such no otherwise, or further, than it can be spared from our current expences, towards which it is commonly, in whole or in part, taken. We can for our present purpose reckon only on so much of it, as might otherwise be employed towards lessening the capital of our debt. We have now had twelve years of peace, in which time I reckon, that we have discharged about eight millions of that capital. This will therefore at an average give us by the year two thirds of a million, or something more than six hundred thousand pounds. This is what we may look to for one of our resources. But we have likewise another, which is the land tax. That is now at three shillings in the pound, but it is sometimes at four. We may therefore count, in case of exigency, on one shilling more, that is on half a million. These two sums amount together, to about one million one hundred thousand pounds. These are our resources, and without borrowing, these are all.

Let us next turn in our thoughts, whether these eleven hundred thousand pounds a year, being a little more than a tenth part of our present income, are likely to be sufficient for this American occasion. Fleets and armies, ships of war and regiments are the means, the tip staves and the constables, which are to execute the measures in question. A million goes but a very little way with us in such articles. This business must in it include a supposition, that all our ancient colonies on that continent, may, in the progress of it, be combined and united in one common association, interest and defence. There can be no reasonable hopes of success, nothing but mortification and disappointment directly in view by proceeding on any plan, which does not comprehend the probability of that circumstance. What a field is then here opened? Is our million or eleven hundred thousand pounds to furnish us there likewise? However, these things concern only our expences. Let us consider the other side of our situation; how much our income is at the same time, likely to be lessened. Four millions sterling yearly of the produce of America; as many of the merchandize of Great Britain; more of debts here at home withheld and kept back from our duties, our customs and our excise. What an operation on the revenue! Is our million one hundred thousand pounds to supply all this besides? How is it possible either on the one hand, that a person having these circumstances before his eyes, should set on foot the present measures against our colonies; or on the other, that any one having capacity or understanding to be at the head of the government and administration of a great kingdom, should so overlook them? This seems to be like not discerning the sun at noon-day, or the moon and the stars by night.

There is from the general condition of our country, but too much reason to apprehend, that the public revenue is, without these additional causes, sinking and decreasing. This could not but add greatly to our difficulties in the situation before described. However it is to be hoped, that this is only surmise and opinion. I shall not take it into the present account; but most assuredly any one at the head of our affairs ought not to forget it in his, if it is true.

But it may be said, that we will in the supposed exigency, borrow, as our predecessors have done before us. I answer, that this may very probably be then out of our power. I will not go upon a general discussion, whether we should enter into another war, with the same credit we have hitherto had; although we may have but too much reason to reflect on that subject. But the consideration properly before us, is, what *would* be the state of our credit, under a revolt and separation of our settlements in America, that great and essential source of our riches and revenue? Loans and money advanced to us, have as yet been reckoned equally secure, there has been no doubt made of the regular payment of the interest, nor in consequence, of a public market for the principal, whether we should ourselves happen to be more or less successful, on any occasion wherein we were at the time concerned, and for which they were borrowed. They were as safe under the defeats and disappointments of the war before, as upon the victories and conquests of the last. But things could not in this case but be much changed. The security of millions lent, must depend upon the future chance and fortune of war. It might be made a doubt, what fruits would for some years to come be received, from provinces mangled and mutilated in a severe contest, decided to their disadvantage, should these at last return to us again; but no one could overlook, what must be the case should the event terminate against us, and end, after an expence of much treasure and blood, in so fatal and inestimable a loss on our side, as that of these colonies would be. However, no Man knows, whether this affair might run into a very long trial. A general breach and defection of these colonies, would cut the sinews of our power. We could not, most probably, in such a situation, long continue to provide and pay the interest of our most enormous debt already incurred and subsisting. It need not be repeated, that it is the assistance received from their commerce and produce, which enables us now to do it. Deprived of that, it will be but to little purpose for us to be inventing new Funds at home. We have enow of them already. More would only run foul of one another. We may, in that day, without the operations of a war in America, without the sending or supplying fleets or armies, at a distance, without creating new debts, new Funds and new taxes, have, at our own homes, from our actual situation, business on our hands, but too sufficient to engage and employ us.

But it may be asked, what will be the consequence should we from these causes, become unable to pay the interest of our present debt. I will be bold to say, that there is no man living wise enough to answer that question in its extent. Experience teaches men; but there is no preceding history or tradition, of any state or nation whatsoever, which can throw sufficient light on that proposition. There never was before in the world, such a debt contracted, or subsisting, as the British. Letters and books are older than money, I mean than gold and silver commonly current, and having their weight known by a stamp. But there is no occasion to ransack ancient times on this subject. The discovery of Mexico and Peru, and the possession of them by the Spaniards is the era from whence we are to date the beginning of the present plenty in Europe, of these two precious metals, which command often individuals, and sometimes commonwealths and kingdoms. The art of Funding was formerly very confined. It is a succession of English administrations, which has carried it to an extent never before known among men. It is a new experiment in a state. There is no example of it in the annals of mankind. We are at a loss where to look for the consequences of such an unprecedented and unheard of deficiency, or bankruptcy, as this would prove. However, we cannot but have before our eyes, disorder, anarchy, and confusion; the monied interest of the nation banded against the landed, and the landed against the monied; rich monied men brought to beggary, and the land drained of the utmost farthing which can be forced from it; every one catching, rending and providing for the present moment; our manufactures and commerce at a stand; the middling people emigrating out of our country, and the poor in famine, or in sedition; foreigners pressing for their demands, and the Dutch particularly in rage, and almost in madness for their countless millions, trusted and hazarded in our country; perhaps at the same time our navy unmanned, and our army in mutiny for want of pay. Who can withal tell the end; for the debt, the burthen, and the demand will ever remain? There was a time, when the Romans had formerly withdrawn themselves from this island, that the possessions became here, through the weakness and helplessness of those remaining, the prize and the prey of all plunderers, pirates, robbers, and conquerors, who came and seized upon them; until that these people themselves, the Danes, the Saxons, and the Normans replenished and strengthened again the country. Whether the like scenes, will, on the same spot be once more acted, or what issue awaits us, he only knows in whose hands these events are. But we must necessarily expect that the distant, or detached parts of our empire, will fall from us; the stronger and the bigger will probably provide for and govern themselves, the weaker and the lesser sink away, or seek another master. I don't at all mean, that they have any inclination so to do, where we give no cause or provocation; but the reins of government will, in such a conjuncture, of course, and of themselves drop out of our hands; we shall no longer be able to hold them. No man can tell, whether Great Britain itself might, at that time continue in one, or whether it may again be split and divided into two. There have not been wanting endeavours towards that end. I don't now pretend to decide at whose door this principally lies. It is not perhaps one man, or one party only, that is in fault. There have been on one hand, most unjust and cruel persecutions. High and strong resentments of these, are no otherwise than natural and warrantable. But they have in one respect been carried to an unreasonable extent. Reflections have been made and continued, where they are totally ungrounded and unmerited. They have hitherto been borne with a national good sense, that brings more honour to the parties, than all the ribaldry in the world can ever do them discredit. But who knows, how their effects may be felt in such a time, as is before described? What a situation! Britain, or England left alone, with a debt of a hundred and forty millions sterling on its head! How can any one have before his eyes such an event, yet run on the road, which leads directly towards it? We need not, perhaps be nice in measuring our force with that of the Americans; the evil of such a day, will but too sufficiently decide the contest.

But all is not yet said which this subject demands. I have hitherto only considered us and our colonies as engaged between ourselves, not a word has been said of any foreign state meddling in the matter. That is yet behind. We must look upon our colonies, in the light of the provinces of Holland, when they contended with Spain. The wish, the hand of every man will be against us. I will not enter into a general discourse of politics, how far it may be for the common good of mankind, to split great states into small ones, to divide them into a size fit to profit and benefit others, but not to overbear or distress them. Let us consider the subject by examples familiar to us. Mexico and Peru are more distant from Great Britain, than our colonies of North America, from Spain, or France; but were those in a state of defection and separation from the Spaniards, I wonder, whether we should find a way to approach them, or to avail ourselves in any manner of that circumstance. France was pretty well plumed in the last war; but, nevertheless, were the reviving or beginning settlements of Pondicherry, of Mauritius and Madagascar, disjoined from it, or its own continent broken once more into several different parts and separate governments, would our endeavours contribute to unite them? Should Batavia, the Spice Islands, and the Cape of Good Hope, revolt from the United Provinces, would not Englishmen try to profit by the conjuncture? I will not touch on the Brazils, *that* may be a tender point. But would none of all mankind, neither French, or Spaniards, or Dutch, or Portuguese, or Danes, or Swedes, to say nothing of the Russians, or of the new maritime state of Prussia; would none of them all, give, directly, or indirectly aid, assistance, encouragement, countenance, or protection to our colonies? Would they not trade or traffick with them, would they supply them with nothing wherewith to defend themselves or offend us? Is it very practicable to watch and guard such immense coasts, or do we with all the navy of England, in our ports find this so easy, with respect to those only of Kent and Sussex at home? Did neither England or France, support formerly the seven United Provinces in their breach with Spain? Have the French at this time afforded no essential assistance to the Turks, nor another nation to the Russians, while each continues at peace with the enemies of their respective friends? Are the independence of the British colonies in North America, and their disjunction from Great Britain, no object to other nations; are not they in particular as much so to France, as this Turkish and Russian squabble? Was that nation formerly ever wanting to Scotland, or insensible of its interest in assisting that division? I don't at all mean hereby to signify any attempts or endeavours of other Governments to take possession of these colonies, or any inability in them to defend themselves from that circumstance; but I mean the general desire and inclination, which there would assuredly be in all Europe, to see them disjoined from our nation, and become absolute, distinct, unconnected, independent states and governments in larger or smaller portions, and more or less like the present states of Holland, as it should happen. Were there in sight such a condition with respect to Mexico and Peru, or the Dutch settlements in the East-Indies, would not the English, without insisting on becoming themselves matters thereof, be most abundantly contented with their general advantage resulting therefrom? It cannot be doubted, but that there will be found a conduct and actions consequent and correspondent to such universal and almost unanimous views and wishes of mankind.

This is all said on supposition of peace. But what if one or more of the greatest powers in Europe, should in a most critical and difficult moment, declare war against us? Have France and Spain forgot the loss of Canada, and Georgia, and the many defeats and disgraces received in their last contest with us? Have they, for their honour or. interest, no desire of revenge, nor that that those provinces should again return to their own crowns? On whom does it depend; whether it shall in the case supposed, be war or peace? Is this to be determined at London, or at Madrid, or Versailles? Is it in the power and in the breast of ourselves, or of those, who are most our rivals, and whose enmity may be said to be hardly yet cooled? Are four years passed since we had two alarms? Is one year gone since we had one? Should there now be happily at the head of one or other government a Personage inclined to peace; yet how uncertain are the days of every mortal, and how are Princes, Ministers, or States tempted into action by circumstances, opportunities and advantages? Let us well weigh what it is for a private man, but much more for a great nation to part with the means of their prosperity out of their own hands, and to place it in the power and determination of those, of whom they have, on account of a long and ancient rivalship, and the continuance of many bloody wars, the utmost reason to be suspicious and jealous.

We cannot too much consider or reflect upon what happened between Spain and the Dutch Provinces at their breach and separation. The Spanish Government consisted at that time, of Spain, of Portugal, of Mexico and Peru, and other provinces of America, of the Spanish and Portuguese, being all the European settlements at that time in the East-Indies, and of Flanders, making seventeen provinces, whereof those now united, and then revolted were only seven. How unequal a match! But yet the battle was not to the strong. The story, and event of their war, are well known. I am not about to repeat them. How little did in the beginning, the Spaniards, or Portuguese, or even the Dutch themselves, dream that the latter, would, before long, strip and divest the former, of the chief, of these their settlements in the East-Indies, and make them their own? They, were nevertheless different nations, spoke different languages, had different customs, and religions, inconsistent together, and were themselves, before the end, extremely odious to one another. The Dutch obtained nothing except by force, victory and conquest. But surely we are well aware, how different things may, in these respects be between us and the Americans, and how much to the advantage of the latter. We are one nation with the same language, the same manners, and the same religion. Their seamen, their soldiers, their people are ours, and ours theirs. How easy will be the transition, or the change of dependence, protection, or government, between one and the other! Our people do already, and at this moment, seek with them shelter and refuge from their domestic poverty and misery. Should ever these our provinces in the events of chance and time, come, to look us in the face with any near equality, would it then be a very strange thing, if they should cause a general revolt of all, or of almost all the seamen of the British Empire? These might not look upon themselves as engaging or acting against their country, but as choosing between two parts of it. They will, at their pleasure distribute the titles of unreasonable and unjust, of injured and oppressed. The best terms, and the best treatment will not fail to carry the greater numbers. There is perhaps on the one side towards this brave and deserving body of men, a most cruel, unjust and impolitic practice which has long cried for vengeance, and which cannot fail to be one day heard, and at that moment, perhaps as likely as at any other. It is in every one's discourse, that something of the same kind may happen with respect to our common soldiery; I will not therefore dwell on that point. But what part might our Islands in the West Indies take at such a juncture? To whom are they the nearest, or on whom do they most depend for their lumber, and other necessary circumstances of their trade? Would there be in the East Indies the same necessity of conquest as the Dutch found? Might more equal conditions, or independence itself be no temptation to one or the other, or might it in that day be thought a great sin to change the words Old England for New? There is one point so important, so critical, that I hardly know either how to mention, or how to be silent on it. Suppose that Ireland itself, I mean the protestant, opulent and ruling part of Ireland, should grow jealous; should begin to make comparisons between the state, situation and relation of the Americans towards us, and their own? —but I will pass by this subject. However, I know so well the openness, the frankness and generosity of that nation, as to be fully assured, that there are at least, none of that country who advise or urge at this time, the present measures, with any distant or double view, to forward and hasten the independence of Ireland, and that, not at its own, but at the cost and hazard of America. The human heart can hardly be conceived to conceal such mysteries. But were it otherwise, our administration would no doubt be sensible of it, and instead of being imposed upon, be the more upon their guard.

Unhappy are the people, who pursue those steps that their friends most fear, and their enemies most wish. Were the cabinets of Versailles and Madrid, or any other the most jealous of the power and prosperity of Great Britain, united in council, and that they had it in their option to drive and push us for their own advantage, upon some ruinous and destructive measure, what would they choose before this very one, which we are now of ourselves so fatally and so madly running upon?

It is sometimes said, that Providence blinds the understanding of those, whom it destines to destruction. When things are ripe for that end, men often provoke and hasten their own fate. But God forbid, that any one being at the helm of this state, should ever not fully and repeatedly consider, or that he should, from any unhappy impulse, scruple or hesitate to stay and to stop such measures, as may in their consequences make his master to sit uneasy on his throne, nor suffer him himself to lay down his head upon his pillow, without bearing on it the curses of his country, but which may throw all the parts of the British empire into such disorder and confusion, that neither he nor any man shall be able to guide, or hold the reins of its government.

I cannot guess into whose hands these sheets may fall, or how they may be received. It is not a Prince alone, who may in these abject times be surrounded with flattery; a minister may not want his share of it. It is withal but a poor satisfaction for a private person to wish, in the waste and havock of his country, that it may be remembered, that there was not wanting one who laid freely and plainly before the public, and those governing it, the risk and likelihood of these fatal events and circumstances. But it is to be hoped, that better and more substantial effects will follow, should these things be truth and reason, which are here advanced. It is at the same time the furthest from my meaning, that futurity can be foreseen, or that it is permitted to look into the book of the time to come. There is nothing certain in human affairs. But in incidents of this prodigious importance, in the fate of states and of kingdoms, in dangers of this transcendent magnitude, probability takes the place of certainty and every prudent ruler ought to shun and avoid the one, with almost as much caution, as he would the other, nor can I finish this subject, without once more repeating, that our present debt puts us into a situation, in which no nation ever was before.

I know that some people affect to magnify the debts of France, but they are hardly worth speaking of in comparison of ours. I don't believe, that they exceeded, at the utmost, fifteen millions sterling, when the Regent Duke of Orleans took the method of the Missisippi, to cancel and annihilate them. The wants of Lewis the fourteenth had been great, but his credit was as small. What can the present King have contracted since, to be compared to the debt of Great Britain? Where is the credit? Does any one believe the Dutch concerns of that kind, to be equal in France to what they are in England, or has France itself supplied the rest? However I will only observe more, that the French debt consists in great measure of arrears of pensions, places, posts, and other grants, which the same hand withholds, as conferred; but that our debt was all received in millions sterling.

As to what has been said that great men moving in a public sphere, are above the rules of right and wrong. He must be unworthy to hold the helm of any government, who is so ignorant of the facts and incidents before his time, or so blind to those about him, as not to observe and perceive, that good and virtuous actions, I mean, such as are really so, without the false colours of flattery and obsequiousness, produce in general and national matters, their proper and correspondent effects. We have not, indeed, before our eyes, in that case, the formalities of a trial and a sentence, the judge in his robes, or the apparatus of an execution; but due consequences do from the general and original law given to the world, follow a good or evil conduct in public concerns, with much more certainty, justice, and impartiality, than they do by the means of municipal laws in private. But I desire to explain, that it is not the piety of a bigot on his knees, or the prayers even of a devout Prince, that will stay or turn the general course and order of the world. Had that been the case, our Henry the sixth, would not have fallen in a prison, by the hand of an assassin, nor Charles the first suffered on a scaffold, by the ax of the executioner, nor James the second have led the latter part of his life in banishment. These were all remarkably both devout and unfortunate Princes. I don't at present enter into the consideration of what reward personal piety will meet with in another place; but it is the public good, a love and regard for that, and attention to it, a constant resolution never to take, directly, or indirectly, by the means either of force, or of corruption, the property of the subject at will, and at pleasure, but to employ the prerogatives and the powers entrusted by the people, only for their welfare and happiness; which are the true trial and touchstone of the conduct of Princes and Ministers, as such. These naturally produce affection, loyalty, fidelity, attachment, and support. But should any man, or number of men, be regardless of the good or condition of others, trample on their rights, lay unjust hands on their properties, treat them rather like the beasts of the fields than as their fellows and equals, should they support themselves herein with the sword, and a superiority of power; the great Author of mankind, and of their welfare and happiness, has so linked and chained together causes and effects, that these things will certainly turn to the detriment and disadvantage of them and theirs who do them; sometimes by a silent and hardly observable course of things, and sometimes with long forbearance and at a great distance; but sometimes likewise at the moment, and upon the occasion, with direct and immediate resistance, and a common confusion, wherein the authors of the mischief are themselves involved, and wherein they often fall a prey and a sacrifice. The ways of Providence, and the course of futurity are unsearchable; but were any man to presume to divine, how justice and injustice, and the general morality of the universe, may possibly, in the present case operate, it would perhaps be; that Right will strongly unite, cement and combine, by a mutual association and assistance, those, who shall act under its banners; while Wrong, shall naturally, and on the contrary, confound and weaken with disunion, dissention and disturbances among themselves, those, by whom it shall have been unhappily adopted. These, are, on each side, the suitable, and as it were, the necessary consequences of their own choice; but there appear some untoward and threatening signs, that the Hand of Heaven, will, on the occasion, be heavy and severe, when, woe, to the party, which shall abide it?

If any thing can, in this case enhance the importance of the great stake, which we are about to venture, it must be a comparison of the very little profit, that we are going to contend for. The Americans are willing and consenting to give us all they have, provided that we will accept it with our right hand, but we are obstinate to risk every thing both of theirs and of our own, rather than not to take it with our left. Our whole object is on this occasion, no more, than the difference between those two propositions. Our Americans have now no gold or silver. It comes all to the mother country. It would equally do so, did they receive as much again. They keep none for their own currency; they use themselves, paper for that, and send us all the other. One would be amazed to think, what men, or administration can desire. Cannot we be contented with all, and do we insist on having more than all?

But it will be said we want to tax them. I ask why? It must be answered, because we are bent upon getting their money. I repeat again, we have it already. But says a ways and means man; we must have it in the shape of taxes. No other will serve our purpose. I reply once more, that we have it really in that shape; for cannot we, and don't we tax it when it comes hither, and is not that the same thing? Are there not taxes enow to take it, as soon as it gets to Britain, or why don't you ask for more if there are not? Who says you nay here? I will be bold to say, that there is at this time raised on Great Britain, nothing less than ten millions sterling a year; besides the collection, which it need not be said, is a very considerable sum more. Our specie has never been used to be reckoned at above twenty millions. It is said, that about three millions and a quarter of guineas have on occasion of the light gold been brought into the bank. Let our currency be calculated on that ground, and we shall according to any just reasoning thereon, appear to raise within the year, by taxes, including the collection, a sum at least equal to half of the whole specie and current coin of the kingdom; a prodigious proportion and perhaps incredible, were we not to examine into particulars.

Should it be said, that a circulating guinea cannot but pay twenty different taxes in a year, some might possibly be at first surprised at it. But how far short will that, on a more minute examination, be found of the truth? Let us consider only the course of a shilling for a very short time. A chairman pays out of it for his pot of porter. How many taxes does that include; the new and old taxes on beer and malt, and the tax on hops? They are more than I have time to reckon. His wife sends next morning to the shop for her tea and sugar. How many more are there? I will leave them to be counted by those better acquainted with the book of rates than I am. But here are a considerable number gone thro', out of one single shilling, by the time that a porter has got his beer over night, and his wife her breakfast the next morning. There remains then a third part of the money to run the gauntlet again, in the service of the man, at dinner time. However they do not perhaps amount quite to twenty; but so is likewise the time a good deal short of a year, and the money much less than a guinea. But this is not taking the matter in the strongest light. There is a chain and union of taxes, which operate insensibly and almost beyond imagination. Go into a Shoemaker's shop. Buy a pair of shoes there. How many taxes does any one in effect pay then? The Journeyman Shoemaker must put into his day's labour, and consequently there must be laid upon the shoes made by him, all the taxes, which he and his family pay in the mean time, for his salt, for his soap, for his coals, for his candles, for his linen, and for the very shoes worn by him, his wife, and his children, and for very many other things. These are all just so much money out of his pocket, and he must be repaid them by his daily labour, which is his only means. He cannot otherwise live; there would be no shoes, and men must go without them. But it is not the immediate taxes of the Shoemaker only, which go upon his manufacture, but those likewise of his tradesmen. The price of his clothes is enhanced by the taxes, which the Taylor and the Weaver paid, while they were making and weaving them; however, not by theirs only, but by those likewise of the persons working for them in their turn, and so on. These must all be put on the shoes. Insomuch that the whole, fully pursued and observed, makes a series and combination, fit to put Newton, or Demoivre, at a stand.[3] A poor guinea, or shilling, cannot, in England, put its head, if I may so express myself, out of any man's pocket, but that an army of those catchpoles are ready to seize upon it, where ever it stirs. The matter being then viewed in these lights, it seems no longer strange, if we raise a revenue equal to the half of our currency, or more. This is a prodigious operation, and surely sufficient to satisfy any administration whatsoever. Let us therefore content ourselves with getting hither the American money. That is our business. We know what to do with it here. This is the very land of taxes. It is now coming on as fast, as it can. Don't let us move Heaven and Earth, only to disturb it in its passage. Let us have the least patience, and fall to work upon it at home. We are certain, that it will be here, and that it will then be taxed, and, as it were, taxed upon taxed. The rest is with all submission, to my superiors, no better at the bottom, than a childish fancy, and impatience, and owing only to the want of a full reflection, and consideration on the subject.

I have yet something to add on this head; which is, that were the Irish and the Americans, both of them unanimously to cry out to us, to spare their lives, and to take all they have; to beg of us to send them such another army of tax-gatherers, as our own, and with them a copy of our code of revenue laws; I will be bold to say, that it would nevertheless be in us the worst policy in the world, and totally contrary to our own interest, to take them at their words, and to do in the least degree any such thing. We see the Thames flowing constantly into the ocean, and yet always full. It need not be said, that the rain and the dew are the causes of this, which first fall and fertilize the earth, and then replenish that noble river. Were those two stopped or dried up, it would not be long, before we should pass over, dry-shod, at London Bridge. Were they so only in part, the stream would then likewise lower in proportion. What our whole debt to foreigners amounts to, no one may probably know with exactness; but the more it has been enquired into, the higher it has always appeared. However, the interest of it is a current, which runs perpetually into the Continent. We do not indeed, see it with our eyes, as we do the Thames; otherwise we love money, so much better than we do water, that we might perhaps be less indifferent about it, than we are. It passes imperceptibly, but nevertheless surely, and without ceasing. What are then the causes which supply it? I answer, those two great sources of Ireland and America. These first, water and fructify with their most benignant current, the whole island of Great Britain, and then finish their course in the discharge of our debt abroad. Their way is no more visible than that of the interest itself, of our debt, but it is alike certain and constant. Stop, or dry up these and you will as surely stop, or dry up the funds of our debts, as withholding the rain, or the dew of Heaven would lessen and lower the stream of the river Thames. Taxes will do this. They are the bane of commerce and of agriculture. They affect the Merchant, the Manufacturer, the Planter, the Farmer, and the Labourer. Our America is not of an age to support their operation. The things from above, keep their course in spite of man, for his benefit and advantage. It is God's very great mercy, that the dew and the rain, do not depend on Administrations, they would otherwise have undoubtedly been taxed and dried long ago. But it is not so, with what is of our own fabrick or production. We have a great power over riches and treasure. Governments can effectually cut off the wells and the springs of these. We have only to look abroad in the world, to be abundantly convinced of that truth. The example of Great Britain, will not prove the contrary. It was when, and while we were not taxed, as we now are, that we prospered, grew great and rich. Those times gave us strength, to bear for a while, the burthens since imposed upon us. It is from the Revolution, that our prodigious taxes have begun. They were laid by degrees, and so must their effects be perceived. They don't operate like a storm, or a whirlwind. Let us give them a fair and full trial, before we declare, that we are not undone by them. It will then be time enough to make ourselves a model for others. I ask, whether it is not our own actual difficulties brought on by these very taxes, which do now, at this instant urge us upon our colonies, and which are the cause of all the present contest and disorder. It is one of the first principles in commerce, not to burthen the means and materials of manufactures. It would be nipping the fruit in the bud. The same reasoning holds here. Let us keep our hands from these two great causes and sources of our treasure and wealth. They have hitherto wonderfully supplied and supported us. They may continue so to do, if we will suffer them.

But it may be said, that we have at home great and profitable manufactures, and our woolen one in particular; whereby we stand less in need of distant assistance. That is very true; but so is it likewise, that we have on the continent very many expences and demands for money besides the interest of our debt. We shall be very fortunate, if we can, with the means of all our richest resources, make at the year's end an even accompt.

But it may be asked, what are we then to do? We are pressed with our domestic burthens and incumbrances. These put us first on the measure of stamps in America, wherein we did not succeed. These induced us afterwards to make demands on the India company, wherein we had rather better fortune. It is these, which have again brought us back to our attack on America. How are we either to stand under them, or to march forwards? Is it safe to rest as we are? What course are we to take if it is not? This is, perhaps, as serious a proposition, as one Englishman can put to another. No man laments more than the writer of these sheets, that twelve years of peace are now elapsed, without any thing being done, without any establishment being made, which may enable us to maintain another war, or perhaps even in peace support long the present very heavy pressure, under which we labour. We are in the mean time daily liable to be engaged in war. We have now had an uncommon interval of peace. It was but a very few years ago, that we were on the brink of a rupture with Spain, which would undoubtedly have been attended by one with France. How can any minister sleep in peace, who has on his hands the care of a great government, and the welfare of many millions of people, while public affairs are in a condition so very unprepared for an event, which may at any moment happen, and which may, in our present situation, bring with it consequences of an importance hardly to be conceived? Surely they think on these things, whose duty most demands it of them. It is impossible, that such concerns of ours can be left only to chance, and hazard, or as it were, to the fortuitous concourse of atoms. One would think there could hardly be a man in Britain, minister or any other, not perpetually employed at the plough, but who must daily revolve in his mind, the present circumstances of his country, our burthens, our debts, and our expences, and at the same time cast in his own breast, what must be the best means of our supporting ourselves under them, whether in war or in peace. There is an issue, which some men have in view, and which I will not express, we may be assured, however, that they do but very superficially consider the matter, who imagine, that this will, in our case, take place without the utter ruin and confusion of every thing. All is, notwithstanding, as yet tranquility and sunshine with us. We possess a great and fine country; we have most noble and beneficial dependencies; we have a fleet; we have an army; we have several hundred thousands, and perhaps near a million of men capable of bearing arms in their own defence; we have a revenue, with a surplus above the interest of our debts and expences. Surely there is yet an opportunity to find some plan; to settle some establishment, whereon things may rest safely and securely, and the public and all reasonable persons be satisfied, that they do so. There is however no time to be lost. It may be too late to prepare, as it were, in the day of battle, and at the moment when our difficulties press strongly upon us. But this is of itself a very wide field, and one of the greatest of considerations, nor is it my immediate subject. But the measures now carrying on will not effect it or any thing towards it. No surrounding dangers or difficulties are a good reason for running down a precipice; our fate can but lead us thither at last. However no other end can happen to us from the way, which we are now in, if we persevere and proceed in it.

This seems to be a sufficient answer to the point before us. However I will not so turn my back on this question, as not freely and frankly to propose, what, I trust, will at least be more effectual for our purpose, as well as more easily carried into execution, than what we are now driving at. I mean to do almost directly the contrary of what we are about, that is to give a greater liberty and latitude of trade both to Ireland and to America, to America including our West India islands. That is my proposition. We are the seat and center of government. This is our strength. This is our advantage. This is what we are to preserve. While we retain this, all the money, riches, and treasure of the more distant and dependant parts of our empire cannot fail to flow in upon us. We have nothing to do with little jealousies about this trade or that manufacture; it is the proper business of the rich to spend their money, and of the poor to earn it; the state may well, without meddling in it, leave them to settle the means of that matter with one another. The end of all trades and manufactures must rest with us, while we continue the seat of dominion. It is the necessary consequence of giving the tone and the law. Ambition, pleasure, fashion, business, curiosity, education, trade, and commerce, posts and places possessed abroad by Englishmen, and numberless other causes, will contribute to, and effect it. The island of Jamaica, and our other islands in the West Indies, what money, and commodities equivalent to money, have they sent to England, could the whole be added together? Had they in the time acquired ten times as much, it would all have run the same road. The climate would have driven the possessors from thence, while the seat of empire would have invited them hither. Do not we see the very proprietaries of our northern colonies, living in England as private gentlemen, and have not we sometimes known them voting in minorities of our Lower House of legislature, while they might have been almost as Princes or Kings in their own governments? Were it in the next month to rain over the different parts of Ireland a million of money, how long does any one imagine it would be, before at least nine hundred thousand pounds of it would find its way into England? Have we lately wanted very sufficient proofs, that there remains no abundance of cash in that kingdom? I will not repeat, what has been said of North America; but they have by their paper-money invented the very contrivance of the world, for sending to us every ounce of their gold and silver, did we but know when to be content. Look at the city of London; they neither plant, nor do they sow, nor do they reap, yet Solomon, or his Jerusalem, were not in all their glory, rich and great, like that capital of our dominions. The money of our whole empire is remitted thither, as the blood runs to the heart. Our great body politic is preserved and nourished, by the dispersion and circulation of it again from thence. This is the constant and never failing course of things. But the case is much more strong, if we take Great Britain itself, whereof London is only a part. That would retain a considerable share of what it receives, did not the interest of our debt carry it out, as fast as it comes in. This is the issue and the drain, which prevents us from perceiving ourselves more enriched and replenished from the vast quantity of treasure perpetually arriving to us from many parts. This may perhaps be the reason, why we are less sensible, less attentive, and perhaps sometimes less grateful, on the occasion. But that is all our own fault, our own doing. We have none to thank for it but ourselves. We ought not, on that account, to esteem these supplies the less, for had we not them, it would be much worse with us. Nothing could follow but our last decease and dissolution, as a state. These must and will take place, whenever the others will stop. However these things don't require much reasoning. We have the world before us for an example. Such are every where the effects between the center and other parts of a government, although perhaps in no case more so than in that of Great Britain, on account of certain circumstances and causes attending that empire, which are particularly suited to produce them. This is our point, if we are but sensible of our true interest; let us but preserve this our great and sacred prerogative, the other benefits and advantages will of course follow, even while we are asleep.

I shall use no words to prove that this arrangement will bring a greater influx of treasure to those, to whose liberty of trade it shall extend. The person the most prejudiced, or the most short-sighted in the case, will not dispute that with me. I will venture to presume on that point. This will therefore attach to us our dependencies, at the same time, that it enriches us ourselves. It will strengthen and fasten the bond and union between us. It will confirm our superiority, while it increases the fruits of it. It will bring us more spoils and profits than

[91]

conquest, although it will operate by love and affection. It will require neither fleets or armies, to enforce it; we need fear no revolts, no defections, or confederacies on the account of it. How happy would it be, if all the circumstances of the other plan, would in the same manner answer and play into the hands of each other! When will men be contented to do others no more mischief, than what will turn to their own benefit? States and Ministers will have advanced, no mean way in policy as well as in morality, when they shall once have learned to confine all their evil towards others, within that circle. It is the very perverseness of folly, to suppose, that men can serve themselves only by oppressing others. But here, on the contrary, the hand of nature itself works with us. Freedom of trade is our foundation; no wonder then that so many blessings coincide together. There is open before us, a rich and wide field; we have only to enter and reap the harvest, which is ripe and plentiful. This proposal rests therefore on three points; to wit, that it will bring a greater influx of treasure into our outward dominions; that this must enrich the center of empire; which cannot therefore, likewise but increase its revenue. These are short propositions, and no way perplexed. Let them be well examined. All falls to the ground, which has been said on the subject, if any one of them be false or mistaken; but should they, on the contrary, be all of them most evident, most certain, and indisputable, let any man, and the greatest in trust, the most consider, how he can answer to Ireland, to the Colonies, to his Country at home, to his King himself, in the concern of his revenue, and his exchequer, the refusing his attention and assistance to a measure, so very practicable, and at the same time so universally beneficial and salutary.

This is the more, and much more necessary, on account of the present condition of Ireland. The late enquiry concerning their linen manufacture, the public history of their emigrations, and the state of their credit at the beginning of their present Session of Parliament, have made that sufficiently known. I shall not pretend to describe it. England, has, perhaps, from that Island, reaped more real benefit, than Spain ever did from Mexico, or Peru. Spain, gains, indeed, from those possessions great riches, of silver and gold; but she has dearly purchased them, at the price of her inhabitants and people at home. Whereas Ireland affords us in many ways, a very advantageous assistance and support of men, while we receive from her at the same time, a constant most rich influx and supply of money. We now so depend on these things, and can so ill do without them, and are by these means so united with our sister Island, that should she on any account unhappily sink, she cannot but like a mill-stone, fastened about our necks, carry us down along with her. Should her condition grow worse, who knows but it may turn to rage and despair, and either have an effect on her Legislature, or that the majority thereof, may be hardly able to manage and govern their own state. I am unwilling to point out such possibilities; but it will not be long health and wealth in England, should any irretrievable mischief happen in Ireland. A moderate remedy, might, however, now be timely, for what may in futurity be beyond redress. A greater liberty and latitude of trade is the proper assistance in the case. It is what Ireland itself wishes and desires. It will at the same time be of more benefit to us than to them. France is beating us out of the trades of Turkey, of Spain, and even of Portugal. Let but loose the Irish, and they will do as much for them, and likewise for some others. It is Great Britain, which withholds the hand of Ireland, and not the nature of things, that confines it. Let us but consent, and they will soon stretch out their right hand, into many a market in the world, where it now never appears, and having done so, they will immediately pay to us, with their left, the money gained there, as surely, as that we are born Englishmen. I don't point out particulars; lights will not be wanting in that respect, whenever there shall be an inclination to demand them. I don't moreover mean to signify, that any opening of the commerce of Ireland, and America, recommended within the compass of these sheets, will, of itself, be adequate to all the demands of our present situation. That will in all appearance require a new and universal arrangement of our taxes and comerce, wherein Great Britain herself must bear a most material part. No man can say, that all the money in Europe, is equal to our national debt, nor can therefore any provision be sufficient, but what may produce effects answerable to such a very great necessity. Some plan seems to be demanded, which may bring into Great Britain a good part of all the gold and silver now current in the world. Nothing less, will perhaps, do our business. The practicability of this, cannot but appear a doubtful problem. Were all states whatsoever formed on a constitution the most advantageous for commerce, whereof each is capable, it is evident, that they would then share among them those two precious metals, in so near a proportion, that no one could therein have over the rest any very great superiority. But this is exceedingly wide of the case. No one state is so constituted; but on the contrary, almost all governments whatever are framed and act on principles directly opposite thereto. This gives a very great opportunity for extreme difference and disproportion in that respect. It is perhaps, on the availing ourselves thereof, that depends the future welfare of our country, and the safety, the stability, and the very subsistence of our state. The Dutch are a small people, or at least have but a very confined territory, and that defended with difficulty from the sea. They have, nevertheless, done a great deal, in the way which we are speaking of. They are certainly therein at the head of all mankind. However, it is evident, and might be easily pointed out, that they are yet far short of perfection. There is good room for others to go beyond, and especially for a state which has such advantages as Great Britain. However, what degree of advantage the nature of things will admit of, on this head, or how to attain thereto, are not questions of this present instant. I have said thus much, led to it by my subject, together with the interest of the Public therein, and the necessity, which I am persuaded, that my country is, at this time under, of finding, and carrying into execution, some such great, general, and salutary measure. Happy will be the hand, that shall in the first place prevent the ruin, whereon we are now running. We must begin there. That is the object directly before us. Let us next enlarge the trade of Ireland and America. This will do a great deal. It may withal lead us towards a more universal plan, with which it cannot, at the same time but coincide. It will, withal be well, that this double benefit of these two parts of our country, went hand in hand together. The present state of Ireland makes it absolutely and immediately necessary, for the one, and the interest of Great Britain, requires it for both.

I don't enter into particulars concerning the stopping up the port of Boston, or the new laws given to Massachusetts Bay. However I must observe, that the alteration of their charter, and of their civil government is not temporary, like the other provisions, but perpetual. The breaking of charters, is making the worst war upon mankind. It involves the innocent, and those yet unborn. Every thing depends with men on their constitution of government. Such a measure is therefore wantonly laying waste the territories of the earth, and, I speak it with reverence, but it is even forbidding Providence itself to make mankind happy thereon, unless he shall for the undoing the works of unreasonable and illjudging men, perform immediate miracles and suspend or counteract his own laws of nature, which is surely not to be supposed or expected. As for those who refuse, or impede law and justice for blood, let them be well aware, that they don't thereby bring it on their own heads, or warrant private men to be themselves their own avengers. However the whole will be received in America as a declaration of war, and depend upon the same issue. It must be by force and conquest if they submit. It is probably not a month or a year, that will finally determine this affair. The flame may break out immediately, or the fire may smother until some fatal opportunity of our being engaged in a foreign war, or some other such occasion. The authors of these measures no doubt expect that the removal of the custom-house and the suspension of the trade of Boston will bring these people on their knees, and force them to submit to the rest of our measures. It is evident, that this is their idea. They might have been well informed and instructed, and ought to have been so before they proceeded so far. They may nevertheless find themselves much mistaken in the event, however forward they are to hazard, on their opinion, the welfare and prosperity of their country. It is no wonder, that some men cannot, even at the distance of America, bear a Democratical constitution. But they ought to know the history of the world better than to be ignorant of the strength and force of such a form of government, and how strenuously, and almost wonderfully, people living under one, have sometimes exerted themselves, in defence of their rights and liberties, and how fatally it has ended with many a man and many a state, who have entered into quarrels, wars and contests with them.

Some say, that all the contradiction and opposition of America, originates from home, and that it is only the faction of England, which catches there. Nothing, perhaps, testifies a greater ignorance of the true state of that country, than such a notion. What is all the spirit of patriotism, or of liberty, now left in England, more than the last snuff of an expiring lamp? It is not longer than three and thirty years ago, that it was otherwise with us. But who can say whether the same flame, the same sacred flame, may not at this time burn brightly and strongly in America, which once show'd forth such wonders in Greece and in Rome, and from whose ashes it still enlightens a great part of mankind, I mean, all who are not sunk in ignorance or barbarity. They have certainly three excellent and free forms of government, and which partake, perhaps, in some degree, of the principles, whereon were framed the ancient ones of those eminent cities. They are themselves, as yet, a new and uncorrupted people. They carried with them formerly, the spirit of liberty from England, at the time that it was in its greatest purity and perfection there, nor has it since degenerated by the climate. Whoever shall judge of their temper by that at home, and proceed accordingly, will perhaps in the end be scorched by that flame, which he may find to burn too powerfully for him, and of the nature, and of the means to extinguish which, he was totally ignorant.

I have now considered the rectitude, the practicability and the profit to be expected from our present measures, and have gone so far as to offer another measure instead. I hope, that I have proved my propositions to a great degree of clearness and certainty. I don't know what to do more on this subject, unless I should propose something, which might convince and satisfy, without the trouble of reason and argument. This seems difficult. However I will not despair. Let me be permitted to try my hand in that case. I will recommend, and so far as becomes me, desire and request, that every one, when he considers of this subject, and especially before he uses any hard words, or passes any harsh laws, will place himelf in America; will imagine himself born, bred, resident, and having all his concerns and fortune there. I don't mean in the light of a Governor, or of one who seeks to recommend and advance himself here, at the expence of his country-men in that part of the world; but as one, who has no other views or interest, except in the common good of his colony, or continent. Let then any such man candidly and fairly ask himself in his own breast, what he should in that situation, think of being taxed at Westminster; and let no man on this occasion throw a stone, whose heart does not plainly and roundly answer him with its assent. I may make too free with Ministers of State; but I would particularly press this on those, whose desires, passions and inclinations are followed by effects, and who hold, perhaps, at this moment, in their hands, the fate of Great Britain, and of North America. This, I say, is, a proposition without a syllogism; but which, if properly brought home, and en-forced by every man, upon himself, may, perhaps, penetrate, move, and soften more than all the arguments and earnestness, which I have hitherto used.

I would willingly try this experiment of transposition upon a late transaction, wherein some people's opinions, seem to be affected by locality. Certain letters (see letters of Governor Hutchinson, &c.) have been published of an American Governor and Lieutenant Governor; and a third person, together with remarks, and the speech of a learned and ingenious gentleman. They are offered as an appeal to the public, against the colony of Massachusetts Bay. These cannot, therefore, but be themselves likewise the object of a public consideration. I have, by the touchstone of locality, a mind to examine and question, some of this learned gentleman's reasoning. It is now but between eighty and ninety years, since we of this country banished our King. On what ground did we do it? It will be answered; that we did not like his actions; for that they tended to deprive us of our best rights and properties. That we did it as Englishmen, on the constitution of England. Who was the common judge between us and him? There was no common judge. We judged for ourselves. He was our King, our magistrate, our trustee. When we found him to fail in the essential points of these offices, we took another. This was our right, as Englishmen. But we set aside one of his daughters, from her turn, in the succession, and appointed instead—a person, who had no title by birth. The King's horse threw him, and the lady succeeded. But that was chance. It might in a course of nature very well have happened, that she never had been Queen. What had she done? She had taken a remarkable part in the revolution, and was totally unexceptionable. But there were in one scale, the welfare and happiness of many millions of people, and in the other, the advancement of only one lady, although a deserving one. There was therefore no equality, the latter could not but kick the beam. I answer, that I subscribe to this with my hand and my heart. But this is one side of the medal. Let us turn the reverse. An American Governor is not so big as a King; he don't wear a crown, nor bear a sceptre, not sit on a throne, nor is worshipped on the knee, nor has a navy, nor an army, nor makes Bishops, nor judges, nor is his civil list perhaps above a thousand pounds a year. He seems to be much more responsible and more removeable, than a King. Suppose then that one of our colonies should take the strongest exceptions to their Governor, and desire to change him; would they, in that case, be permitted to judge for themselves? No. Why not? Because they are Americans. Who are to judge for them? We. Why so? Because we are Englishmen. But would their application be to us, a sufficient cause for removal? Perhaps not; but on the contrary, a reason to continue him at present, and to promote and advance him afterwards. That has been the case before, and may probably be so again. But why is the measure which we mete to them, so different from that, which we measure to ourselves? Because we are Englishmen and they are Americans. This must be owned to be perfectly just and satisfactory, and the Americans are the most unreasonable men in the world, if they don't see it exactly in the same light.

But suppose that the representative body of the province should make the complaint? The answer would then be, that there was no accuser, or if any one chose to speak latin, no *delator*. Suppose that they complain of falsehood and treachery towards the province? That would be no charge, no *crimen*. Suppose they give in evidence, the party's own letters? That would compleat the thing; for there would then be no evidence, no *testis*. But will this hold water? Admirably; with respect to America, and in latin.

It is strongly disputed, whether these American letters are of a public or a private nature. This may not, in itself, be a very important point. However let us endeavour to settle it, since it lies in our way. Whatever concerns and affects the interests, the welfare, and happiness of a whole people, is, and must be of a public nature, whether papers, letters, or any other thing whatsoever. Good and evil are not matters of law or of logic. They are the most, if not the only essential circumstances of the world. They are what every thing else refers to. They stamp an eternal mark and difference on all things, which even imagination cannot cancel or erase. The enjoyment of the one, and the avoiding of the other, is the very end of our being, and likewise of all the beings which do, or which even can be supposed to exist, and which have a sense and perception of them. Whatever, therefore, relates to the general good or evil of a people, is of a public nature. It is that circumstance which makes it so. The terms are as good as synonymous. Whatever concerns, on the contrary, only this or that individual, is of a private nature. It is confined to one or other's happiness or welfare; to one or other's good and evil. Here is again the true unerring distinction. These things seem clear to the greatest degree of intuitive certainty. It is strange to be forced to reason about them. However we are told otherwise. If some compliments happen in a letter, to be made to an old lady, it changes the essence of every thing; *she* contracts and confines the whole matter, and all becomes of a private nature; although the chief subject of that very letter should be to advise, and point out the means of altering the charter, and of new modeling the constitution of a colony, and that there should be recommended therein, the finding some way, according to its own language, "to TAKE OFF the original incendiaries," lest they should "continue to instil their poison into the minds of the people;"

[98]

but the mention of the *old lady*, makes it all private (see Mr. Wedderburne's speech, page 94, and letter of Mr. A. Oliver, Feb. 13, 1769).[4] But suppose that these letters were really meant and intended to produce public effects; what will that do? Nothing at all. If the person to whom they were written, had not at that moment a place, it signifies nothing; although he might have had a post before, and might look for one again, and although he might have communicated these letters to others, for the very purpose of affecting the public. All this will be of no importance, if the person did not happen to have a place at the time. Would not one be tempted to think, that as some endeavour to leave no property in America, others have a mind to banish all human reason out of American affairs?

But let us take this matter in another light. Suppose a Prince to have been the subject of these letters, instead of a people, and his conduct and character to have therein been so freely treated and censured, instead of theirs, and the divesting him of his power and dignity, so plainly mentioned and recommended, instead of depriving them of their rights and privileges, and the *taking him off* proposed, instead of the *taking off* some of them, what would have been the consequence? High Treason. But might not these have been private letters of friendship, and the receiver have secreted and concealed them? There is no such thing as private letters in the case. No civilities sent to the fairest Lady in the land, can make them so. The person receiving, must, at his own peril carry them to a Secretary of State, or to a Justice of the Peace, or to some other Magistrate; we don't otherwise want a word for him, which is misprision of treason. But who would take notice of such a thing? Let Mr. Attorney, or Mr. Solicitor answer that. But on what ground is all this? Because the Prince is supposed to be the public person, and to represent the whole people, and that what relates to him may affect them. But there are bad Princes, and writing against them, is sometimes writing in support, and in the interests of the Public, and of the People. No such plea, or proposition is ever suffered. It would, on the contrary, be an additional crime, even to make, or to offer it. But does any one, by representing a body, acquire more prerogative than belong to that body itself, or are the public more affected through a third person, than immediately in themselves? Yes, just so. Say a word against a Prince and beware of informations, inditements, fines, prisons, scaffolds and gibbets. These are the strongest arguments in the world, and I never knew any man get the better, in disputing with them. But

[99]

abuse a people from morning till night, and every one knows, that the rule and the law is; let them mend their manners, if it is true; let them despise it, and leave it to fall on the author, if it is not—I am at the feet of Gamaliel. I desire only to learn. I shall not contradict the doctrine concerning a Prince, and I subscribe, heartily, to that about a People. Should these commonwealths of America, ever become as strong and independent, as they are now weak and dependent, and should they, in their greatness and glory, remember a word of the humblest and the meanest, but not the least sincere, or the least disinterested of their friends and advocates, it will be, never to employ force and power, against reason and argument; to leave those instruments to such as choose to make use of them, but to believe *truth* to be ever the real interest of the People, and the Public; and that no other incense, or sacrifice, should ever be offered at the altars of that goddess, but the pure oblation of a freedom of thinking, speaking, and writing. But here it cannot well fail to be observed, that should these people, whose distresses are now pleaded, ever come to be masters, both of themselves and of others, to be glutted with power and riches; that they will certainly run the race of the rest of mankind, and learn in their turn, tyranny and injustice, as their betters and their predecessors have done before them. I answer, no man perhaps believes this, more than myself; however, that this is not now the case. But it is hoped, that neither will there, in that day, be wanting some honest man, who will endeavour to make them blush at such a conduct, if he shall not be able to dissuade and divert them from it. However, I would willingly in my turn, now ask, whether this last observation is also local, and confined to America, or whether it extends itself likewise to Great Britain?

It is not reason and argument; it is this locality which operates on the present occasion. It is this only that makes many men easy and indifferent in the case, about right and wrong, justice, and injustice. Were my countrymen, now in England, dipped once in the River Delaware, I dare say, that it would make an almost miraculous change in their opinions. If some, who might be named, were transposed into Assembly Men, they would perhaps be as ready to repeal certain late laws as ever they were to pass them. However, I will not go back again to topicks, which seem, sufficient to awake the most lethargic Englishman, out of his soundest sleep; but I desire to put a case relating to this locality itself, and its power and effects.

At the beginning of the last century, there lived a gentleman of the name of Fawkes. He hired a house and some cellars, and other apartments in Westminster. We will suppose that he had a lease of them; a lease is, for the time, as good as a purchase; it might not indeed be stamped, but stamps were not then in fashion, it was good without. He bought some gunpowder. It is to be believed, that he paid honestly for it. He could, perhaps, have produced a receipt for it. He placed it in the cellars, or other apartments hired by him. He had, indeed, a mind to amuse himself with blowing up the Legislature of Great Britain. He met with his reward. But, suppose that he, and Garnet, and the rest of their associates, instead of falling into the hands of an English Jury, had been tried at Rome, before the Consistory Court, or at any other Court there, they would no doubt have found an *advocate*. That is no other than the duty of the profession. I won't take upon me to say, whether he would in this case have flourished about private property, trespass, or forcible entry; but whatever turn the Italian council had thought proper to give the cause of his clients, has any one seriously, the least doubt, but that they would have been cleared and acquitted, and probably by the Court of Rome itself, in good time, preferred and promoted. As it happened, nothing remained for them but the honour of Martyrdom, which, however, some of them are said to have attained. So much can a difference of climate do, and such force have prejudice, prepossession and locality. But Garnet and Fawkes, and their friends were fools, Jesuits, as some of them were. They did not understand their trade. A certain northern Prince of our time, and perhaps some others, have found better ways of blowing up Legislatures than with gunpowder; which don't make a quarter of the crack and combustion, but which are ten times more effectual.

But our colonies might be well enough, were it not for Dr. Franklin, who has with a brand, lighted from the clouds, set fire to all America. No Governments ever care to acknowledge the people to be fairly against them. For whatever may be the case with the opinions of the multitude, in abstruse and refined matters, which but little concern them, nor do they much trouble themselves about; yet the end, and therefore the touchstone and trial of all Government being their welfare and happiness, there is hardly common modesty in affecting to despise and refuse their sense concerning their own good and evil, their own feelings, benefits, or sufferings. It is in these things, that the voice of the People is said to approach, that of their Maker. The sycophants of Ministers, endeavour therefore to throw on the artifice and influence of individuals, all discontent, or dissatisfaction of the Public. Mr. Wilkes moves England, and Dr. Franklin America; as if we had here no feeling, but through the first, and they had there neither eyes, or ears, but by the latter. It were happy for mankind, if administrations procured their own votes and majorities with as much fairness, as the voice of the people is commonly obtained. I wonder, whether we should then have heard of any government in Europe indebted in the sum of an hundred and forty millions sterling; or be at this moment under the alarm of a parent state attacking its own colonies, or of a great empire setting at work its fleets and armies only to throw the parts of itself into mischief and confusion? It is idle and childish to be crying out against this or that private person. The truth is, that whenever governments heap up combustibles, there will always be found a hand to put the match to them, or these would heat and fire of themselves, if they were not.

But is not Mr. W.'s Philippic against the Doctor a capital performance? I am sure that I have not the least inclination to depreciate the ingenuity of that learned gentleman, whose argument I have been making so free with. But the being charmed with spruce expressions, or a smartness of invective, where the subject makes against the privileges or the liberties of a people, what is it better, than if a parcel of prisoners or of galley slaves, were so abject as to take a pleasure in the rattling, or as it were, in the music of their chains?

I am drawing towards an end of my career. However I will first say something to the Americans themselves. I observe them to charge sometimes on the British subjects, in general, the measures with which they are aggrieved. Herein they do us wrong. I may venture to affirm, that there would not be hurt the hair of the head of an American, were it to be voted by all our country. Every one must remember, the universal satisfaction produced by the repeal of the stamp act, and it would no doubt be the same again, were the present measures discharged and remitted. But it often happens, that representatives and their constituents, are in the most essential and the most important points, diametrically opposite to one another. I don't pretend to account for this. It is a fatality. But the Americans should consider, that two different parts of a country may be oppressed by one and the same hand. Administrations have been squandering and running us in debt at home, until our whole substance is wasted and consumed. It may now be coming to their turn. But *procul a Jove, procul a fulmine*. Great Britain is first brought to its extremity. Let any of our dependencies compare their burthens with ours, and then complain of the nation, if they shall find that ours are the lighter. I don't mean to make a merit of this; but let them suppose the same strong hand to be upon us both, when they shall have been convinced, how little we are in this respect to be envied.

I am unwilling to take my leave without saying likewise one word to my countrymen of England. It is not only riches and power, men and money, which the centre of government receives from the detached parts of its dominions, but likewise credit and honour in the world. The Scotch and the Irish are as good men as any in Europe. This is well known, wherever they seek service and establishments, and the which they are left to do, in more parts than is for the benefit of Great Britain. Our countrymen of America have not yet so figured in our quarter of the globe; but it is hardly a compliment to place them clearly at the head of their own, the offspring of all other people there included. If there are any spoiled children of our national family, it must be the English themselves; unless that riches and luxury mend the manners of men. But nevertheless, being so, the seat of empire, and all commands issuing from our capital, and our name being forward, the actions, the merits, the figure, the reputation, and the glory of all our countrymen whatsoever, and wheresoever, do exceedingly redound to us, and to the credit of England, and of Englishmen. In return for these things, they desire no more than a just sense and acknowledgment of them. Whether we do make this return, whether these circumstances have always the weight with us, which they merit, Englishmen will best determine by examining into their own breasts. But this we may be assured of; that the good will, affection, and attachment of our countrymen, spread throughout our common empire, will be our firmest strength and security, if it shall be our lot to continue in our present splendor and prosperity; as likewise that the same cannot but be our best support and assistance, wherewith to weather the storms of fate and fortune, if Heaven shall on the contrary have any reverse, or times of difficulty and distress in store for us.

I have now finished, unless it may be a few words with respect to the author himself. He hopes, that should, in the warmth of writing, any inadvertencies or inaccuracies have fallen from him, that they will be readily overlooked; he is persuaded, there are none such as affect his argument. He has wrote with freedom, but he trusts without offence; he has no personal views whatsoever, in any thing that he has advanced or offered; he has no interest in any distant part of the British dominions, neither in Scotland, Ireland, or America; he has neither trade or traffick with them, nor a foot of land in any of them. His concerns, his property, his family, his friendships, his affections, every thing most dear to him, center in South Britain. He has no intercourse or connexion with any man that either is, that ever was, or who to the best of his knowledge desires to be a minister. He is totally indifferent, who shall be at the head of our affairs, any otherwise than as the public may be concerned in it. He would not perhaps, in his humble situation, accept of any place or post, high or low, which the King has to confer, great and powerful as he is. He wishes only, that these sheets may be read, as they are written, with the purest and most disinterested intentions, for the good, the greatness, and the prosperity of our whole empire; for the union, harmony, and preservation of all its parts; and for the particular interest, safety, peace, welfare, and happiness of England.

FINIS

NOTES

[1] William Molyneux (1656–98), author of *The Case of Ireland Being Bound by Acts of Parliament in England Stated* (1698), an assertion of the legislative dependence of the Irish parliament; and Sir Edward Poynings (1459–1521), Lord Deputy of Ireland, who in 1494 extracted from the Irish Parliament legislation making Irish administration dependent upon the English Crown and Privy Council, most notably a measure providing that no act of the Irish Parliament should be valid until accepted by the English Privy Council.

[2] Rome's letter, dated "Narraganset, Dec. 22, 1767," was quoted by Solicitor General Alexander Wedderburn in his bitter attack upon Franklin at the hearing on Massachusetts' petition for the dismissal of Governor Hutchinson, January 29, 1774. The letter was appended to Wedderburn's "Speech" and printed in *The Letters of Governor Hutchinson, and Lieut. Governor Oliver, &c., Printed at Boston, and Remarks Thereon, With the Assembly's Address, And the Proceedings of the Lords Committee of Council, Together With the Substance of Mr. Wedderburn's Speech Relating to Those Letters and the Report of the Lords Committee to His Majesty in Council* (London, 1774), p. 123–134.

[3] Abraham De Moivre (1667–1754), French mathematician.

[4] The reference is to *The Letters of Governor Hutchinson*. The passage from Oliver's letter is found on p. 29.

Catharine Macaulay

O F THOSE in England who spoke in behalf of America against the policies of the North Ministry on the eve of the American Revolution, none achieved greater contemporary renown than Catharine Macaulay. With the appearance in 1763 of the first of her eight volumes on *The History of England From the Accession of James I to That of the Brunswick Line* she had won instant fame. Acclaimed by a modern scholar as the greatest woman England had produced, she had written "the shameful story" of the Stuarts with a vigorously Whiggish slant that appealed to Whig oligarchs who believed they faced an ominously Tory current in the reign of George III. Her work was well received in political and literary circles both in England and abroad, and she was seen by many as a latter-day Brutus who defended liberty and smote tyrants wherever they appeared. Having achieved fame as a historian, she repeatedly entered the ranks of radical writers and became noted as a controversialist whose pamphlets were vigorous and uncompromising. Twice, in 1770 and 1790, she sallied forth against Edmund Burke to challenge first his *Thoughts on the Present Discontents* and later his *Reflections on the Revolution in France.*

Born Catharine Sawbridge of a well-established Kent family, she was the sister of John Sawbridge, a liberal alderman, sheriff, Member of Parliament, and Lord Mayor of London. At the age of 29 she married George Macaulay, a Scots physician 15 years her senior.[1] Macaulay encouraged her work and provided a measure of security and stability that enabled her to launch a literary career, but their marriage ended abruptly with his death six years later. Mrs. Macaulay subsequently immersed herself in her historical studies, but found the time to write several radical pamphlets. She scandalized her contemporaries and undermined her reputation in England when, as a matron of 47, she married William Graham, a young man of 21 who lacked redeeming social standing. Abroad, however, Mrs. Macaulay was still regarded as a woman of genius and a trusted friend of liberty; during the War of Independence, she maintained her contacts with friends and admirers in France and America. In earlier years, probably as an outgrowth of her brother's political activities, she had mixed with the leading English radicals in London. There she had become acquainted with such Americans as Arthur and William Lee, the latter himself an alderman and sheriff of London, who in turn had introduced her to still other Americans who visited the mother country during the 1760's and 1770's. When she visited the United States in 1784, Mrs. Macaulay renewed these contacts. After spending several months in Boston in the Adams circle and cementing a lasting friendship with Mercy Otis Warren, she traveled to New Hampshire, New York, and Philadelphia and paid her respects to George Washington, to whom she was introduced through the Adamses and the Virginia Lees.[2] Her 10-day stay at Mount Vernon, the culmination of a year in America, proved to be "very flattering" to Washington and led to a correspondence that lasted until her death in 1791. Washington's estimate of her as a woman "whose principles are so much and so justly admired by the friends of liberty and of mankind" would have been endorsed by most Americans.[3]

Mrs. Macaulay's *Address to the People of England, Ireland, and Scotland* [4] in 1775 is one of the most vigorous and inflamatory attacks on the Government of George III penned during the 1770's. In contrast to Bishop Shipley's works, for example, the pamphlet is filled with invective and vituperation. Whereas Shipley seems genuinely to have sought moderation and labored to convince officials of the necessity for conciliatory measures, Mrs. Macaulay passionately denounced the government and exhorted British citizens to work for the defeat of their leaders. Although her American readers must have drawn inspiration from her tirade, publication of the *Address* in England contributed little to the cause of those who sought to close the widening breach with America.

The purpose of the pamphlet was to alert "the People of England, Ireland, and Scotland" to the danger of the parliamentary oppression which threatened them, and to arouse them to political activity before their "supineness" enabled the Ministry to strip them entirely of the same political rights that the Americans had recently lost. Viewing the cause of America as the cause of Englishmen, she lamented the "guilty acquiescence" of her countrymen in permitting the destruction of the Canadian Assembly and the closing of the Port of Boston. She attempted to inflame her readers against the introduction of "Popery" into the dangerously enlarged Catholic Province of Quebec. She drew heavily upon James Burgh's *Political Disquisitions*—a work which was rapidly becoming a favorite of both English and American political radicals—to rivet attention on the effects of vice, corruption, and ministerial abuses of power.

Two solutions to Britain's plight were specifically mentioned. First, the people should require "tests" of candidates for office similar to those required by the electors of London and Middlesex County to ensure that Members of Parliament would remain responsible to the will of the electorate. Second, the system of septennial Parliaments should be overturned, although Mrs. Macaulay failed to state whether she desired annual elections or a return to triennial Parliaments. The impact of her appeal, however, is to be found not in the content of her recommendations so much as in her unrestrained denunciation of the Government and the vigor of her prose.

NOTES

[1] Much of the information in this introduction was drawn from Mildred C. Beckwith's unpublished doctoral dissertation, "Catharine Macaulay, Eighteenth-Century English Rebel," Ohio State University, 1953; and Lucy Martin Donnelly, "The Celebrated Mrs. Macaulay," *William and Mary Quarterly*, 3d series, 6: 173–207 (April 1949).

[2] In commemoration of her services to the American cause before the War for Independence, Mrs. Macaulay's *Address to the People of England, Ireland, and Scotland* was serialized in Powar's Boston *American Herald* on October 4, 11, and 18, 1784, while she was in Massachusetts.

[3] Mrs. Macaulay's friendship with Washington can be traced in *The Writings of George Washington*, edited by John C. Fitzpatrick (Washington, 1931–44), vol. 28, p. 370–371; vol. 29, p. 316–317; vol. 30, p. 495–498; vol. 31, p. 213–214, p. 316–317. For evidence of her earlier contacts with prominent Americans see *Letters of Benjamin Rush* (Princeton, 1951), vol. 1, p. 69–72, and *Adams Family Correspondence* (Cambridge, Mass., 1963), vol. 1, p. 177–179, both edited by Lyman C. Butterfield, as well as her letter of September 11, 1774, to John Adams, Adams Family Papers, reel 344.

[4] The text reprinted here was taken from a microcard copy, filmed for the *Early American Imprints* series, of a pamphlet printed in New York by John Holt and owned by the Library Company of Philadelphia. In addition to this microcopy, the Library of Congress has one copy of the first and two copies of

the second London editions. In *American Independence, the Growth of an Idea,* an excellent bibliographic study of American political pamphlets from 1764 to 1776, Thomas R. Adams notes that copies of Holt's edition are at the Library Company of Philadelphia, the Historical Society of Pennsylvania, and the Connecticut Historical Society. Holt used the second London edition of the pamphlet, which contains a few minor variations from the first edition.

Title page reproduced from the collections of the Library Company of Philadelphia.

AN
ADDRESS
TO THE
PEOPLE
OF

England, *Ireland,* and *Scotland,*

ON THE PRESENT

Important Crisis of AFFAIRS.

BY
CATHARINE MACAULAY.

The THIRD EDITION.

LONDON: Printed.
NEW-YORK: Reprinted by John Holt, in *Water Street.*

M,DCC,LXXV.

AN
ADDRESS, &c.

THE advantage of a second opportunity to correct a mistake, when the first has been neglected, is a happiness which few individuals, or bodies of men, experience; and a blessing which, if it oftener occurred in the affairs of life, would enable most of us to avoid the greater part of the misery which at present appears inseparable from the human state.

The electors of this kingdom, however, have shewn themselves incorrigible, by recently abusing what the author of *The Patriot* justly calls a high dignity, and an important trust; and this after a ruinous experience of the effects of a former ill-placed confidence.

It is not to be supposed, that either the beauty of justice, the interests of liberty, or the welfare of individuals, as united to the common good, can have any avail with men, who, at this important crisis of British affairs, could reject the wise example set them by the city of London, and the county of Middlesex, in requiring a test from those they elected into the representative office;[1] a test which, had it been generally taken, and religiously observed, would have dispersed the dark cloud which hangs over the empire, restored the former splendor of the nation, and given a renewed strength, vigour, and purity, to the British constitution.

Among the body of Electors, however, there are undoubtedly many who, by the most cruel of undue influences, that influence which the opulent exert over the needy, have in a manner been constrained to act contrary to judgment and inclination; while there are others who have been misled by their ignorance, and the sophistry of men of better understanding. To these, and that large body of my countrymen who are unjustly debarred the privilege of election, and, except by petition and remonstrance, have no legal means of opposing the measures of government, I address myself, on the present momentous occasion.

[113]

It can be no secret to any of you, my friends and fellow citizens, that the ministry, after having exhausted all those ample sources of corruption which your own tameness under oppressive taxes has afforded, either fearing the unbiassed judgment of the people, or impatient at the slow, but steady progress of despotism, have attempted to wrest from our American Colonists every privilege necessary to freemen—privileges which they hold from the authority of their charters, and the principles of the constitution.

With an entire supineness, England, Scotland, and Ireland, have seen the Americans, year by year, stripped of the most valuable of their rights; and, to the eternal shame of this country, the stamp act, by which they were to be taxed in an arbitrary manner, met with no opposition, except from those who are particularly concerned, that the commercial intercourse between Great-Britain and her Colonies should meet with no interruption.

With the same guilty acquiescence, my countrymen, you have seen the last Parliament finish their venal course, with passing two acts for shutting up the Port of Boston, for indemnifying the murderers of the inhabitants of the Massachusets Bay, and changing their chartered constitution of government: And to shew that none of the fundamental principles of our boasted constitution are held sacred by the government, the same Parliament, without any interruption either by petition or remonstrance, passed another act for changing the government of Quebec; in which the Popish religion, instead of being tolerated as stipulated by the treaty of peace, is established; in which the Canadians are deprived of the right to an assembly, and of trial by jury; in which the English laws in civil cases are abolished, the French laws established, and the crown empowered to erect arbitrary courts of judicature; and in which, for the purpose of enlarging the bounds where despotism is to have its full sway, the limits of that province are extended so as to comprehend those vast regions that lie adjoining to the northerly and westerly bounds of our colonies.

The anxious desire of preserving that harmony which had so long and so happily existed between the Parent State and her Colonies, occasioned the Americans to bear, with an almost blameable patience, the innovations which were continually made on their liberty, till the ministry, who imagined their moderation proceeded from ignorance and cowardice, by depriving them of almost every part of their rights which remained unviolated, have raised a spirit beyond the Atlantic, which may either recover the opportunities *we* have lost of restoring the breaches which for near a century have been making in our constitution, or of sinking us into the lowest abyss of national misery.

In these times of general discontent, when almost every act of our Governors, excites a jealousy and apprehension, in all those who make the interests of the community their care, there are several among us who, dazzled with the sunshine of a court, or fattening on the spoils of the people, have used their utmost endeavours to darken your understandings on those subjects, which, at this time, it is particularly your business to be acquainted with. There are others who, whilst they have the words Freedom, Constitution, and Privileges, continually in their mouths, are using every mean in their power to render those limitations useless, which have from time to time been erected by our ancestors, as mitigations of that barbarous system of despotism imposed by the Norman tyrant, on the inhabitants of this island.

These men attempt to persuade you, that those who appear the most anxious for the safety of their country, are the least interested in its welfare. They have had the insolence to tell you, though in contradiction to the evidence of your feelings, that all goes well, that your Governors faithfully fulfil the duties of their office, and that there are no grievances worthy to be complained of, but those which arise from that spirit of faction which, more or less, must ever exist in a limited monarchy. These men have told you, that you are no judges of the state of your political happiness; that you are made of too inflammable materials to be trusted with the knowledge of your injuries, even if you have suffered any; and that those who appeal to you, do it only with the intention to betray you. They have told you that Quebec, being on the other side of the Atlantic, it is of little consequence to you what religion is there established; that the Canada bill only secures to the inhabitants of that province privileges which were stipulated to them on the yielding the place to the English; and that those are as bad as Papists, who refuse to any people the enjoyment of their religion.

These men have attempted to divert you from the exacting a test as the rule of parliamentary conduct, and to bring into suspicion those who have been willing to enter into salutary engagements. They have told you, that such candidates, by promising more than they were able to perform, only meant to delude you by an empty clamour of ineffectual zeal. These men, in asserting that you are too profligate, too needy, and too ignorant to be adequate judges of your own business, endeavour to throw disgrace and contempt on those who have made an indefinite promise of obeying the mandates of their constituents.

These men have asserted, that unlimited obedience is stipulated in the acceptance of protection; and though such an assertion involves you and the subjects of every state in unlimited slavery, and unlimited slavery excludes every idea of right and power, yet they have also told you, that it is in vindication of your authority that your Governors have exerted an arbitrary power over your brethren in America.

In order to confound your ideas on the merits of the dispute, and to stifle your feelings of humanity, they have told you, that the Americans, though neither adequately or inadequately represented in the case of taxation, stand on the same predicament with yourselves, and that there is no more injustice in inflicting a severe punishment on the whole town of Boston, for the supposed offence of a few of its inhabitants, than in the bombarding a town in the possession of an enemy, when, by such an act of hostility, a few of our own people dwelling in the town, might accidentally be destroyed.

This, my friends and fellow citizens, is treating you, indeed, according to the appellations of ignorant and profligate, so freely given you; but as there are many of you, who, I trust, deserve not these severe terms of reproach, I shall appeal to that measure of understanding which the Almighty has given in common to man, and endeavour to convince you of the falsehood of these assertions.

Men who are rid of the numerous ills which narrow circumstances occasion, and this by pensions taken from the public treasure, may, from a selfishness inseparable from human nature, fancy that the times cannot be better; but that it is the mere delusion of those who rejoice at your expence, your own experience must, I think, fully shew you. Let the once-opulent trader, let the starving mechanic, bear witness to this truth, that our commerce has been declining with hasty steps for these last ten years. Let the numerous half-famished poor which we meet at every turn in our streets; let the needy gentry, whose honest independent ancestors have handed down to them a moderate income, and who find that income yearly sinking from bare sufficiency to poverty, bear witness, that the high price of all the necessaries of life, with the oppressive burden of our taxes, are very weighty evils.

Though men of true virtue, my fellow citizens, (that is, men who have a just regard for the rights of nature, for the general happiness of the human species, and for the happiness of their countrymen in particular) will not willingly associate with those of looser principles, yet they will undoubtedly endeavour to stop the career of that government, whose impolitic measures are every day adding numbers to the wretched mass of the ignorant, the needy, and the profligate.

To oppose government with success, such honest individuals must make use of the assistance of the multitude, and consequently, of good and bad citizens, of the rich and the poor, the learned and the unlearned, of the wise and the foolish, that is, of every man who will cooperate with them in their designs, whether he be led to such cooperation by the principle of justice, by interest, or by passion.

Though Quebec is situated beyond the Atlantic, my fellow citizens, you are still to remember that it is part of the British empire; and that, though a toleration of all religions, where such indulgence can be used with safety to the welfare of the community, is undoubtedly laudable, because agreeable to the principles of justice and the rights of nature, yet the establishment of Popery, which is a very different thing from the toleration of it, is, for very just and wise reasons, altogether incompatible with the fundamental principles of our constitution.

I will, however, wave a subject which must ever be an invidious one while there are so many of us in communion with the Roman church, and which is perhaps impertinent, because it carries with it the appearance of a remote danger, while so many nearer mischiefs demand our present and our earnest attention.

It is not the establishment of the Popish religion in Quebec (even to the exclusion of a toleration to the Protestants except by favour of the crown, and this at a time when the test, and other arbitrary acts restraining the rights of conscience, hang over the heads of our own Dissenters) of which we now complain.[2] Our present objection is not to that which the Canadians enjoy, but to that of which they are deprived. It is not the preservation, but the violation of the Royal Word, which stands the foremost in our list of grievances.

In the act for the government of the province of Quebec, my friends and fellow citizens, we read despotism in every line. The deluded Canadians, instead of being put in possession of all the privileges and immunities of English subjects, according to his Majesty's proclamation in 1763, are indeed favoured with the full possession of their religion, as long as his Majesty, who is at the head of their church, is graciously inclined to continue to them such indulgence; yet in respect both to their civil and religious rights, they are in a more abject state of slavery than when they were under the French government.

The conquests of foreign nations are dangerous triumphs, even to the liberty of republican states; but in limited monarchies, when on the conquered are imposed laws, opposite and hostile to the limitations of power in these governments, it never fails of subjecting the conquerors to the same measure of slavery which they have imposed on the conquered.

Had the government of Charles the Fifth been confined to the sovereignty of Spain, the Spaniards might to this day have preserved a greater degree of freedom than any other of the European nations.

It was the Canada bill, and other transactions of the government, which equally threatened your security and welfare; that engaged the city of London, and the county of Middlesex, to exact from those they elected into the representative office, an engagement, by which their members were bound to endeavour, to the utmost of their abilities, the repeal of the unconstitutional laws respecting America which passed in the last session of the last parliament. And as septennial parliaments are found to be the root from whence all our political grievances spring, they were also bound to endeavour the restoration of our ancient Privileges in respect to the duration of parliaments.

Surely, my friends and fellow citizens, this is a conduct which, at such a crisis of our affairs, was laudable and necessary, and a conduct which, if all the electors of Great-Britain had followed, we should not now have been at the eve of a civil war with America; nor such an interruption have been given to our commerce, as threatens the immediate ruin of thousands of families.

Surely, in such a state of our affairs, no honest and enlightened man could have refused binding himself to such endeavours; and though the obeying every mandate of constituents may, in some very extraordinary conjuncture of opinions and circumstances, be wrong, yet at a time when the representatives had affected an intire independency on, or rather an absolute sovereignty over their constituents, this might be a sufficient reason for many worthy men, as a far lesser evil, to submit to an indefinite obligation of obedience.

Power is regarded by all men as the greatest of temporal advantages. The support given to power, therefore, is an obligation; and, consequently, the protection given by governors to subjects, a positive duty. The subject can only be bound to obedience on the considerations of public good; but the Sovereign, on these considerations, and a thousand others equally binding, is tied to the exact observance of the laws of that constitution under which he holds his power.

The assertion that "Americans, tho' neither adequately, or inadequately represented, stand on the same predicament with yourselves," is too glaring a falsehood to deceive you; and I shall not affront your understanding so much as to fancy you can suppose that the positive punishment of the whole town of Boston, for the offence of a few individuals, when those individuals might have been prosecuted according to law, can be a case similar to the running the hazard of hurting a few citizens in the attempt of re-taking one of our own towns from the enemy.

I have hitherto endeavoured to prevent your being misled by the sophistry of those who have an interest in deceiving you. I shall now give you some of the judicious observations of one of your best friends, in regard to the conduct of your government towards America.

"Before the taxing of the unrepresented colonies in America was thought of (says Mr. Burgh*) the Ministry ought to have reduced exorbitant salaries, abated or abolished excessive perquisites, annihilated useless places, stopped iniquitous pensions, withheld electioneering expences, and bribes for votes in the house, reduced an odious and devouring army, and taxed vice, luxury, gaming, and public diversions: This would have brought into the treasury ten times more than could have ever been expected from taxing, by force and authority, the unrepresented Colonies. "Even a conquered city has time given it to raise the contributions laid upon it, and may raise it in its own way. We have treated our Colonies worse than conquered countries. Neither Wales nor Ireland are taxed unheard and unrepresented in the British parliament, as the Colonies: Wales sends members to parliament, and Ireland has done so; and as Ireland is not now represented in the British parliament, neither is it taxed in the British parliament.

"It is frivolous to alledge, that because the Mother Country has been at expences for the colonies, therefore the British Parliament may tax them, without allowing them any legal opportunity of remonstrating against the oppression. The mother country

---

* *Political Disquisitions*, page 313, *et seq.*

has spent her blood and her treasure in supporting, at different times, France against Spain, and Spain against France, Prussia against Hungary, and Hungary against Prussia, and so on without end. Does this give our parliament a right to tax all Europe? "What difference is there between the British parliament's taxing America, and the French court's laying England under contribution? The French Court could but do this if they had conquered England. Have we conquered our Colonies?"

This excellent author shews how the Americans, if there had been a necessity for such a measure, might have been taxed by our parliament, without violating the right of representation; but, with the Bishop of St. Asaph, who speaks on this subject in a manner which must convince every man whose prejudices are only founded in ignorance, he is of opinion, that the most beneficial way of taxing the Colonies is the obliging them to an exclusive commerce with us.

To all the restrictions laid on their trade, the Americans declare they will ever readily submit; and this on the generous consideration that they are supposed to be for the benefit and advantage of the whole empire.

At the same time, my friends and fellow citizens, the Americans declare, that if you will not concur with your own, and their enemies, to oppress them, that is, if you will not concur with men whose every act of administration are so many evidences of a formed design to enslave the whole empire, they will ever esteem an union with you their glory and their happiness.

That they will be ever ready to contribute all in their power towards the welfare of the empire; and that they will consider your enemies as their enemies, and hold your interests as dear to them as their own.

They exhort you for the sake of that honour and justice for which this nation was once renowned, they entreat you by all those ties of common interest which are inseparable from the subjects of free states, not to suffer your enemies to effect your slavery, in their ruin. They set before you in the strongest colours, all those disadvantages which must attend that large independent power the sovereigns of Great-Britain will gain by the means of taxing, in an arbitrary manner, the Americans; and they invite you, for these cogent reasons, to join with them in every legal method to disappoint the designs of our common foes.

It is not impossible, that after having tamely suffered the government, by a yearly increase of taxes, to beggar yourselves and your posterity, you may be led away with the delusive hope, that the Ministry, when they have the power to pick the pockets of your American brethren, will have the moderation to save those of their countrymen.

If these are your thoughts, my fellow citizens, little have you studied your own natures, and the experience of all ages, which must have convinced you, that the want of power is the only limitation to the exertion of human selfishness; but should you be contented to bid defiance to the warnings of common policy, should you be contented to be slaves on the hope that the Americans will bear the greater part of the burden of your enormous taxes, be assured, that such an alternative will never be in your power. No, if a civil war commences between Great-Britain and her Colonies, either the mother country, by one great exertion, may ruin both herself and America, or the Americans, by a lingering contest, will gain an independency; and in this case, all those advantages which you for some time have enjoyed by our colonies, and advantages which have hitherto preserved you from a national bankruptcy, must for ever have an end; and whilst a new, a flourishing, and an extensive empire of freemen is established on the other side the Atlantic, you, with the loss of all those blessings you have received by the unrivalled state of your commerce, will be left to the bare possession of your foggy islands; and this under the sway of a domestic despot, or you will become the provinces of some powerful European state.

If a long succession of abused prosperity should, my friends and fellow citizens, have entirely deprived you of that virtue, the renown of which makes you even at this day respectable among all the nations of the civilized world; if neither the principles of justice, or generosity have any weight with you, let me conjure you to take into consideration the interests of your safety and preservation. Suffer me again to remind you of the imminent danger of your situation. Your Ministers, by attacking the rights of all America, have effected that which the malicious policy of more judicious minds would have avoided. Your colonists, convinced that their safety depends on their harmony, are now united in one strong bond of union; nor will it be in the power of a Machiavel to take any advantage of those feuds and jealousies which formerly subsisted among them, and which exposed their liberties to more real danger than all the fleets and armies we are able to send against them. Your Ministers also, deceived by present appearances, vainly imagine, because our rivals in Europe are encouraging us to engage beyond the possibility of a retreat, that they will reject the opportunity when it offers, of putting a final end to the greatness and the glory of our empire; but if, by the imprudent measures of the government, the public expences increase, or the public income decrease to such a degree that the public revenue fail, and you be rendered unable to pay the interest of your debt, then will no longer be delayed the day, and the hour of your destruction; then will you become an easy prey to the courts of France and Spain, who, you may depend upon it, will fall upon you as soon as they see you fairly engaged in a war with your Colonists; and, according to what is foretold you in a late publication, that conjuncture will prove the latest and the uttermost of your prosperity, your peace, and, in all probability, of your existence, as an independent state and nation.

Rouse, my countrymen! rouse from that state of guilty dissipation in which you have too long remained, and in which, if you longer continue, you are lost for ever. Rouse! and unite in one general effort; till, by your unanimous and repeated addresses to the throne, and to both houses of parliament, you draw the attention of every part of the government to their own interests, and to the dangerous state of the British empire.

FINIS

NOTES

¹ The interest of London radicals in the American issue in 1774 and 1775 should be viewed in the perspective of perennial attempts of reformers to make the House of Commons more responsive to the electorate. In the aftermath of John Wilkes' expulsion from his Middlesex seat in 1769, demands were formulated for shorter Parliaments and the imposition of a test upon candidates standing for election that would bind them to instructions from their constituents. In the 1774 elections Wilkes himself had formulated and accepted such a pledge and led a slate of candidates (including John Sawbridge, Mrs. Macaulay's brother) who followed his example. The failure of voters throughout the counties to follow the lead of London and Middlesex County, where pledged candidates did well at the polls, led to Mrs. Macaulay's outburst against "the electors of this Kingdom." See Ian Christie's *Myth and Reality in Late-Eighteenth-Century British Politics and Other Papers* (Berkeley and Los Angeles, 1970), p. 246–259.

Parentheses supplied for clarity.

John Cartwright

J OHN Cartwright (1740–1824), "regarded in his own lifetime as the Father of Parliamentary Reform," was converted to a career of radical political reform by the American crisis in 1774.[1] *American Independence*, the earliest of Cartwright's 80 political tracts, was his first direct intellectual confrontation with the American problem. His contact with America dated from the preceding decade, however, when he was a young naval officer assigned to the Newfoundland station. There, as Deputy Commissary to the Vice-Admiralty Court, he began to interest himself in the land, the inhabitants, and the practical problems of imperial administration in America, revealing the active mind and broad curiosity that characterized his later work.[2] Cartwright returned home in 1770 to recover his health, and the convalescence provided him with the leisure and relief from official duties that enabled him to develop ideas about the Colonies and the authority of the British Government. These he began to systematize as the imperial crisis worsened, particularly in the aftermath of the Boston Tea Party. Early in 1776 he received an unsolicited and highly desired offer of a naval appointment from Lord Howe, under whom he had served during the Seven Years' War. He had already become so committed to the American cause and to the principles of reform, however, that he declined the opportunity for advancement rather than compromise his political principles.[3]

Cartwright's essays on American independence were published in H.S. Woodfall's London *Public Advertiser* between March 20 and April 14, 1774. They appeared as a series of 10 letters "To the Legislature," under the pseudonym "Constitution." The essays were republished in August, with an "Epistle Dedicatory" and a preface by Woodfall. It was this edition that was reprinted by Robert Bell at Philadelphia in 1776. A second London edition had been issued in

1775, containing two additional "letters," a 26-page "Letter to Edmund Burke," a 31-page "Postscript," and a 19-page draft bill for restoring peace to America, but Bell was unable to obtain a copy of that edition for American readers. These discursive additions added little new substance to Cartwright's original effort.

Cartwright's letters on the American issue, which were but a prelude to his more famous work on parliamentary reform, *Take Your Choice* (1776), are characterized by a radical simplicity that marked nearly all his work. During his entire life his appeal was to ultimate principles—"the plain maxims of the law of nature"—and to abstract rights—"the title to liberty is the immediate gift of God." He repeatedly attacked the opportunist doctrines and arguments from expediency that were commonly used by leaders of both Whig and Tory leanings, quarreling with moderate critics of ministerial policy such as Josiah Tucker and Edmund Burke. Cartwright was often assailed by his opponents as being obstinate and hopelessly impractical, but he was never deterred from speaking out against wrongs where he perceived them, even when personal losses such as abandonment of his naval career were involved. "Moderation in conduct is wisdom, but moderation in principle is dishonour, and moderation in justice is injustice." [4]

Although Cartwright's essays are often prolix and tedious, they are also strewn with striking phrases, insights, and arguments which had a natural appeal to Americans and must be judged in that context. In the first "letter," a discussion of taxation and representative government, he condemns those who attempt to uphold Parliament's right to tax the Colonies by appealing to the past. In a few lines he characteristically sweeps away all claims that rest on mere precedent. To Cartwright no free man may be taxed without his consent. The proposition requires no proof and cannot be controverted by resort to contrary precedents. It is a maxim of the law of nature. And it makes no difference whether "such a maxim was received and acquiesced in only yesterday, or a thousand years ago . . . . Truth is not the less truth, though mankind were in ignorance of it until lately."

Similarly he goes on to circumvent the arguments of many writers by questioning the authority of those learned merely in the law who would deny the ability of a man of common sense to judge such matters for himself. "The gospel of civil as well as religious salvation 'is hid from the wise and prudent, and revealed unto babes.'" Men may safely ignore "political Popes, who would fain have us distrust our common sense and our feelings, and believe implicitly in their infallibility." It is wrong to "consider the liberty of mankind in the same light as an estate or chattel, and go about to prove or disprove their right to it by the letter of grants and charters, by custom and usage, and by municipal statutes." The liberty of mankind is not to be found among "mouldy parchments, nor in the cobwebs of a casuist's brain," it is "the universal gift of God." "Let us then hear no more of a right in our present-constituted parliament to govern the Americans, as being derived from any former exercise of this sovereignty."

Although many English leaders were scornful of such assertions, few Americans could have quarreled with these sentiments. The impatience reflected in Cartwright's uncompromising tone was shared by many Americans who had themselves grown weary of constructing new defenses for their rights to meet each new provocation from Parliament. Not the least consequence of the decade of controversy with the mother country had been a growing American tendency to abandon fine-spun arguments in favor of sweeping claims resting on fundamental principles incapable of misinterpretation or distortion. But his limited appeal in England was part and parcel of this same radicalism, which in Cartwright outran even that of most of his American readers. As he stripped from Parliament the right to tax the Colonies, he also rejected slavery "in all its forms," applying the same arguments employed by Americans against Britain to denounce the claims of slaveholders to their slaves.

Cartwright's basic political principles were stated in the first two essays, in which he effectively denied unlimited parliamentary sovereignty. Perhaps too few readers persevered to follow him patiently over the terrain he covered in the later essays, which dealt with the reciprocal obligations of the Colonies, regulation of commerce, parallels drawn from the Irish problem, and colonial representation in Parliament. He struck a new note in the sixth "letter" when he interrupted his discourse to answer Dean Josiah Tucker, whose political tracts, Cartwright explained, had fallen into his hands precisely at that point.[5] Even though both Tucker and Cartwright advocated American independence, they had reached that position by such different routes that Cartwright felt compelled to refute Tucker's arguments. Tucker assumed Britain's *right* to rule the Colonies and advocated only withholding its exercise. "While he thinks we are entitled to govern, [he] foresees and demonstrates the fatal consequences of attempting it," Cartwright noted. He went on to score the dean's failure to discover "the fallaciousness of his original positions of parliamentary right to govern the colonies." With less effect, Cartwright devoted his seventh essay to one of Tucker's earlier tracts on colonial trade, and in the eighth and ninth he analyzed the dean's various recommendations for dealing with the Americans. Foreseeing that the separation of the Colonies was likely to be accompanied by a bitterness and hostility inimical to the interests of both America and Britain, Cartwright offered, in the 10th essay, the outline of a bill to effect a mutually beneficial separation.

While he might have considered much of Cartwright's work obscure and the frequent references to Tucker labored, the American reader nonetheless must have found more than enough eye-catching passages to confirm his belief that the Colonies had taken the only course available in their struggle with Britain. Calling England an "extravagant country, immersed in dissipation and corruption," Cartwright praised American leaders for withstanding the temptation to betray their rights. He pleaded with Englishmen to imagine how they themselves would have responded to the persecutions that Americans had endured and concluded with a sweeping defense of the "good citizens" of Boston who had accepted their obligation to resist tyranny with force. Considering their provocations, they had displayed "singular wisdom" and "remarkable temper and forbearance." To Cartwright, the leaders of the Boston Tea Party were "a band of virtuous patriots, whose names, once made public will doubtless be held in eternal veneration by their countrymen." It was a striking piece of prophecy. Such words, falling on the ears of men torn by doubts and struggling to maintain unity in the face of increased criticism at home and abroad, must have been a powerful antidote to despair. Surely Cartwright's essays offered aid and comfort to Americans then girding themselves for the trials of 1776.

NOTES

[1] The quotation above and much of the factual data contained in this introduction were drawn from information and references in Naomi Helen Churgin's unpublished doctoral dissertation, "Major John Cartwright: A Study in Radical Parliamentary Reform, 1774–1824," Columbia University, 1963. The opening quote is from the introduction, p. i.

[2] Cartwright was the brother of the inventor, Edmund Cartwright, and apparently shared many of his brother's interests and aptitudes.

[3] This episode, together with his correspondence on the subject with Lord Howe, for whom he had great respect, is recounted by Frances Cartwright in *The Life and Correspondence of Major Cartwright* (London, 1826; reprinted New York, 1969), vol. 1, p. 71–81.

[4] A concise discussion of Cartwright's political principles may be found in C. B. Roylance Kent's *The English Radicals* (London, 1899), p. 69–73.

[5] Josiah Tucker, *Four Tracts, Together With Two Sermons, On Political and Commercial Subjects* (Gloucester, 1774).

AMERICAN·INDEPENDENCE

THE

INTEREST AND GLORY

OF

GREAT BRITAIN;

CONTAINING

ARGUMENTS which prove, that not only in TAXATION, but in TRADE, MANUFACTURES, and GOVERNMENT, the Colonies are entitled to an entire Independency on the BRITISH LEGISLATURE; and that it can only be by a formal DECLARATION of thefe Rights, and forming thereupon a friendly LEAGUE with them, that the true and lafting Welfare of both Countries can be promoted.

In a SERIES of LETTERS to the LEGISLATURE.

It is not to be hoped, in the corrupt State of Human Nature, that any Nation will be fubject to another, any longer than it finds its own Account in it, and cannot help itfelf.

No Creatures fuck the Teats of their Dams longer than they can draw Milk from thence, or can provide themfelves with better Food; nor will any Country continue their fubjection to another, only becaufe their great Grand-Mothers were acquainted. This is the courfe of human affairs, and all wife States will always have it before their eyes.

Trenchard on Plantations and Colonies, in Cato's Letters, No. 106.

PHILADELPHIA,

Printed and Sold by ROBERT BELL, in Third-Street.

MDCCLXXVI.

N.B. In this Work are included copious Notes; containing Reflections on the Boston and Quebec Acts; and a full Justification of the People of Boston, for destroying the British-taxed Tea; submitted to the Judgment, not of those who have none but borrowed Party-opinions, but of the Candid and Honest.[1]

AMERICAN
INDEPENDENCE

To the LEGISLATURE
LETTER I.

March 20, 1774.

EVEN the most ignorant perceive this to be a crisis of the utmost importance to Great-Britain, and to North America: but it doth not appear that the most sage have yet formed a plan of proceedings that is likely to give content to both parties. With deference to the sentiments of others, and with a sincere desire of rendering a service to my country, permit me to offer a few thoughts on the subject, and to throw some hints in your way, which I do not perceive to have been as yet started by any political writer. It is most deeply to be lamented, that passion and prejudice, pride and self-interest, have evidently too much influence over the minds of most men, to suffer them to decide impartially and equitably in such delicate conjunctures as the present. We want now to discover, and to establish a principle of lasting union between our colonies and the mother country; while the measures of administration, the deliberations in parliament, the sentiments of political writers, and the language of the people at large, all tend to prove, that the most probable event will be mutual jealousy, animosity, and strife.

It is the misfortune of this country, surely without necessity, that schemes of reformation, and plans of a great and comprehensive nature, for the general benefit of the people, are rarely or never formed before hand in the peaceful closet of a provident minister; and, it is as unusual for them to attain their completion by dispassionate contemplation, and the calm determinations of wisdom. On the contrary, we suffer every trivial error and irregularity to ripen into mischief before we think of reformation; when we undertake it at last with minds heated to fermentation, and we perform it with rashness and violence. Let not, however, on this great occasion, any thing so intemperate and faulty mark your deliberations, nor leave a stain upon your measures. Reflect, that the fate of empires is now in suspence, and that the balance is in your hands. No patriots of any age or country ever had a nobler opportunity of immortalizing their fame; nor, what is infinitely more to be desired, of obtaining the inward reward of self-approbation for having given happiness to millions. Remember your duty to mankind; remember your duty to God. Let not the breath of anger or resentment sully your councils; let not jealousy or ambition poison your breasts, nor hang upon your tongues. Be calm, contemplative, candid, prudent, wise; let justice and benevolence rule your hearts; in one word, be Christians! embracing with love and charity your American brethren; and consulting their happiness equally with your own.

The two grand questions now to be decided are; 1. Whether or not the British parliament or legislature, hath the right of sovereignty over North America? And, 2. Whether or not a British parliament hath a right to tax the North Americans*?

Although the latter question be properly involved in the former†, since taxation is a part of legislation, yet being extremely simple and well understood, I shall consider it first, in order to get rid of it; so as it may not embarrass our discussion of the other, which it will be necessary for us to treat with all possible perspicuity. As for those who, with great warmth, maintain the right of parliament to tax the North Americans, surely they are rather to be pitied than argued with! Must they not be totally ignorant of the principles of that inestimable constitution, under which they have the happiness to live? How then shall we expect them to be acquainted with the principles of the law of nature, from whence they flow? When I meet a man inclined towards this opinion, I do not contradict him; and I beseech him to avoid disputation above all things. I beg of him also to divest himself totally of every previous inclination for seeing the point in this or in that light; to consult immediately the great Mr. Locke, and other authors of note, and after a careful examination of the arguments for and against the question, to decide upon it himself impartially and honestly. I remind him likewise, that it is his interest, as well as for the advantage of his country, that he should discover the truth: but a matter of total indifferency on which side it lies. If this fail to set him right, I do not dispute with him myself, nor do I assume the countenance or manner of an opponent; but I intimate to him, that, were he of my opinion, it would afford him great satisfaction of mind; since it gives me a consistency of sentiment, by which I see every right of legislation perfectly consonant with the freedom and the happiness of mankind; and I then simply state my reasons for holding it. I have ever found this appeal to a man's own heart and understanding, the most successful way of enlightening the one, and improving the other. Very few indeed of those with whom I have thus reasoned, on the present subject of American taxation, have gone away unsatisfied, or found a necessity of reading, in order to be convinced: but ignorance and obstinacy, heated by former debate, have sometimes rendered my endeavours ineffectual; and such as were notorious for a vicious ambition, or servility to the ruling powers, have generally remained immoveable, though without producing one just or wise argument in support of their sentiments, or rather their assertions. Such men are not aware how much they lay open to the light that part of their characters they always mean to hide; and that there is as much dishonesty in that disposition which denies an evident truth, as in that which gives a false evidence, or takes a purse. It would have required no learning, but only common sense and common honesty, to have known that a man hath no property, in that which another 'can *by right* take from him *without his consent,*' had not the world been pestered with writers of corrupt hearts, who, for wicked ends, have brought this clear proposition into dispute, and involved it in a casuistical jargon, which persons of plain sense, and too busy or too indolent for reflection, are apt to mistake for learning and superior skill; and to compliment it, first with doubting, and then denying upon trust, what they once understood and believed. But I trust, that characters so weak as these, so profligate as those, will have no influence with the British legislature; that its deliberations will be carried on with too much wisdom and too much dignity to give a hearing to the drivelings of shallow and impudent praters; or to suffer the unseemly violence of furious and tyrannical spirits, to discompose that serenity and divestment from passion, which ought ever to be observed in the presence of his Majesty, and in the awful councils of the nation. Here I must express my concern, that it should seem to be thought by very sensible men, that it is necessary to appeal to ancient times, in order to ascertain the right of a free subject not to be taxed without his consent, either in person or by representation. With as much reason might we go about to prove, that no ancient King had a right to take from every subject at his good pleasure, an eye or an ear. It is sufficient that we know any maxim in our law, to be at the same time a maxim of the law of nature, or demonstrably deducible from its fundamental principles. What is it to the purpose, whether such a maxim was received and acquiesced in only yesterday, or a thousand years ago? Truth is not the less truth, though mankind were in ignorance of it until lately. No mathematician, in demonstrating an astronomical problem, thinks it necessary to prove the properties of a triangle, a circle, or an ellipsis; why then should the politician waste his time and embarrass his argument, with proving principles and axioms universally assented to by all just reasoners? not but that a maxim carries more weight and authority with it, as this of the necessary connection between taxation and representation, when we find it has been the uniform sentiment of all ages; and references to antient times, and to various histories, serve very properly to illustrate political arguments; sometimes facilitating their reception among the timid and suspicious, who are apt to shrink at bold and honest truths, to which they have not been familiarized.

NOTES, &c. to LETTER I.

*Let me recommend to the reader's perusal, an excellent pamphlet, under the title of Letters from a Farmer in Pennsylvania, to the inhabitants of the British Colonies. It is printed for Almon.

† I think a noble Lord has lately asserted the contrary; but we shall probably be of the same sentiment, when we come to an explanation of our words. I here mean that just legislation only which is founded on liberty, and in which the people, either personally, or by their representatives, have a share. Every other species of legislation, being clearly an infringement on the inherent rights of mankind, is totally excluded from my ideas of government; so that confining myself to a free government, where the people have a share, it still appears to me, that taxation is a part, and included in the general idea of legislation. If it be the sole province and exclusive right of that branch, which consists of the people or their representatives, to grant money for the support of government; yet taxation is not completed, nor can it be carried into execution, until the other branches of the constitution have given their concurrence. A mere free gift of the Commons, without an act of legislation, would not be a *tax*; and we must remember, that though it be wisely provided, that in all taxations, the Commons alone shall *give and grant*, yet, that the Lords are not exempt from *paying*. May we not therefore say, with propriety, that taxation is a part of legislation.

LETTER II.

TO every man of candour, I apprehend it must be evident, that 'Parliament hath not the rights of sovereignty over his Majesty's American Subjects.' Every species, indeed of declamation and sophistry, have been made use of in order to shew that it hath, because it gratifies the pride of Englishmen in general, to think that, that legislature, in which they feel themselves to have a share, should govern half the world: but there are not wanting an honest few who think more justly and more generously. Amongst this number, a writer who subscribes himself A. B. in the Public Advertiser of the 22d, deserves the thanks of every friend to freedom. Except in his idea of the country of America, having been by the prerogative the property of the crown, which, in the sense of the passage, signifies the *King exclusively*, I entirely agree with him in sentiment. He hath clearly and elegantly refuted the notion of parliamentary sovereignty; he has, with a generous warmth becoming an Englishman, appealed to the manly sense and to the virtue of his countrymen*. It would be an endless, as well as an useless work, to follow the many daily writers along all the mazes they wander through, in order to assert the sovereignty of parliament, and to justify administration in the harsh measures they are now carrying into execution. Notwithstanding their laboured and fine-spun performances, there is in reality no difficulty in the case. We have no need of profound learning, nor an intimate acquaintance with antiquity, nor even of the history of the respective provinces and their different origins; neither do we want copies of grants, charters, or acts of parliament, in order to judge of the question before us. If we comprehend but the most well known principles of the English constitution; if we comprehend but a few of the plain maxims of the law of nature, and the clearest doctrines of Christianity, all which are so simple and plain, as to be understood by hundreds, nay thousands, of plain men who know not that they are possessed of so useful a treasure, we have knowledge enough on this occasion. The only requisite wanting beyond this, is a heart strictly devoted to truth and virtue, without which we shall never understand any doctrine that does not soothe our passions.

The gospel of civil as well as religious salvation 'is hid from the wise and prudent, and revealed unto babes;' that is, unto those who are not puffed up with vanity and false learning, nor blinded by pride, ambition, and self-interest, but whose minds are in a state of humility and innocence. But we have our political Popes, who would fain have us distrust our common sense and our feelings, and believe implicitly in their infallibility; nor do I doubt, but they would prove as faithful guardians of civil, as the Roman Pope is of religious, liberty, was it once put into their hands.

It is a capital error in the reasonings of several writers on this subject, that they consider the liberty of mankind in the same light as an estate of chattel, and go about to prove or disprove their right to it by the letter of grants and charters, by custom and usage, and by municipal statutes. Hence too we are told, that these men have a right to more, those to less, and some to none at all. But a title to the liberty of mankind is not established on such rotten foundations: 'tis not among mouldy parchments, nor in the cobwebs of a casuist's brain we are to look for it; it is the immediate, the universal gift of God, and the seal of it is that free-will which he hath made the noblest constituent of man's nature. It is not derived from any one, but original in every one; it is inherent and unalienable. The most antient inheritance cannot strengthen this right; the want of inheritance cannot impair it. The child of a slave is as free-born, according to the law of nature, as he who could trace a free ancestry up to the creation. Slavery in all its forms, in all its degrees, is an outrageous violation of the rights of mankind; an odious degradation of human nature. It is utterly impossible that any human being can be without a title to liberty, except he himself hath forfeited it by crimes which make him dangerous to society.

Let us then hear no more of a right in our present-constituted parliament to govern the Americans, as being derived from any former exercise of this sovereignty, from the original dependence and protection of the emigrants and infant colonies, or from the tenour of grants and charters! The respective governments in America, are no longer dependent colonies; they are independent nations. Not that I allow they ever were otherways then free (although dependent) in the most absolute sense: All their original constitutions either were, or ought to have been on the true principles of freedom. They are not to be deprived of it as a man would lose an estate, by a flaw in their title; for I have already proved, that their title can have no flaw.

Those who are so fond of placing them metaphorically in the relation of children to a parent state, and thence are childish enough to argue for a blind filial obedience, should recollect, that the power of a parent, even during childhood, doth not extend to any act of tyranny or injustice; and totally ceases when the child arrives at years of maturity. Then, as to the *property* of a child, a parent cannot take it from him even *with* his consent; and as soon as his independency puts it in his power to give it to his parent, he hath also the power of with-holding it if he think proper. In short, during infancy, he must be protected agreable to the laws of equity; when arrived at manhood, he is free, and becomes his own protector. But analogy not being the safe road of reason, we resign it again, after this short excursion, to those who carelessly range the fields of politics for amusement; but are not solicitous, as we are, of reaching the abodes of truth and freedom.

The Americans, in common with the whole race of man, have indisputably an inherent right to liberty; and to be governed by such laws as shall best provide for the continuance of that liberty, and for securing their property. These are the hinges on which turn the welfare and happiness of society; these are the true, the only ends of civil government. But how are they to be obtained under the sovereignty of a British Parliament? Are not the legislators of every free state to be bound themselves by the laws they make? And, must they not tax their own purses, together with those of their constituents? Is there any safety for the people without these ties upon their legislaors? Will a member of the British parliament be bound by any law enacted for, and confined to, America? Must the purses of the Americans be at his mercy, while his own shall be exempt from every taxation he may vote? What English school-boy, so ignorant of the constitution, as to admit these absurdities! He must first go out into the world, and, by the help of a little political sophistry, unlearn his common-sense, and even his A B C.

The secure enjoyment of liberty and property, in which consist the welfare and happiness of a people, being the true ends of all civil government; this is the foundation alone on which we must argue concerning who have a right to govern. The answer is obvious and short. The rights of sovereignty reside in the people themselves; that is, they have a right to chuse their own governors. Minds that do not feel the force of self-evidences may deny the truth of this simple proposition: but they may be assured, that if they set themselves about controverting it, they will only bewilder themselves in their own subtleties, without telling us any thing that will benefit mankind. Don't we all acknowledge, that the Americans are a free people? But how are they free, if they cannot choose their own governors; if their laws be not enacted by their own representatives? In what doth our freedom consist if not in these very rights as the essence of it? In these rights which we have so often asserted, for which we have so often bled! That people cannot be free who are *not* governed by their own consent. Those who are governed by their own consent, *choose their own governors*. This is indispensably requisite towards the welfare and happiness of every people; it is an unalterable law of nature; that is, it is the law of God.

NOTES, &c. to LETTER II.

* The letter alluded to, is so well worth preserving, and so much to our present purpose, that I shall take the liberty of transcribing it for the use of my reader.

"The daily papers abound so much in idle declamation against the northern colonies, that it is not surprising, such admirable reasons are advanced in most companies, where the conversation turns upon this important topic, why force should be used to bring them to obedience. Neither is it much to be wondered at, that the people of England are so unanimous in their opinions. The same motives, which induce their rulers to abridge their privileges, make the people of England willing to abridge the liberties of America. The subjects of the King of Great-Britain consider themselves as the sovereigns of his Majesty's American subjects; for, if the House of Commons have a legislative power over the colonies, the people of England must have the same right ultimately, as the House derive all their power from the people by election. But it would be worth an enquiry how the people of England obtained this sovereignty. Was it by the free concessions of the American provinces? By no means; or, did it result from the spirit of the English laws or government upon the migration of oppressed religionists and their settlement in those regions, which, by the prerogative, were the property of the crown,† and which the King, by the same prerogative, had the power of alienating without the consent of the people of England, particularly when such alienation was made to a part of his own subjects? It would be difficult to shew that this was the case, and I believe it has never been attempted. That the King should have the sovereignty of the colonies is but reasonable, is consistent with the spirit of the English laws. If English subjects settle upon the lands of the crown out of this realm, with the King's permission and consent, they do not thereby become a state independent of the kingly power; as they were subjects in England, so are they subjects in

[140]

their new country; but they do not become subjects of subjects; despicable indeed would be their situation were such the case. On the contrary, they have the same rights which they had before, and the same sovereign executive power. The rights of Englishmen are not confined to this little spot of land; but they follow the person as a shadow follows the substance; however, it may vary its situation, whether it goes North, West, East, or South. The House of Commons can claim no power of imposing laws on the colonists, for they derive no such power by election. The power of the Commons of Great Britain is circumscribed; from the spirit of the laws, they have only a legislative power, and that power, bears relation to the purpose for which it was given; which was to impose laws upon the people of Great-Britain, but by no means the people of America, because the power of the electors extended only to themselves. The three orders united, i.e. the parliament have a most extensive power over the subjects of Great-Britain, because every power in the state meets in that body: but considered with respect to the Colonies, their pretension to such a power there clashes with the legislatures of those Colonies, they can never subsist together in the same place. As to the relation of parent and child, in which Great-Britain and the colonies are said to stand by some ingenious men, I confess it would be a tolerable good figure in a rhetorical flourish, or would sound very prettily in metre; but with submission, when the rights of many opulent and populous provinces are in question, something more than a simile or allusion ought to decide it. Let Englishmen, who have been admired for ages, for their regard to liberty, blush, when it is now said, that, by superior force, they would deprive three or four millions of their fellow-subjects of those rights and privileges to which they are so attached themselves. How depraved a mind would that individual be said to possess, who would defend his property at the risk of his life, exclaim against the aggressor as a lawless invader, and yet, at the same time, or a moment afterwards, behave in the same unjustifiable manner to his neighbour. Is this the people, will foreigners cry, who are so fond of liberty? No; we have always mistaken them: they are selfish, arbitrary, and tyrannical, fond of the privileges they enjoy; but they would exclude the rest of the world, nay, their fellow subjects, from the same advantages—advantages which they have hitherto enjoyed in common with Englishmen. Is this the people so celebrated for humanity? No; they are most inhuman: they invade the most precious rights a human being can enjoy, and would render the rest of mankind miserable servile wretches. 'Tis really strange, the national character of Englishmen should have been so much mistaken!"

A.B.

Tuesday, March 22, 1774.

† Although the King, by his prerogative, be vested with the power of making grants, it is only officially; and, I am of opinion, that ever since a legislative authority hath been established in any colony, his Majesty's prerogative of making grants within the same, ought in strictness, to have been in his official capacity, as first magistrate of that colony, and not as

first magistrate of England or Great-Britain. As the people of Great-Britain have no power beyond themselves, nor a shadow of a right in the soil of North America, so it is inconsistent with reason to admit, that the King can derive from them a power of granting away those lands; more especially on any conditions, which should give them a title to sovereignty over their American kindred, who have as good a right to freedom and independency as themselves.

LETTER III.

March 24, 1774.

AT the same Time that I hold that "Parliament hath not the Rights of Sovereignty over his Majesty's American Subjects," and that "these rights reside in themselves," I do not mean to promote an ungrateful forsaking of the mother country by her children, to sever and estrange the sons from the fathers; but where filial duty and obedience ceases, to substitute in its stead a brotherly affection, a manly and independent friendship, which naturally takes place where the parent hath truly loved and exercised his authority for the sole end of promoting the welfare of the child, without a view to self interest, or the gratification of pride, ambition, or other vicious passion. I would consider the American governments, like that of Ireland, as sister kingdoms; and I would cement a lasting union with them as between the separate branches of one great family.* We know that it is impossible to effect such a family union, if the arrogance of the elder branch expect to govern the others, or even demand their homage; and how much more so, if it demand the use of their purses at its own descretion, as a return for former assistance, or under pretence of maintaining the honor and interest of the whole combined family. But while every one is left independent, and no other influence is made use of but that of sincere brotherly affection, a reciprocation of good offices, and a fair representation of the general advantage of the whole, there is little doubt but that all will be ready to contribute their respective shares, and that due respect and deference will ever be paid to the elder house. Family pride, no less than those advantages which result from unions of such a nature, will produce this effect, except we be ashamed of our family. I hope a selfish and

[142]

tyrannical spirit in the English, will not make the Americans ashamed of their descent: but illustration is misleading us again into the tempting, but unsure, path of analogy. Let us quit it once more before we lose sight of the direct road.

Every one of those writers, who endeavour to support the pretensions of parliament to the sovereign of America by any shew of abstract reasoning, have, so far as they have fallen under my observation, either sat out upon defective premises, or from good ones, have drawn false conclusions; as needs must be in this case, until truth become a changeling. Plain sense, and an ingenuous mind, are sufficient to guard any one against their sophistry: but we have need of a little more penetration, and to be somewhat conversant in affairs, when we would dispute with a different sort, who plunge headlong into the depths of politics, and hurry us unprepared into all the intricacies of commerce; placing at once before our eyes, in an indirect point of view, that multiplicity of wheels within wheels, pulleys upon pulleys, and springs upon springs, which belong to the complicated machines of government and trade, instead of directing our attention to the first principles of motion, and the few master springs, on whose movements all the rest depend in a regular order and subordination. By these means they endeavour to confound, when they cannot convince us. But these are dishonest arts, the common tricks of designing men in every sphere. They are too stale and hackneyed, however, to impose upon men of sound and cultivated understandings. These know, that government and trade, as well as every science whatever, are established on a very small number of fundamental principles of the utmost simplicity, since they must be self-evident, or they are no principles at all; and they know also, that those who mean honestly, do always ultimately refer every maxim, by clear inferences, to some one or other of these simple, self-evident principles. All the subtleties and refinements, all the arguments that the wit of men can invent, will never be sufficient to justify any species of arbitrary dominion, while we retain a knowledge of this short and simple proposition—"the good of society is the end of civil government;" nor will they ever justify a discretionary taxation by a prince or government, the people being unrepresented, so long as we know, that "a man hath no property in that which another can by right take from him without his consent."

One of the most specious arguments made use of in support of a sovereign power in parliament over the Americans, is that drawn from a supposed necessity of equipping a powerful armament at a short notice, for the protection of the *whole empire*, as these gentlemen will have it: hereupon we are asked, if his Majesty is to have imposed upon him the arduous task of first obtaining a majority in two Houses of Commons in Europe, and about thirty provincial assemblies in America, before he can raise the necessary supplies? and the interrogators seem to plume themselves much upon the impossibility of carrying on the executive part of government under such restraints. Let me in return ask how we draw supplies from Ireland? Are they voted in the British House of Commons? Then, in the first place, I answer, that if an empire be too large, and its parts too widely separated by immense oceans, or other impediments, to admit of being governed on the principles essentially belonging to all free governments, it is an overgrown empire, and ought to be divided before it fall to pieces. The welfare and happiness of mankind supercede every other possible claim or pretension to govern. When we find ourselves subject to a distant power, which cannot possibly govern us on any other principles than those of tyranny, we have an inherent right, by the law of nature, and it is an indispensible duty to ourselves and to our posterity, to shake off such an unjust yoke, and to erect a free government amongst ourselves. Those degenerate Englishmen, who are now seeking to enslave the Americans, would ill brook the government of the Emperor of Germany, if by any means he should lawfully inherit the crown of these kingdoms, and make Vienna the seat of government. Would they suffer themselves to be taxed by German ministers or German diets? Would they not say to their sovereign, "either come and reside amongst us, or delegate to your Vice-roy all the prerogatives of the crown, and leave us, in conjunction with him alone, to tax and to govern ourselves according to our own just laws, and the rights of a free people?" Can any language be plainer? Can any doctrine be more intelligible or more equitable? But, in answer to the above interrogatory, I have another answer as intelligible as this.

Establish the mode of governing which these persons contend for, and there will still be the same inevitable delay, with regard to the American supplies, as they would have us believe is peculiar to the mode which the people there claim a right to exercise. For though a British Parliament might *vote* them with their usual alacrity, yet we must send to America to *collect* them. And if our armament cannot go on without first sending so far for this collection, its operations might as well be suspended a few days or a few weeks longer, in order to obtain it on *British*, rather than on *Prussian*, principles.† But the truth is, we should not defer the equipment of any necessary armament one moment on this account. Do we at present wait for the assembling of Parliament, and a vote of supplies, before we arm in any just cause in which the safety, the interest or honour of the state is concerned? Doth not the executive branch of government, by virtue of its own powers and in discharge of its duty, put the state in a posture of defence upon every alarm without loss of time, and then apply to parliament for its approbation and support? Is it ever withheld in a just cause? hath the government no resources, no ways and means of its own, for discharging or contracting for the future discharge of, these prompt expences of the state? If the uncertainty of meeting with like support from America, as they find in Great-Britain, should be a clog upon our ministers in their warlike projects, might it not be fortunate for the people of both countries? Would it not make them extremely cautious and prudent how they involved us in continental politics and in German wars? No ingenuous man will, however, entertain a serious doubt of the readiness of the Americans to contribute their share to every necessary expence of government, so long as they shall find themselves in possession of their freedom.‡

They *must* contribute their share; that is to say, they must preserve their own existence as a people, and defend their own property, under any form of government whatever. When men tell us, that an enlightened and free people are refractory; that they will not contribute their proportion of taxes; that at the hazard of their lives by the sword or the halter, they oppose and seek to subvert the government, and this for a succession of years; they tell us, with a moral certainty, though perhaps without meaning it, that they feel some real oppressions, some real invasions made on their rights or liberties; for no other causes ever did, or ever will, produce a general and permanent opposition in the whole body of a people towards their governors. When we remark likewise, that, in the present contest, there is no religious zeal of persecution; no national antipathy or rancour, but quite the reverse; no introduction of a new code of laws by a foreign conqueror; no imaginary pretender to weaken the allegiance of the people towards their sovereign; nor indeed any one cause of dissatisfaction, but the avowed one; and that, on the part of the people, clearly justified on the obvious principles of the English constitution, can we hesitate a moment to pronounce what ought to be done? We ought to allow the Americans to tax themselves as an inseparable adjunct to freedom.

NOTES, &c. to LETTER III.

* It is not my meaning, that the American colonies should feel the effects of that narrow, and, may I not call it, barbarous policy, by which this country hath conducted herself towards her sister Ireland. Besides the liberty of raising her own taxes, and that share of legislation which she enjoys in her own parliament, I must confess, I see no reason why her trade should not be as free as that of Great-Britain. Nature seems to have formed her for an union with the greater island. This once effected, on a liberal plan of equality in trade and freedom, any future jealousy would be an instance of that folly which is exposed in the fable of the belly and members. Humanity, wisdom, and virtue dictate an union. Should Ireland then rival us in trade, (which *I fear* it would never be in a condition to do) I know of no consequences but good ones. It might possibly tend to abate our luxury and extravagance, by a more equal division of wealth, and of circulating money in the two kingdoms; at the same time, that it would excite an industrious emulation in commerce, to the mutual benefit of both countries; and, consequently, augment the numbers of useful people, the riches and strength of the united state.

† If the British parliament will not relinquish its arbitrary sovereignty, let it not, however, double the injury by such oppressions, needless even to its own unjust policy.

‡ I make use of the word *freedom* in this place, although I am arguing on a supposition of the British parliament continuing to exercise a sovereign power over the Americans, which I hold to be tyrannical in its principle; because the Americans themselves are as yet not averse to it, and universally breathe towards it none but sentiments of respect and submission, so long as it shall not be exercised to tax or to oppress them. Perhaps I may be asked, why do I, while the Americans are thus submissively inclined towards parliamentary sovereignty, officiously endeavour to withdraw their respect and obedience; therefore, as a general answer on this head, let me say once for all, that it is the dictate of my conscience; the same as it would be to warn any individual against ignorantly or heedlessly acquiescing in any selfish, crafty, or unjust pretentions of another person, which, in its natural and unavoidable consequences, must end in his own distress, and the ruin of his children, and all this without even benefiting his oppressor; but, on the contrary, rendering him criminal and unhappy, and preparing the way for his hasty downfall. If an ordinary regard to justice, and the duties of humanity, would have required this at our hands, in a case where only a few individuals were concerned, how much more is it the duty of a good citizen to sound the alarm, when he sees millions, and successions of millions thro' future ages, in danger of sinking into slavery, with all its attendant curses! and I moreover think it my duty, to seize this occasion, of advancing my opinions against the supposed and pretended right of sovereignty in the British parliament over America, because too many writers,

through misjudgment, disingenuousness, or a base prostitution to the lust of tyrannic power, have taken advantage of this acquiescence on the part of the colonists, and of this principle with regard to the sovereignty being so generally acknowledged, as a good political axiom; to deduce from it a right in parliament even to *tax* the colonies. Thus, by proving *too much,* they raised a suspicion, that their first principles were unsound, and their leading proposition a mere sophism; and, upon examination, the reader, I flatter myself, finds them to be so. Leave our adversaries but possessed of this intrenched ground of *parliamentary sovereignty,* and the event of the contest, concerning the right of *taxation* will be doubtful; at least, they will so long be enabled to make a shew of maintaining the dispute; but when truth and fair argument have forced this feeble intrenchment, as I cannot but think they have now done, they will soon be driven out of the field; and the standard of freedom, supported by the hand of justice, be fixed there for ever.

LETTER IV.

March 25, 1774.

SOME theorists make a proposal to allow the Americans a representation in the British Parliament, in order to justify our taxation of them; but from the small number of such representatives, which I have understood to be proposed, and their being restricted from voting as some would have them, in any but American questions, I should fear that this proposal proceeded from a sense of shame, as not appearing to preserve even the common forms of justice, rather than from a strict and sacred regard to justice itself; or on a supposition, that this representation should be an adequate one, how would it be possible for the American representatives to serve their constituents in a proper manner. Could they, during every recess of Parliament, visit their respective counties, as the members can in Great-Britain? Could they, by a post letter, in a day or two, communicate to, or receive from, their constituents all necessary intelligence? or, could they meet and consult with them on all emergencies at a short notice? Must they reside a thousand or fifteen hundred leagues from their estates and compting-houses, in order to serve their country in parliament? Surely so weak a system of government must have been the visionary suggestion of a dream! But we may rest assured, that while the Americans are themselves awake, they will never consent to it. Will they trust their property, their freedom, their dearest rights, their every thing, in the hands of exiles, sent half way to the Antipodes, in order to sit in council for their government! Sent to reside in a luxurious, extravagant country, immersed in dissipation and corruption, and exposed to every temptation to betray them! Believe me, they are not so senseless. In the imaginations of these visionaries, the vast Atlantic is no more, I presume, than a mere ferry.

Those who have thought proper to indulge themselves in the way of declamation, tell us of the mighty things done for the Americans by the mother country, and make a great cry of their rebellion and ingratitude. Nay, they are silly enough to urge these obligations as so many irrefragable reasons why the Americans are bound to obey the British parliament: on this foundation they build our right of sovereignty. But who ever heard of a suit prosecuted in any English court of justice for ingratitude? Is a frugal son, out of his little competency, and to the prejudice of his own children, obliged, by any law of England, or of nature, to minister to the extravagancies of a proud, luxurious parent, and in what degree that parent shall direct? Do the obligations of friendship deprive the person obliged of his future freedom and independency? Doth not an attempt to enslave, cancel, in a moment, every former obligation? These declaimers should keep in mind, that voluntary good offices are moral and religious, not civil or political, obligations. We may safely admit the whole catalogue of them in their full force, without thereby affording parliament the most shadowy pretension to the rights of sovereignty over the Americans: but, in justice to the character of that people, we must positively deny their existence; for they have been amply repaid in a profitable commerce to this country. Men must surely be lost to a sense of common decency, who would impose upon us as truth, that the part which government hath ever taken, in settling and assisting the American colonies, was solely or primarily to benefit the settlers; whereby they have been laid under this vast load of obligation to the mother country, which nothing less than a surrender of their liberty can cancel. Every honest, unprejudiced man, who will reason, and not wrangle, must acknowledge, that government's first object was, as indeed it always ought to be, to extend the commerce of this kingdom. This was the end: the countenance and assistance given to American settlers, was only the means, and therefore could be no more than a secondary consideration. When the colonies were in danger of falling a prey to France, was it pure *affection* and *generos-*

ity towards *them*, or *jealousy of that ambitious power*, which caused Great-Britain to take up arms? Did not her own existence depend on the preservation of her American colonies? so that, though we do not mean to say affection, for her kindred had no share in moving her to draw her sword, yet, we presume, it will be admitted, that *her own* safety, *her own* interest, *her own* honor, were the only motives that could have engaged her to proceed such lengths, at that juncture; and this will the more evidently appear, when we consider, that according to her notions of her right to the sovereignty, she saw the protection of her colonies, literally in the light of self-defence, and the more heartily undertook it accordingly. Surely, it must be a very bad title to dominion, which is built upon an error of her judgment, and a political selfishness. Had the *Hanoverians*, or *Dutch*, the *Prussians, Portuguese*, or *Hungarians*; Had even the very *French*, with whom she fought, at that time stood in the place of her American colonies, she would, on the same principles, have been as lavish of her blood and treasure in their support, as *every one of them* hath heretofore experienced; and yet our opponents in argument, would not have maintained, that services of this kind, done to any such state, would have entitled this kingdom to the same right of ruling and of taxing it, as they contend for upon the same principle in the case of America. America, therefore, is not ungrateful; but is not rather Great-Britain unwise, ambitious, and tyrannical? The obligations, in fact, were mutual, and as equivalent as the nature of things would admit; so that it would be a very nice, perhaps an impossible, but certainly an useless speculation, to decide which party hath been most benefited. The attempt is insidious, and he who makes it, is no friend either to America or Great-Britain.

Many definitions of government have been given us, and a multitude of arguments employed, in order to shew the well known necessity of one central supreme power being somewhere lodged in every empire, which shall be all sufficient of itself to perform the whole of legislation, and consequently taxation, as an essential part of it. But this will make nothing for the claims of parliament to the sovereignty of America. On the reverse, it only points out more strongly the error which most people have fallen into in their notion of the British empire. They will have it, that the British empire comprehends within it all his Majesty's dominions in America; whereas the American governments, except that of Newfoundland, are independent nations, having within themselves the rights and the actual powers of legislation, which cannot be taken from them, and lodged in the hands of British legislators, without a manifest wrong, and the subverting of so many free governments. Here we shall be told, that our Kings, in granting them their original charters and privileges, only exercised a prerogative which they derived from the constitution; wherefore the Americans are still dependent upon, and owe allegiance, not to the King alone, but to the state of Great-Britain. But still I maintain, that the inherent rights of mankind, above all, their freedom, are not to depend on casuistical niceties and logical distinctions, (which, by the way, must be false, when they would disprove these rights) but are theirs independently of all the Kings, all the governments in the universe. Kings and constitutions of government are the creatures, not the creators, of these rights. They are held immediately of God himself, who gave them. Had the original charters to the American settlers been granted on the express and sole condition of acknowledging the sovereignty of parliament, even all that would not have bettered our present title one jot; for freedom, notwithstanding all that sophistry may say to the contrary, cannot be alienated by any human creature; much less can he enslave his posterity; and, therefore, such a contract could only be binding, so far and so long as freedom should not be infringed by it; but, with regard to a virtue in it, of depriving a future people, many nations, of their freedom, it would be null and void in its own nature to all intents and purposes; and 'tis a mockery to our common-sense, to plead it as an authority to this end.

It is a mistaken notion, that planting of colonies, and extending of empire, are necessarily one and the same thing. Even the *intention* of the planters will not make it so, where the rights of mankind, and the nature of things are not adapted to it; where growing colonies are so situated and so circumstanced, that, in the nature of things, they cannot be governed by the parent state on the principles of justice and freedom; it is surely paying little respect to our understandings, and shocks every feeling of a free mind, to assert, that they must nevertheless submit to its oppressive rule. Having denied that America, when we drop the popular language, and speak correctly, is a part of the British empire, it will naturally be expected I should say what are, and where are its limits. The British empire, then, I hold to be confined to the British Isles*, and to the various *settlements and factories of our trade* in the different parts of the world, including *the government of Newfoundland;* together with the garrisons of *Gibral-*

ter and *Minorca*. As to the West India islands, they, as well as the continental colonies, certainly have a right to their independency, whenever they shall think proper to demand it, as they contain within themselves every necessary of legislation; but, if it be their choice, to acknowledge the sovereignty of the British Parliament, as I apprehend it may, because, I believe, it will be their *interest*, I see no objection in that case to its being exercised. If it be true, as I believe all writers agree, that they would be depopulated, was it not for annual supplies of white men as well as blacks, this, and some other arguments, drawn from West-Indian manners and sentiments, seem to indicate, that it is not in their nature, nor perhaps in their wish, to support an independency; nor ought we to forget, that their soil itself points out to them dependency, supplying only the means of effeminacy, luxury, and intoxication, while for *bread*, and the *necessaries of life*, its inhabitants must depend upon other countries. It matters not how much, in the nature of trading settlements, our first colonies might have been, (though were not in fact) nor at what period they might be said to become independent nations: it matters not that they were orginally planted and protected by the government of this country, (I admit this planting; I make no reservation of those who fled from *persecution* and *want*) nor what were the intentions of government in so doing; for, having in them (the people of those colonies) the inherent and unalienable rights of freemen, they had therein the rights of independency, whenever they should think proper to assert them. Doth a man, who furnishes a young indigent relation with every necessary, who settles him in a trading accompting-house, who supplies him with money, and supports him with every species of protection whereby he prospers in the world, and raises a fortune; doth the man, I say, to whom he owes all this, obtain thereby a right, a legal title, to take from him, without his consent, a single shilling of this fortune? men of slavish principles would have us believe, that the rights of private persons, of subjects, being mean and insignificant considerations, are level with the capacities of, and may be comprehended by the people; but that the sublime and mysterious rights of empire are only to be judged of, and determined upon, by those who govern, and by those to whom these mysteries are confidentially revealed, in order to be treated of with due profundity and unintelligibility, not to enlighten the people, but to impress them with a proper respect for things so awful and sacred. True enough it is, that what hath too frequently been written concerning them, hath not been level with the capacities of the people, nor with any other capacities; for no man can understand what hath no sense or meaning, what is palpable nonsense.

NOTE, &c. to LETTER IV.

* I say British Isles, since I consider Ireland as naturally a dependent upon Great-Britain, until an union shall take place, and make her an equal. In barbarous times, she might have remained separate and independent; but such a state would now be inconsistent with the self preservation of the larger kingdom, and therefore the law of nature dictates an union, or a curb.

LETTER V.

March 26, 1774.

IT is demanded, with an air of confidence and imaginary triumph, 'Were not the first settlers in America British subjects? Did they not settle under the sanction of grants and charters? Hath not the kingdom, at all times, put itself to great expences in their support, and favoured them with many peculiar advantages in trade? Was not the last most expensive war undertaken solely on their account? Can any one be so absurd, as to imagine the kingdom intended to nurse and erect so many independent nations instead of enlarging her own dominion? Ought not the Americans to repay us part of the expences of the war in particular, in order to enable us to discharge some part of that enormous debt it occasioned? and contribute their proportion towards the general expences of the whole empire'? To most of these questions, my arguments have already answered. Now, let me ask, in my turn,—Have any of the nations of the earth, especially the free ones, become what they are, in consequence of the *intentions*, and by a regular plan for that purpose, of the governments of those countries from which they are respectively descended? When we speak of the Greeks as an Egyptian colony, or of the Carthaginians as a colony of Phœnicians, do we the less consider them as free nations? or imagine that the mother countries had a right to govern or to tax them, because the first settlers had once stood in the relation of subjects to those states? Let the *intention* of government, in planting a colony, be what it may, 'tis impossible it should take away an *inherent unalienable* right; such, for instance, as freedom. But what Britain principally intended, she hath certainly obtained—an extension of commerce. Again, let me ask, hath not Providence usually carried on its gracious designs of making great nations, and peopling new regions, contrary to the councils of the wise ones of this world? While we are plotting and contriving, toiling and sweating, treating and waging war, in order to gratify our own self-interest and pride, by extending our commerce, and enlarging our empire beyond all bounds, Providence takes care to frustrate our foolish and wicked projects, and often brings about the reverse of what we think to insure by the depth of our policy, and the strength of our arm. Let us take care that we do not provoke it to make us a scorn and a reproach to America, instead of its arrogant ruler. By adhering strictly to the principles of justice, and the rights of mankind, we may firmly unite and cement together our own interests with those of our sister nations in America, and remain ourselves to the end of time, a powerful and independent state: but let us dread, by a violation of these sacred duties, to pull down upon our devoted heads the mighty ruins of an over-grown empire. Let it be the peculiar glory of this free, this enlightened, this christian kingdom, to extend the influence of her religion and laws, not the limits of her empire! Nor let her entertain one anxious thought concerning the hackneyed notion of the progress of empire westward. Who are these presumptuous unfolders of the decrees of fate, these revealers of the hidden councils of God, that doom Great-Britain to a speedy fall, when empire shall have fixed its seat in America? Are the dispensations of Divine Providence so uniform and regular, as to become the object of science and proud philosophy? to be foretold by man, or calculated like the movement and appearance of a comet? Our *philosophical prophets* pretend to judge from similar causes producing similar effects: but they ought to know, that in *all essentials*, there is *yet* very little or no similitude between the state of Great-Britain and any antient empire whatever: and I am not without faith, that there will always be wisdom and virtue enough in this happy island, to prevent its ever coming within that predicament. It behoves her, however, for instruction, to have a constant retrospect to them and their fate. Let her maturely reflect on the insatiable avarice and ambition, the enormous, the gigantic wickedness of bloody Rome. Let her consider also the Grecian, the Persian, and Assyrian empires, and carefully mark the grand causes of their overthrow. They were all erected on the rotten foundations of *Idolatry* and *tyranny*, (the very seed-plots of hell) they all fell the victims of their own mad ambition, and a lust of rule, that nothing could satiate less then the dominion of the whole earth. Where is the similitude! Our religion, being a divine revelation, is confessedly perfect; and the law of nature, no less divine, being the immoveable basis of our political fabric, the very soul of our constitution, this also is *perfect*. I say perfect, absolutely perfect; for, whenever it hath the appearance of being otherwise, it is only from the want of a right interpretation, or a close adherence to its true principles. It is this immutable, this divine standard, we have to refer to in all our deviations, that hath preserved our constitution through all ages, and improved it till it is become the admiration and envy of all nations*. This is a principle of renovation and recovery from all corruption and decays; this is a principle of immortality! No other constitution ever had the same, or at least never preserved it until it was sufficiently understood, and properly valued by the people. This has, under a most singular Providence, been our peculiar blessing. I trust it will be the blessing of our posterity to the latest generations; and that, when we shall have given birth, and the birthrights of freemen, to as many independent states as can find habitations on the vast American continent, that Britain still will be great and free; the respected mother, the model, the glory of them all! and I will, I must indulge the fond hope, that the pure religion, and the perfect constitution of Britain, will gradually spread themselves over all America; and in every other part of the globe† so enlighten and operate upon the minds of men, as to become the chief instruments in the Hands of Almighty God of bringing about, in his due time, that universality of christianity, that harmony and happiness among the nations of the earth, which are intimated in the prophetic writings. Those prophetic intimations themselves, the peculiar fitness of the causes to the effects, together with a great variety of circumstances, that seem evidently tending towards this point, convince me, that it may be rationally hoped for; while all the arguments brought to shew the probability of America becoming the seat of a mighty conquering empire, to which Britain shall, in length of time, be a province, appear to my apprehension, to be destitute of any foundation of the smallest degree of probability.

We are told, that empire hath been observed to make its progress westward; that every empire hath had its infancy, its youth, its vigour, its declension, its death; and that they necessarily follow each other with the same certainty as in the frail life of man; and lastly, we are reminded, that Great-Britain hath past her meridian, and empire is now rising fast in America. To the first, I answer, that empire must needs have travelled westward from its source, except Europe had remained a desert; that it also travelled East, South, and North, as well as West, witness China, Indostan, Abyssinia, Russia; and that it hath already been in America, witness Peru and Mexico; and that it hath also taken retrograde courses, witness Turkey and the Persian empire under Nadir Shah; and with regard to modern Europe, I can see no probability why it may not remain to the end of time, divided in proportions, not much differing from the present. To the second argument, I have only to say, that analogical reasoning is always very fallacious, and that there is no analogy between things *mortal* and *immortal*. To the third, I must repeat, that Great-Britain, having in her constitution the principles of renovation and recovery, from corruption and decay, and the seeds of immortality (which no other state ever had) is in no great danger of a declension, so long as this World is likely to last; and that the British North American states having, all of them, christianity void of persecution, as a light from Heaven; British freedom as a soul, and a spirit of commerce as the breath of life; it must be thought next to an impossibility that any one of them should ever swallow up all the rest, and then extend its conquests beyond the Atlantic and Pacific Oceans. The times for "heroes and demigods" are past; and the phrenzy for universal empire is somewhat out of date and out of countenance. They prevailed, and only could prevail, when the minds of men were in a proper tone for such extravagancies; when *the advantages of commerce, the true principles and ends of government, and the religion of peace and pure virtue*, were either wholly or very imperfectly known: besides, no searcher into prophecy hath yet discovered in the womb of time, an empire that is to be so formidable to the liberties of the world; and, if it be true, that the species, as well as the individuals of mankind, obtains knowledge, wisdom, and virtue progressively, its latter days will, according to the nature of things, and by means of the divine assistance that hath been vouchsafed it, to all appearance, be more wise, peaceable, and pious, than the earlier periods of its existence. To this end let every one labour; and his own happiness at least, if not the general happiness of mankind, will most assuredly be his reward.

Notes, &c. to Letter V.

* "I wish," says Lord Camden, "the maxim of Machiavel was followed, that of examining a constitution, at certain periods, according to its first principles, this would correct abuses, and supply defects." In this wish, every man, who hath a just sense of our inestimable constitution, will most devoutly join his Lordship. It is true, however, as intimated above, that our wise ancestors did, from time to time, avail themselves of such an examination, as occasion offered, and circumstances would admit. If the effects have been so great and so happy, ought we not to improve upon their example, and instead of suffering abuses to run on uncorrected, until they threaten a general ruin, would it be more than common sense, and common prudence, to adopt a *regular and periodical inquest*, for this most salutary purpose? Who so learned in the law and the constitution; who more the friend of both; who therefore so fit as his Lordship, for the generous task of framing a proper bill on this occasion? As it is his Lordship's proposal, where else shall we look for a volunteer; knowing his eloquence and senatorial abilities, on whom else could we rely, with so much confidence and hope, for obtaining so great a blessing?

† We are now sending a code of British laws to our settlements in India, and establishing courts to administer them.

LETTER VI.

March 27, 1774.

WHEN we talk of asserting our sovereignty over the Americans, do we foresee to what fatal lengths it will carry us? Are not those nations encreasing with astonishing rapidity? Must they not, in the nature of things, cover in a few ages that immense continent like a swarm of bees? Do we vainly imagine, that we can then hold the reins of government, and hurl our thunders on the heads of the disobedient? Where are we to stop? or, shall we pretend to circumscribe American populations? To say, 'thus far shall ye go, and no farther?' No! Swollen indeed must we be with the pride of dominion, and drunk with the fumes, if we can foolishly imagine these things*. It is high

[156]

time that we opened our eyes to the unintentional encroachments we have been making upon the liberties of mankind, and to the necessity of setting bounds to our dominion. Without the American continent, the British empire will be large enough in all reason. But if government persist in maintaining our sovereignty there, it may possibly occasion our own destruction, but can be productive of no good to us, either present, or future. After all that has been done to alarm the Americans for their rights as free men, and calling up their attention to a thorough investigation of them; after the flame of opposition hath been kindled in every breast, and now animates them as one man, it will be in vain to steer any middle course; to adopt measures for *light oppressions* and compelling obedience to laws *moderately tyrannical.* We must either relinquish at once our claim to sovereignty, or fix on their neck with strong hand the galling yoke of slavery. We must either conquer ourselves or them. Justice, wisdom, humanity, and religion leave us without a doubt which to prefer; and, should the latter be determined on, woe be to Great-Britain! We may, indeed, by means of fleets and armies, maintain a precarious tyranny over the Americans for a while; but the most shallow politicians must foresee what this would end in†. It would expose us to the certain attacks of all our European rivals; and, when we found the necessity of courting the assistance of the Americans, we should deservedly find them the bitterest of our enemies. With the nations of Europe we contend for commerce, for glory, and some imaginary objects; with those of America, the contest would be for the dearest rights, the very dignity of humanity. After the struggles of interest and prowess, a tolerable reconciliation may take place, but eternal enmity and hate always succeed those between a free people and their tyrants. From the spirit of freedom, which hath in all ages glowed in the bosoms of true Englishmen, and which hath brought to its present perfection our glorious constitution in defiance of every attempt to crush it; we ought to know, that until we can extinguish this spirit in the breasts of the Americans, and eradicate from their very nature its first and noblest principles, self-preservation and free-will, that all our efforts to bow them down in subjection to our authority must finally be ineffectual, and will recoil sooner or later perhaps with tenfold retribution upon ourselves. There are some politicians who think, that present expediency is a sufficient justification of any measures; and who, from the ideas of re-imbursing ourselves for the charges of the last war, of supplying the present exigencies of the state, and securing our power over the American commerce, make no scruple to bid us draw the accursed sword, and enslave our children and our brethren. But, be it known to them, that though our very existence as a nation, depended on violating the express laws of God, it must not be done. And if their ignorance, which may be implied from the folly of their proposal, hath not yet made the discovery, let them be told that policy, national as well as individual, must have justice and the laws of God for its basis, or, 'tis the policy of villains, the policy of sots and fools. Can the legislature of Great-Britain, I once more ask, govern the Americans on the true principles of freedom? For the reasons I have already given, I believe it to be impossible‡. As to their reimbursing us the sums of money spent on their account in the last war, they will do it, if we act wisely and justly, in the only way it is possible they should, and in the only way we expected of them when we undertook the war; that is, by a commerce beneficial to this kingdom. And by leaving them to their own independency, the charges of government may be greatly retrenched.

Thus far had I written, when the political tracts of a reverend Dean fell into my hands.[2] They amply supply all the examples and explanations necessary to illustrate my principles, and shew to a demonstration the absolute necessity, in a political light, of relinquishing our claims to the sovereignty of America; to which the whole tenour of my letters point, and with which they are to conclude. But I am far from subscribing to this gentleman's doctrine as to the rights of sovereignty. If I could acknowledge the truth of that, I should very much doubt of the propriety of his proposed separation of America from Great-Britain; for giving up one's right, cannot be thought a good rule for promoting his interest. But in this case, as is very frequent, his common-sense hath been obliged to subdue his learning before he arrived at truth. While metaphysical refinements teach him to think, that Britain hath a right to govern America, the invincible force of truth extorts from him an acknowledgment that she must, if governed by true policy, relinquish it. 'Tis a pity so able a writer had not discovered that the Americans have a right to choose their own governors, and thence inforced the necessity of his proposed separation as a religious duty, no less than a measure of national policy. In so doing, he would have been consistent; there would then have been no obscurity nor would his sentiments of right and expediency have been at variance; but his conclusion would naturally and evidently have flowed from his premises, supported by that trite, but true and most excellent maxim, that honesty is the best policy. But, perhaps, some may be of opinion, that the propriety of a separation is more strongly enforced, by its appearing to be the only result he could possibly arrive at through the medium of opinions that pointed the direct contrary way. The same opinions have, in all other writers, led them only to consider, by what means the unity of the whole British empire (taking in America) might be best preserved; how the supreme legislative power might be best supported, and enforce obedience to the utmost bounds of this vast dominion. Every project for this purpose (without a single exception) being embarrassed with a fundamental incompatibility, a radical error in supporting a right, where, in truth, there is none, hath been visionary, oppressive, sanguinary, and totally impracticable; so difficult it is to strive against the stream of nature and truth.

The Dean, with more good sense, with an extensive insight into the human heart, and the springs of commerce, and with the temper of a philosophic, uninterested looker-on, hath nobly abandoned the full persuasion of his own mind on the point of right; and, while he thinks we are entitled to govern, foresees and demonstrates the fatal consequences of attempting it. He accordingly advises us to separate in good humour, and trusts to our mutual interests for its producing, in fact, a real and sincere union, and this, he says, is "the only means of living in peace and harmony with them."

In the whole course of his work, wherever the dispute of right is not immediately in view, his reasonings flow spontaneously, and in spite of himself, from the feelings of right in his own heart. In page 12, he says, 'For I am not for charging our colonies in particular with being sinners above others, because, I believe, (and if I am wrong, let the histories of all colonies, whether antient or modern, from the days of Thucydides down to the present time, confute me if it can; I say, 'till that is done, I believe) that it is the nature of them all to aspire after independence, and to set up for themselves as soon as ever they find that they are able to subsist without being beholding to the mother-country. And if our Americans have expressed themselves sooner on this head than others have done, or in a more direct and daring manner, this ought not to be imputed to any greater malignity, or ingratitude in them than in others, but to that bold, free constitution, which is the prerogative and boast of us all. We ourselves derive our origin from those very Saxons who inhabited the lower parts of Germany, &c." What can more fully prove the right of independence in colonies, too far removed to be governed on the principles of freedom by the mother country, than this universal, this uniform, invariable feeling of all mankind, in all ages, than that "it is the nature of them all to aspire after it." Shall we reject the unvarying testimony of nature speaking home to our hearts, and pin our faith upon the fine-spun, cobweb subtleties of our learned casuists and court-lawyers? or shall we, with more safety, rely upon the letter of an old musty charter, penned before this question was so much as thought of? Hath nature left herself so much without a witness to the truth in the human breast, that we must give ourselves wholly up to the direction of such blind guides as these? Fie! fie! If much learning hath not made us mad, it hath at least in this, and many similar cases, made us ignorant. It is to be lamented, that such a blaze of truth, as there is in the above observation, did not discover to the writer the fallaciousness of his original position of parliamentary right to govern the colonies; when all the while, it is the express, the sole purport of this work to prove, that parliament in continuing to assert this right, cannot promote either the welfare of Great-Britain or America.

Notes, &c. to Letter VI.

* I find it is one of the avowed principles of the Quebec Act, by the accounts of its ablest advocates, to check as much as possible, all population in the *upper* and *interior country*, at the back of the colonies. (See a pamphlet entitled, The Justice and Policy of the late Act of Parliament, for making more effectual provision for the government of the Province of Quebec, asserted and proved, page 43; and an Appeal to the Public, stating and considering the objections to the Quebec Bill, page 46). At the same time that I honour all the *real* humanity, shewn in this act to the Canadians; I most heartily condemn the general *policy* of it, with regard to the other Colonies. The evils complained of in the above-mentioned unsettled country, and made the lame pretence for enlarging so extravagantly the province of Quebec, by the annexation of the whole of it, are evils wholly occasioned by the inactivity and omissions of government for twelve years past; if it be true, that it is *the want of laws*, which introduces disorder into any society; and they are, with great injustice charged upon the bordering Colonies, as *legislative states*; (in which light, I find, they are to be considered by their enemies, whenever it may serve a turn to their disadvantage. See the appeal above mentioned, page 50.) and as an artful pretence for denying them leave of settlement, and that share in the peltry trade which they are most advantageously situated for enjoying. Provided Great Britain had no people to spare, for sending out colonies to occupy that desolate country, I can see no right she had to hinder the

American states from so doing, except by *voluntary agreement between her and them*, unless she claim a power of counteracting God's first benediction to mankind. "Be fruitful and multiply, and replenish the earth and subdue it." But notwithstanding it is the language of this act, that 'immense tracts of the earth shall remain desert and unpeopled, in order that the British parliament may maintain an usurped sovereignty over a multitude of populous nations, beyond one of the grand watery divisions of the Globe;' yet in the end, it will prove to have no more virtue in it, towards stemming the overflowings of the Colonies, than had the royal mandate of the wise Canutus, when in order to confound his evil counsellors, he magisterially forbad the swelling tide of the ocean to approach his feet. A chain of feeble forts in a wilderness, or the pronouncing this wilderness to be part of the province of Quebec, will form a mighty barrier truly, against the swarms that will one day pour westward, from the too populous states upon the sea coast! I do not, however, deny, that even *this* mode of preventing anarchy, bloodshed, and cruelty for the present, is not better than none; but I think this is not the *right* way. To have consented, under our own guaranty, to a partition of this country amongst the bordering colonies, according to their respective situations, and as far as the just claims of the Indians would admit, would have been at once an act of justice and wise policy; or, if the enlargement of these respective colonies would be impolitic, on account of the future balance of power on that continent, and the general arbitration of Great-Britain hereafter spoken of, then it might have been stipulated with them, that their several emigrants into this desert country, should be independent of them, and left to form a new state or new states, under laws to be given them for a free government on their first settlement, and suitable limitations of country, for the sake of preserving the future equilibrium and general peace. There cannot be a worse, or more narrow policy, than to give any check to American population; for, by those means, Britain will lose so many customers for her manufactures, and the colonies, by having their emigrations restrained, will be under a necessity of employing her hands in manufactures, instead of agriculture. We know the consequences.

† The infatuated people of this country, are not sparing of their ridicule and illiberal jests on the Bostonians, now the iron hand of power hath got them in its grasp. No man of sense ever doubted the *present* power of Great Britain, to crush any one opposing colony, or, possibly, to trample on the united necks of them all; but this arrogance and injustice she will assuredly repent. I wish it may not be in sackcloth and ashes. I wish it may not be very soon.

‡ In framing the Quebec Act, it were much to have been desired, that none of the other Colonies had been so much as thought of, it might then, perhaps, have breathed pure wisdom and benevolence; but, having interwoven in it that fatal policy, which is daily sowing the seeds of discord between Great-Britain and America, I am inclined to think, it is justly censurable in a high degree; and that it is far less beneficial to the Canadians than it ought to be. Although it may be very true, that they are at present incapable of receiving all the rights and privileges, and the full liberty of British subjects, yet that will be no justification of us, for intailing on their posterity so much servitude

to an arbitrary power, as by this act is vested in the governor and council; all at the appointment of the crown *during pleasure*. To have had an assembly, wherein the people should have been represented, they had an undoubted right; to deny it them is tyrannical, and a mere evasion, to insinuate the impracticability of such a plan. Surely that power, which now totally deprives them of this essential to freedom, had been exerted more agreeable to the principles of justice and humanity; had it granted them but the rudest model of an assembly, containing within it the seeds of freedom, to have germinated and expanded with their prosperity, and their advancement in arts and knowledge! Those who assert the contrary, must be little acquainted with the origin and rise of almost all the free states that have flourished in the world, and must conceive the Canadians to be more stupid and barbarous than the Hottentots or Samoiedes. As to any intention of our ministers to promote in this act the interests of Popery, I think they may stand freely acquitted of them; and though I am of opinion, the religious part of it might be amended, yet I cannot but smile at the terrors that have been expressed on this occasion, as if his Holiness was at the very door of St. Paul's. No; the error of the legislature hath been in not seeing, that the most perfect freedom in America, is not only compatible with, but is now become necessary to, the prosperity of Great-Britain; and its crime, if a crime hath been committed, in seeking to support a tottering tyranny over the antient colonies, by erecting an arbitrary government in Quebec. For the sake of Britons on both sides of the Atlantic equally; for the sake of the Canadians, and for the sake of freedom's holy cause universally, I sincerely hope a little reflection on an end so abominable, and the still more abominable means, will dispose our legislators to retrieve, e're it be too late, such an unconstitutional and alarming step. The act of parliament of which we have been speaking, as well as two other memorable ones, passed since the writer first began to publish these letters separately in a news-paper, are thought by sober and reflecting men, to be melancholy records of human passions and infirmity; affording us most striking admonitions, that in national conduct, as well as in that of individuals, a mistaken principle of action, if not forsaken, or one false step, if unretrieved in time, may easily hurry us on to lengths of folly and wickedness, at which we should once have shuddered with horror, but can afterwards persist in to our utter destruction, regardless of all the miseries we at the same time bring upon others. Will rational and moral beings never learn, that without justice, 'tis impossible there should ever be wisdom in the councils of a nation? or can statesmen believe it will obtain their acquittal at the last tribunal, to plead, that in their private capacity, "they did justice and remembered mercy," though in their public stations, they violated these sacred regards; and through a false notion of serving and aggrandizing their country, they endeavoured to establish tyranny, and to intail on millions and millions, the deadliest curse that can imbitter life? In what light must a truly good and wise man behold a law, which is at once a yoke of bondage to one colony, and a scourge to the rest! Although greater miseries, previously endufed, together with an ignorance in the value of, and the requisites to, freedom, may cause the poor Canadians, in their present circumstances, to receive it with joy and thankfulness; will that justify towards them, so ungenerous, so mean a policy?

LETTER VII.

March 28, 1774.

SINCE my last letter was sent to the Printer, I have a second time looked into the publication therein referred to; and finding it likely to make a strong impression on its readers, as well as that there is the most striking inconsistency between its foundation and superstructure, I perceive that I cannot well pass it over without a regular though concise examination of its third and fourth tract. These alone being immediately to the point, I shall confine my observations to them, without taking notice of the rest of the book.

In the beginning of the third tract, entitled, "A Letter from a Merchant in London to his Nephew in America," I am sorry to observe an appeal to *the spirit of our constitution* treated with ridicule, and an attempt made to substitute in place of this only genuine authority, *the letter of the statutes,* or even of Magna Charta itself; for these may all be imperfect, though as I have proved in a former letter the spirit of the constitution cannot. A proceeding of this kind in an anonymous writer, or one of no credit, would, I confess, have given me an alarm of danger, and a suspicion of some deep design against the cause of truth: it certainly is very far from being a recommendation of the present work. May we not ask what is meant by removing the appeal from *the spirit of the constitution,* to something which is called "the constitution itself," (page 93 94) and what that something is? It is not defined, nor can I understand what it is, unless it be a something which hath its sole existence in the varying and unsteady letter of the statute law, and therefore may be one thing today, and another tomorrow, as it was once tyranny and popery, and is at present freedom and true religion. If the author will be candid, he must acknowledge, that his distinction of "the constitution itself," from the spirit of the constitution, is unlogical, and a palpable conradiction. How can any thing be set in contradistinction to its essence? That "Magna Charta is the great foundation of English liberties, and the basis of the English constitution," I must positively deny. It is indeed a glorious member of the superstructure, but of itself would, never have existed, had not the constitution already had a basis, and a firm one too. And as to this charter being the "foundation of English liberty," that was evidently otherwise; since it was an exertion

[163]

of this very liberty that produced the charter; extorting it from an encroaching King, as a meer formal declaration of rights, already known to be the constitutional inheritance of every Englishman. Besides I have elsewhere observed, that the original and only real foundations of liberty were, by the Almighty architect, laid together with the foundations of the world, when this right was ingrafted into the nature of man at his creation; and therefore it cannot be held, after the manner of an external property or possession, by charters and titles of human fabrick. We ought to be careful to preserve a gospel purity in our civil as in our religious constitution; for they are both founded on the word of God. If the religious be more express and clear, the civil is more ancient, and no less divine, though only revealed to us by a general and fainter impress on the mind and heart of man. If the Dean will not admit the decrees of Popes and councils as of equal authority with the word of God, he will not surely maintain, that a Magna Charta ought to come in competition with the spirit of a constitution, whose basis is *internal justice and inherent liberty*; a Magna Charta, notoriously known to have been extorted by the sword, and formed and ratified in the heat of a hostile contention. Nor will he, it is to be hoped, plead "the public statutes of the realm," (p.4.) when they militate against the spirit, or gospel purity of the constitution.

And here I must remark, that his quotations of them, in order to prove the sovereignty of parliament, have not the weight of fair evidence in the trial now before the tribunal of the public; since they stand in the place, and in the nature of parties concerned. It is these very "public statutes of the realm," arrogating a right to govern and to tax the Americans which are called in question; therefore their testimony goes for nothing. If the cause be given in their favour, then it will be time enough for them to operate; but if it goes against them, they must all be condemned as usurpations. We are now arguing what is just and right, and *ought to be* practised, not what *has been* practised by those who had the power in their hands; not what they have been pleased, in their declarations to *call* just and right. Although Parliament should enact, that reason and truth should no longer be reason and truth, yet plain and honest people would be apt to call them reason and truth still, and to rely upon them with the same assurance they do at present. Hence it is, and ever will be, a truth as evident and as uncontrovertible as any law of nature can be, that "an American," notwithstanding the ingenuity of this author, and all that has been, or can be said to the contrary, has a right to insist, "that according to the spirit of the constituion, he ought not be taxed without his own consent, given either by himself or by a representative in parliament;" I will not add "chosen by himself;" because that, with regard to each individual, were we disposed to cavil, would lead us into useless and puerile disputations, (p. 93.) Every man of sense admits of the propriety of virtual representation, so far as it answers the ends and purposes of a real one, *but no farther.* I am sincerely sorry to observe a writer, so much entitled to respect as the Dean of Glocester, employ this talents in an endeavour to mislead us into an opinion, that the Americans are virtually represented in the British parliament. It were a suitable and an innocent exercise of parts in a young disputant at college; but will it bear to be gravely debated upon by a political writer! Well might a noble Lord exclaim, "for as to the distinction of a virtual representation, it is so absurd, as not to deserve an answer; I therefore pass it over with contempt." And if authorities are to have their weight, that, I presume of this noble Lord, who presided with so much dignity and lustre, in the noblest court of equity in the world, will be allowed to preponderate against the Dean's, at least in the judgment of every one who reads the tracts before us. If our author had duly weighed the arguments he has quoted from Judge Foster, in his 4th tract, (p. 27.) he would have found, that they made nothing for such a virtual representation *as he contends for.*[3] The Judge, it is plain, was not so irrational as to think of the welfare of *two separate nations* (for so we may surely esteem Britain and America, think as we will of *empire*) inhabiting, with respect one to the other, "the ends of the earth," as being a fit object of consultation to a single national assembly; and that the deputies of one of these nations could be esteemed the representatives of the other. As to the imagination of Great Britain and America being *one empire*, these are only words that serve to blind, to amuse, and to confound inconsiderate reasoners.

How often must it be repeated, that pride, ambition, and lust of dominion, are not, *on any pretence whatsoever*, to be gratified at the expence of nations; and that the *sole end* of civil government is to promote the good of the people? If an empire become too wide and unwieldy for this purpose, I do assert, that by the laws of nature, which are the laws of God, *it is no empire*, that is to say, not a *just* empire. It therefore must be divided, unless we admit that tyranny can be rightfully established, which God forbid! In our own case, I only want it to be done in form, as it is already done in fact, in which the Dean agrees with me; "for says he, (p. 12) an undoubted fact it is, that from the moment in which Canada came into the possession of the English, an end was put to the sovereignty of the mother-country over her colonies*." I must now take notice of one argument, in favour of virtual representation, that our author seems to value himself upon, as of sufficient force to decide the general dispute with the Americans, and, at the same time, the much litigated question of the Middlesex election. We find it in a note, (p. 29) "Surely the nation might have expelled Mr. Wilkes, or have struck his name out of the list of committee, had it been assembled, and had it thought proper so to do. What then should hinder the deputies of the nation from doing the same thing? and which ought to prevail in this case, the nation in general, or the county of Middlesex?" Now, this argument is evidently fallacious; for the House of Commons doth *not* answer to the *imagined committee* of Judge Foster, to which it is here compared; for that was a simple *democratical* council. Our national committee consists of *King* and *Lords*, as well as Commons? and therefore, according to the Dean's premises, that "the nation might have expelled Mr. Wilkes," it is the necessary conclusion, that nothing less than the national committee, namely, our compleat legislature of King, Lords, and Commons, had a right to strike his name out of the list. I entirely agree with this writer, that the member chosen and returned by certain individuals, is the representative of the whole nation; so that what is generally called a virtual, is, in fact, a real representation; but, at the same time, I must say it doth not appear to be very consistent with *the spirit of our constitution,* (if that expression will not give offence) that a Dunwich or an Old Sarum, containing half a dozen cottagers, should have the chusing of as many of these national representatives as a Norwich or a Bristol; nor that a Weymouth should return as great a number as the metropolis, whose citizens, according to our author, (p. 99) form "a body as respectable as the greatest of our colonies with regard to *property*, and superior to many of them with respect to *numbers.*"

Is not this an abuse that calls aloud for reformation? Can any thing be more notorious, than that a great majority of the national representatives are elected by a small number of indigent and corrupt men, who professedly made a trade of voting, and who gratify, in the very act, a sordid self-interest, in direct violation of the rights and interests of the nation collectively. These electors being *primarily* the representatives of the nation, may be called the *elective representatives*; and are answerable to the nation for the exercise of that great trust. If they pervert it from the end for which it was given them, and transfer it to bad men for their own selfish purposes, it is fit *they should be deprived of it*, in order to the establishing a more just and safe mode of electing the *legislative representatives* of the nation. But to return; I am of opinion, the Dean might as well have spared his reproaches of "folly and absurdity" upon the positions of the Americans, concerning their want of an adequate representation, (p. 98) and have omitted his comparison of the state of the city of London, although it "hath long enjoyed, before the colonies were ever thought of, the three-fold power of jurisdiction, legislation, and taxation *in certain cases*; for, if no man in his senses ever yet supposed, that the city of London either was or could be exempted, by her charters, from parliamentary jurisdiction, or parliamentary taxes;" it is full as evident that no man in his senses can see any just similitude, with respect to parliamentary jurisdiction and taxation between *a metropolis*, the very central point of a nation, and *an entire kindred nation*, which hath arisen in the new world, at the distance of three thousand miles from the parent state, and beyond the vast Atlantic Ocean. *It is consistent with the security of the liberty and property of the citizens of London,* to be subject to parliamentary jurisdiction and taxation! but this subjection *would not be consistent* with the security of the American nations. May not a man in his senses believe, that a kindred nation, or a colony, if you please, may be capable of managing its own concerns; and that it is full as likely to do it faithfully as the legislators of its mother country? May not a man in his senses believe, that such a state hath *a right* to appoint the guardians of its own liberties and properties, and to defend them against all invaders, even the legislators of its mother country, without involving himself in either "folly or absurdity?" Would the independency of any colony or kindred nation in America, necessarily create any such confusion, any such inconsistency in the government of Great-Britain, as would follow from the independency of, and a separate supreme legislation in, the capital city?

Note, &c. to Letter VII.

* As justice says it *ought* to be so; good sense will inform us that it *must* be so; notwithstanding the profound policy of the Quebec act.

LETTER VIII.

April 8, 1774.

WHEN our reverend author is not in a jeering humour, he will acknowledge that it is, in reality, "unreasonable, unjust, and cruel," to tax an unrepresented people (for I deny that America is represented at Westminster) against their own consent. (P. 100.) But "strange, exclaims the Dean, that you did not discover these bad things before! Strange, that tho' the British parliament has been, from the beginning, thus *unreasonable*, thus *unjust* and *cruel* towards you, by levying taxes on many commodities, outwards and inwards; nay, by laying an internal tax, the post-tax, for example, on the whole British empire in America; and, what is still worse, by making laws to affect your property, your paper currency, and even to take away life itself if you offended against them: strange and unaccountable, I say, that after you had suffered this so long, you should not have been able to have discovered that you were without representatives in the British parliament, *of your own electing*, till this enlightening tax upon paper opened your eyes! And what a pity is it, that you have been slaves for so many generations, and yet did not know that you were slaves until now." Now, strange and unaccountable as this may appear to the Dean, it has been by means of the very same kind precisely that our eyes have been successively opened to see the just rights of the people, the due limits of authority in their rulers, in every particular in which they are now legally ascertained. A rude and infant nation of husbandmen, having no pressing occasion, is not very logical or critically learned in the law, and all its remote consequences. It must move progressively towards the acquisition of knowledge as well as strength. This knowledge will always be first confined to reflecting individuals, before it will spread at large amongst the people; and many such individuals amongst the Americans, by the Dean's own account, (P. 4, and 5,) have had "their eyes open" these hundred years and upwards. The bulk of a nation must be made to *feel*, before they reason with tolerable accuracy, or lay much stress upon their governors keeping strictly within the pale of just and legal authority. Even self-evident truths are not discerned, until the attention of mankind is called upon by necessity, or some other powerful cause, to examine the subject in which they exist. The divine right of Kings, and their absolute power too, might have remained in the creeds of all nations to this day, had not too liberal an exercise of these powers taught them to reason by making them *feel*. No man in any country, ever thought of scrupulously defining the proper powers of taxation, while he possessed nothing worth taxing; nor of limiting the exercise of such powers, so long as the contributions required were trifling to him, the occasions of raising them apparent to all men, and the application of them known to, and approved by, every individual. It is, when a state begins to rise into some degree of political consequence, and the operations of its government are become too secret and complex to be penetrated by the vulgar eye, and at the same time grow expensive to the people, that they, not knowing what is going forward, and suspicious of some ill towards themselves, begin to investigate the legal powers of taxing, and how far they ought to be exercised; nor shall we exceed the truth, if we add, that all their jealousy and vigilance have been little enough, in the happiest age and nation, for guarding against the king-craft and tyranny of their rulers. While too insignificant to become the objects, or the tools of ambition, they remain in ignorance; it is the alarm of chains, and the dislike of burthens, that "enlighten them and open their eyes." After what has been said, I should hope it was quite unnecessary to refute the feeble arguments we find in p. 101, 102, 103, drawn from the freedom which an American now is permitted to enjoy, of voting for a member of the British parliament. We must remember, however, that he cannot do this without being a *British* freeholder, or holding some property which makes him at least a *British* subject; and it is therefore *as a Briton*, not *as an American*, he is represented. But to trace this rope of sand any farther, would really be to mock my readers, and I have already sufficiently replied to all such sorry subtleties. If the true and proper relation, in which this country stands with regard to the colonies, hath not, in all particulars, been accurately defined by mutual agreement and declaratory laws; but there are to be found some little inconsistencies, as there needs must be in such a connection so long as Great-Britain, through a love of rule, finds means to evade a fair discussion of *the question of right*; which, I pray, is the course that a wise and good man ought to pursue, in order to reconcile all contradictions, and to obtain a just idea of what is fit to be done for the remedying these inconveniences? Ought not the welfare of the whole people, without any partiality for countries, to out-weigh, in his mind, every other consideration? Must it not be his polar star, whenever he ventures upon the dark and deceitful sea of casuistry? Will he, for a moment, believe in the truth of any position or maxim, how antient, how specious soever, that is evidently incompatible with this object? Surely he will not lose sight of the true, the only ends of government, and labour to harden the heart and strengthen the hands of tyranny! Nor will he, surely, disregard the plain and obvious dictates of reason and nature, and, in defence of a bad cause, stoop and strain to catch at every little flaw and defect in forms and precedents! But one false step in reasoning, frequently misleads a good man into opinions and disputations prejudicial to truth. However, when the good of the public shall ultimately appear to be the end he aims at, we must make charitable allowances for his mistakes. Such allowances I am disposed to make to the author of the tracts; but yet as a well-wisher, and in perfect good humour, I must needs say he has indulged too freely a spirit, I will not say a talent, of ridicule; he is too supercilious even to his nephew, and is apt to sneer somewhat out of season, and when a satirical opponent might very easily retort it upon him with double force. Neither doth he appear to me quite so cool, dispassionate and impartial, as becomes a man who takes upon him to elucidate a disputed question on which depends the welfare, perhaps the existence of nations. He must have been a poor casuist, indeed, not to have obtained a victory over an antagonist of his own making: but we need not quarrel with him for beating him, since he shewed him so much mercy and good manners. But doth it not rather favour of disingenuousness, to put the maimed and mutilated arguments of the Americans into the mouth of a wrong-headed ignorant boy? Had it not been more to the advantage of his knowledge and eloquence, to have impressed conviction upon the mind of an experienced and able man, one who was well acquainted with the history, the laws, and the constitution of both Great-Britain and the colonies? But in that case, decency would have confined him to argument, instead of sneer and ridicule, and to a carriage suited to an equal, instead of that supercilious superiority assumed over the booby nephew; and this would have deprived his letter of its principal force and spirit. "But let that pass," and let us proceed to what is more to the purpose.

Our author proves, very satisfactorily, that the cause of contention between us and the colonies, is no recent affair—not the factious contrivance of a Lord Chatham, or a Lord Cambden, as the historians of the day would have it, but existed in no small force so early in the last century as 1670, (p. 5,) and in 1696, (p. 6,) gave occasion to a very remarkable act, for the very purpose chiefly of asserting the sovereignty of parliament. Acts of Parliament do not take place on such occasions until the mischief to be remedied is already at some degree of ripeness; and accordingly it appears, that the colonies had for a considerable time previous to 1696, shown a disposition to doubt, to dispute, and in some sort to oppose the authority of the English Parliament. Their eyes began to be open, and nature made them feel their inherent rights as men, long before they could define them. On the other hand, false definitions of law and right, have as long suppressed the feelings of equity in the minds of those possessed of the power. Let us make true definitions, and consult our true feelings, and we shall then no longer doubt of the right of independence in the Americans; I say true feelings, because, without we are circumspect, we are continually acquiring false ones, as well as false opinions; and the latter has a wonderful power in generating the former. Witness the daily and perpetual severities we see practiced towards children, to the injury both of body and mind, by injudicious parents, who yet want neither humanity nor tenderness, and who act upon principle. A false system begetting false feelings, while they are injuring and punishing their children, they think they are serving them and consulting their true happiness; and they consequently feel self-approbation for a conduct that ought to inspire horror and self-reproof. Now, with regard to our American children and kindred, let us divest ourselves of every interest, of every passion, of every prejudice; let us pluck from our hearts that deep-rooted love of rule, and for a moment put ourselves in their places; and then, deliberately and solemnly laying our hand upon our heart, remembering that we are christians, and answerable at the awful tribunal of the Deity for our very thoughts; let us ask ourselves these plain questions: is not the end of government to the Americans the same as to all other people, that is to say, the welfare and happiness of the society? Can there be welfare and happiness without freedom? Can freedom exist under a taxation, at the discretion of the legislature of another, and that a distant, a luxurious, a necessitous country? Is it agreeable to common-sense to imagine, that an American representation in the British-Parliament could answer the true ends of representation to the people of that country? or, is it possible, according to any plan which human wisdom hath yet conceived, that the Parliament of Great-Britain should govern the many and multiplying nations of America on the true principles of freedom, or without a certainty of sinking herself under the weight of empire? And is it fit that, on the authority of a few logical distinctions, (admitting they were just, which, by the way, they are not) and for the sake of proudly maintaining an absolute, a deceased claim to an empty sovereignty, (for so it is confessed to be, by its advocate the Dean) that we should forget all these considerations, all the ties of consanguinity and affection, all the feelings of humanity, and the divine lessons of our holy religion, and enforce the obedience of the Americans to an odious tyranny by fire and sword?

It is matter of the greatest astonishment to me, that a writer, so learned and so clear sighted as the Dean, should have so far over-looked all arguments of this nature, as to have left himself without a just, a moral reason, as well as a political one, for his proposed separation. As to the matter of fact, concerning the possibility of keeping the sovereignty in our hands, he and I are well agreed, as I have already shewn in my quotation from p. 12; nay, we both agree, that we have it not to keep, that it is already gone, never to be recovered but by conquest, never more to be held but with greater armies, and at a greater expence than ever this country supported in any war. I have also, in a former letter, quoted, what he says in the same page, (12) in order to shew, that it hath ever been the nature of all colonies, in all ages, to aspire after independence, and made my reflections thereupon, so that we may now hasten to the consideration of his five proposals, and to the conclusion of the task we have assigned ourselves. If I have trespassed upon the reader, by a repetition of the same arguments in different places, I would observe, that the few plain and clear arguments, on which this question depends, need to be repeated again and again, and never to be lost sight of; for the enemies of liberty, like the disingenuous foes of religion, are a sort of people, who, conscious that they cannot convince, and determined to wrangle, do not scruple to advance the same stale arguments that have been a thousand and a thousand times refuted before, and if not refuted again, as often as they have the shamelessness to revive them, they insult their adversaries with affected shouts of victory and triumph.

But my manner of treating the subject may, nevertheless, need many apologies. I shall, however, only plead, that these letters have been written as leisure would permit, and sent away to the Printer, without reserved copies to refer to: besides which it may be proper to add, that at the time I am writing this eighth, no more than the two first have made their appearance in the paper. As for the presumption of entering on a subject, without abilities equal to the attempt, I shall only offer, in my defence, that I have been prompted to it through a warm, a passionate love of liberty, and a sincere desire of promoting its cause.

Whatever may be my success, I shall never want the pleasing reflection of having done my duty conscientiously, as a member of society, although in a subordinate degree to greater workmen: and, I hope, it is not uncharitable to think, that if every writer would resign his pen to the same guidance, we should all be agreed very soon, as nearly as would be requisite, and that mankind would then reap such benefits from political disquisitions, as I fear are not likely to take place, while controversy is carried on upon other principles.

LETTER IX.

April 9, 1774.

WE come now to the consideration of our author's final settlements, and in p. 14, we find him thus expressing himself:

'Enough surely has been said on this subject, and the upshot of the whole matter is plainly this: that even the arbitrary and despotic governments of France and Spain (arbitrary, I say, both in temporals and spirituals) maintain their authority over their American colonies but very imperfectly, inasmuch as they cannot restrain them from breaking through those rules and regulations of exclusive trade, for the sake of which all colonies seemed to have been originally founded. What then shall we say in regard to such colonies as are the offspring of a free constitution? And after what manner, and according to what rule, are our own in particular to be governed, without using any force or compulsion, or pursuing any measure repugnant to their own ideas of civil or religious liberty? In short, and to sum up all in one word, how shall we be able to render these colonies more subservient to the interests, and more obedient to the laws and government of the mother country, than they voluntarily chuse to be? After having pondered and revolved the affair over and over, I confess there seems to me to be but the five following proposals which can possibly be made, viz.

'First, To suffer things to go on for a while as they have lately done, in hopes that some favourable opportunity may offer for recovering the jurisdiction of the British legislature over her colonies, and for maintaining the authority of the mother country; or, if these temporizing measures should be found to strengthen and confirm the evil instead of removing it, then,

'Secondly, To attempt to persuade the colonies to send over a certain number of deputies, or representatives, to sit and vote in the British parliament, in order to incorporate America and Great Britain into one common empire; or, if this proposal should be found impracticable, whether on account of the difficulties attending it on this side the Atlantic, or because that the Americans themselves would not concur in such a measure; then,

'Thirdly, to declare open war against them as rebels and revolters; and after having made a perfect conquest of the country, then to govern it by military force and despotic sway; or if this scheme should be judged (as it ought to be) the most destructive, and they least eligible of any; then,

'Fourthly, To propose to consent that America shall become the general seat of empire, and that Great-Britain and Ireland should be governed by viceroys sent over from the court-residencies either at Philadelphia or New-York, or at some other American imperial city; or, if this plan of accommodation should be ill-digested by home-born Englishmen, who, I will venture to affirm, would never submit to such an indignity; then,

'Fifthly, to propose to separate entirely from the colonies, by declaring them to be a free and independent people, over whom we lay no claim, and then by offering to guarentee this freedom and independence against all foreign invaders whomsoever.

'Now, these being all the plans which, in the nature of things, seem capable of being proposed, let us examine each of them in their order.'

I shall not need myself to accompany the Dean throughout this examination, in order to point out the fatal policy of attempting, and total impracticability of executing, any one of the four first of these schemes, since he has done it so effectually himself as to need no assistance. But though I agree with him in the result, that they are all both impolitic and impracticable, yet I differ widely from him in several arguments introduced in the discussion, and no less in the fundamental principles he frequently argues from. When he talks of the mother country governing 'in the manner she ought to do;' (p. 18) and according to the original terms of the constitution, I presume we are to understand the constitution to be some one individual contract between the mother country and her race of colonies, some certain deed signed and sealed between them and her in due form. Is this the same constitution he told us of in p. 94, of which Magna Charta was the basis? But if terms or conditions be the marks of our constitution, it may indeed be a colony charter, a marriage act, a stamp act, or, in short, any act of Parliament; or of the crown either, so that it will be a matter of very little consequence, whether it have Magna Charta for its basis, or any basis at all, besides that of the statute in being. Since he lays so much stress on those original terms, by which the colonies are bound to suffer their respectable mother to govern as he thinks 'she ought to do,' let us warn him not to rely too much upon analogical reasoning, since it is apt to prove too much. If he means that Great-Britain ought to be obeyed by her colonies, because she is their mother, because she produced them, and gave them their law, and that her contracts with them, when in their infancy ought to bind them forever, he would do well to remember, that no civil contract, between a parent and an infant child, affecting the future property of that child, can possibly have any validity, because of the child's being, at the time, in the power of the parent; because it dares not object to it, it cannot reject any terms she may please to dictate. I need not tell our author, that in the eye of the law, and agreeable to the spirit of the constitution, such a contract is esteemed no better than a fraud, or an act of the grossest tyranny.

Before I take my final leave of the four first of our author's proposals, I must make two observations upon what appears on the face of them. In the first place, let me request the reader to mark attentively the obvious sentiment, the unambiguous language of the second proposal. When the Dean is off his guard, and when the mistaken principles he adopted, respecting the sovereignty of parliament over America, are for a moment out of sight, see how naturally, how unavoidably he allows all I contend for! Here he admits, by direct and unavoidable implication, that parliament hath not the rights of sovereignty over America; he admits, that America is not a part of the British empire, or he could not possibly propose 'to atempt to persuade the colonies to send representatives to sit in the British parliament, in order to incorporate America and Great Britain into one common empire.' In the next place, I want to know, when, under the idea of an union, he has proposed to consent, that the seat of empire be transferred from Great Britain to America, why 'every home-born Englishman' should consider it as 'such an indignity.' The answer is plain, because he would become a slave; and while America shall be governed at Westminister, the Americans will be slaves. If our dignity consist in governing other nations against their wills, it is a dignity we ought to be ashamed of; but if it be the genuine offspring, and the associate of our liberty and independence, in God's name let our American kindred enjoy it as well as ourselves.

We now come to the consideration of the Dean's fifth and last proposal of an amicable and friendly separation, concerning which he very justly demands p. 50, 'and, in fact, what is all this but the natural, and even the necessary corollary to be deduced from each of the former reasons and observations? For, if we neither can govern the Americans, nor be governed by them; if we can neither unite with them, nor ought to subdue them, what remains, but to part with them on as friendly terms as we can?' This proposal, and the invincible arguments in its support, make ample amends for all the errors in the foregoing parts of his work. He shews himself to be master of this part of his subject; and it cannot be too much recommended to those whom I address in these letters, and to the people in general, to make themselves well acquainted with what he advances. His much superior knowledge of our American commerce, places the good policy of a separation from America in a much stronger point of light than it was in my power to have done: but I flatter myself, I have sufficiently proved, that we could not have kept that country in subjection without being tyrants. When justice and policy both point the same way, nothing but determined wickedness, or a wilful blindness can occasion us to take a wrong course. With the favour of the reader, I must here repeat one of the first observations I made on the Dean's work, as it strikes me afresh with redoubled force every time I consider it, and that is, that the proposed declaration of the independence of America, is a conclusion in direct opposition to his original premises. In his abstract reasonings on government, and the relation of colonies to the parent state, he falls—the common fate of genius on slippery abstract ground, into an error in fundamentals, laying it down as a principle, that 'parliament hath the rights of sovereignty over America;' and consequently, that 'America is actually a part of the British empire.'

These are the principles he sets out upon; but behold the result of all his subtle, all his laboured reasonings! At the end of a second work upon the subject, and after exhausting the chaotic treasuries of sophistry for arguments in support of these principles, he concludes with a proposal to the legislature, to declare that parliament doth not claim these rights. Nay, but a minute before, and, as I have observed when off his guard, he acknowledges that parliament hath not these rights, and even proposes 'to attempt to persuade the colonies to agree to an union.' There is something too irreconcileable in the idea as before remarked, of giving up one's rights, in order to promote one's interest; but false principles will ever produce fallacious reasonings. How can we possibly say more for an amicable separation from America, than that the absolute necessity of it took, as it were by storm, a mind naturally strong and vigorous, and fortified with all the powers of art against the attack! The Dean, in journeying to the great, the imperial city of truth, whose eternal foundations occupy a rock that overlooks the country around, unfortunately sets off in a mist of prejudice.

Sometimes he takes a direct contrary course; sometimes intervals of a clearer light keep him steady in the right road; but then again, as the density of the mist either totally obstructs his view, or discovers truth in faint glimmerings, he frequently deviates into bye paths and hollow ways, to the danger of being lost, even when near his journey's end. At last, however the sun of conviction bursts forth in meridian blaze, the mist is gone, and he arrives at the eternal city. But after having thus proposed a separation, 'as the only means of living in peace and harmony with the colonies:' and, after having given reasons for it, in opposition to which, I must needs think no man can remain an infidel, who is not at the same time an ideot; our author is, in my opinion, far more faithless, far more hopeless, than at this time there seems cause to be with regard to the execution of his plan. His plan I call it, since he is for aught I know to the contrary, the first who hath taken the pains to propose it publicly, and to explain its advantages, although it has been for some time past a common sentiment amongst discerning and liberalminded men, and to propose it was the first motive to the writing, and the main drift of these letters. It has been more particularly a common sentiment (for indeed invention itself cannot hit on any other plausible expedient) ever since the late noble and indignant conduct* of the Americans in defence of their almost-undermined liberty, as this affords a sufficient demonstration to all intelligent minds, in which the love of liberty and justice retained their influence, that the time is come, that they are determined to be independent of Great-Britain, whether it be with her consent or not.

'I frankly acknowledge,' says our author, p. 63, 'I propose no *present* convenience or advantage to either administration or anti-administration; nay, I firmly believe, that no minister, as things are now circumstanced, will dare to do so much good to his country:' whereas I, on my part, firmly believe, that Lord North is the minister who dares to do this great good to his country. He took the helm in a storm, when no other minister was to be found who could guide it; and he has given us throughout his administration, very ample proofs of his intrepidity. Are we not, at this moment under a general consternation at what may be the consequences of his intrepidity? Shall he dare in a single act that has no precedent, to shock this whole nation? Shall he dare to hurl a rash and misguided vengeance on the town of Boston, and bid a bold defiance to all America, and yet want courage to adopt a measure of the greatest wisdom and goodness; a measure which, to execute, he may esteem the glory of his life? The idea is too contradictory for a character so consistent as his.

There are conjunctures in the affairs of kingdoms when none but an intrepid statesman can stem a head-long torrent of popular zeal, or avert a gathering storm which threatens his authority. If the urgent necessity of the case shall not admit of temperate measures, but shall demand a daring act of temporary violence, such a statesman, if he be wise and virtuous also, will avail himself of the short-lived calm that succeeds the conflict, and before the discontents of the people can break forth afresh with redoubled and irresistable impetuosity, he will effectually remove them, by removing their causes, and by giving them a security against future alarms. I hope that the late bill† will prove only a temporary violence, and that these moments, which are generally thought to be a sullen calm, foreboding some dreadful political convulsion, may be pregnant with more salutary measures and plans of peace.‡ The remembrance of it will, in a moment, be done away, when Great-Britain shall once have done justice to the Americans, by an open declaration of their independence, and by offering them her friendship. Our mutual jealousies will

be buried in oblivion, and, as the Dean foretels, the Americans will
then consider us as 'their protectors, mediators, benefactors.'

NOTES, &c. to LETTER IX.

* I would not have the reader imagine, I mean to justify every tarring and
feathering rioter at Boston, and all disorderly proceedings in America indiscri-
minately. Some of the people, I doubt not, may have been to blame; for the
commonalty of that country must have had a portion of wisdom and patience,
which hath not at any time before been found in the world, had all their
expressions of resentment for ill usage, been confined within the bounds of
moderation. When governors become tyrants, shall we wonder, that an injured
and insulted people become riotous and unruly! Have ambitious and encroaching rulers ever yet thought of rendering *satisfaction*, of making *reparation*, for the cruellest injuries they have so constantly committed; and have
they not always thought themselves wonderfully gracious and condescending,
when they have merely *ceased to oppress?* but if a free people, finding their
humble petitions, and most dutiful remonstrances scattered to the winds with
contempt, being stung with a sense of accumulated wrongs, and feeling an
indignation at being treated like slaves and villains, do but assault the meanest
miscreant in the train of power; 'tis rebellion! felony! treason! Gaols and gibbets, ball and bayonet, must here be the correctives. Is this human polity! Are
these the proceedings of men, of fellow creatures, of fellow christians? When
merely *ceasing to oppress*, is all the reparation required for a long train of
injuries and insults; shall authority, with whom wisdom ought ever to reside,
become deaf to that voice which called her into being, and think it merito-
rious to persist in doing wrong?

So universally have I heard the Bostonians condemned for destroying the
tea, and the action pronounced illegal and rebellious, that I have taken some
pains to examine all the particulars of that affair. Now, to my agreeable disappointment, and to the best of my judgment, instead of an act of rebellion, I
find it one reflecting honour, and stamping the character of good subjects, on
those who performed it; instead of being illegal it appears to me to be warranted by the law of nature, the great original of all human laws, when just.
Those who would wish to think justly, and to speak honestly of this matter,
will do well to examine for themselves. When they shall have so done, with
care and candour, and admitting on my part, for the sake of taking no advantage in the argument, the Bostonian character to be as black as malignantly
represented, I should be glad to propose to them this plain question: 'What
was possible for the most wise and virtuous persons on earth, in the place of
the Bostonians, to have done, in order to have performed their duty to the
utmost towards God and their Country?'—To have shewn a passive obedience
to an unjust act of parliament, in a case of such moment, and of so critical a
nature, would have been treason to their country, and therefore not accepta-
ble, I imagine, to God. I have introduced in various conversations, with sensible men, the same question I here propose, but never yet, I can aver with the

[179]

strictest veracity, have I met with a solution of it, which did not confirm me in an opinion, that as wise and virtuous men, as good citizens, and true patriots, *they could not possibly have acted otherwise than as they did.*

They had only this one alternative; they were driven to this dilemma by their magistrates, *either to suffer an insidious attempt against their sacred rights and liberties to take effect, or to destroy the hated instrument.* Having had *no other choice,* they must necessarily have either *done* this, or *suffered* that. Which ought to have been chosen by every brave and honest man, I leave the reader to determine. 'Tis visionary, even to childishness, to say, they might have permitted the tea to have been landed, and yet have defeated the tax, by unanimously refusing to have purchased it. The conductors of that noble action must have been patriots indeed, and most wonderfully wise, to have left their country, by going this way to work, at the discretion and mercy of the most ignorant and vicious of its inhabitants, to have relied upon the prudence and self-denial of every tea-drinker in America! Besides that the wisdom of each well meaning individual was not to be depended on for foreseeing all the ill consequences of purchasing a pound of tea, nor their resolution in preventing them; I fear there might have been some traitors to the public cause, some tools of government or the India Company, or some suspected persons at least, in whom to have confided, for not setting the example, and using all their cunning to seduce others, would not have argued any extraordinary degree of prudence.

What teacher of morals or politics, ever was lunatic enough to build all his hopes of serving his country, on an expectation of bringing *every individual* of it to be of one mind, and as unanimously to act up to the same rigid principle of virtue? and which of us would care to risk the safety of the city of London from some dreadful calamity, on a confidence that every female, from the fine lady to the washerwoman, every man, from the minister of state down to the blackguard, might be prevailed upon totally to abstain from the use of tea, porter, or gin, *except the temptation was removed out of their way.*

To all my readers, except those unhappy ones, who have learned the fatal art of occasionally closing the mental eye, so as to admit just so much, and no more of the light of truth as their passions and prejudices will bear; I must needs think, it would be reflecting upon their understandings and their ingenuousness, to attempt any farther proof of my proposition, that the Bostonians did what was strictly consonant to right and justice in destroying the tea; but, in order to open the self-closed, winking eyes of the prejudiced, I will propose one more comparison, which, I apprehend, will be admitted as a fair one, since it is agreed on all hands, except by the calm advancers of direct falsehoods and lies, and the bold denyers of demonstration, that with regard to taxation, the colonists, as legitimate shoots from a parent stock of freedom, have at least an equal right to be their own tax-masters as the people of Ireland, which was a conquered, and every one knows, a very rebellious kingdom for many ages.

Let then the reader only substitute Ireland and Dublin, for Massachusett's-Bay and Boston, and try the cause over again in his own mind. If he pleases, we will suppose, that instead of a duty on tea, we should attempt to touch the pockets of the Irish, by a duty on certain stamped papers, being publications of gross immoralities and blasphemies, tending to debauch the minds of the

[180]

people, and fit them for slavery; and that an association of honest citizens of Dublin, more mindful of their duty to God and their country, than of obedience to an ordinance they held to be subversive of their liberties, should find this precious cargo, precisely in a similar situation with the tea at Boston; that the Lord Mayor, the magistrates, and revenue myrmidons, like the Boston governor and officers of Customs, should all absolutely refuse their permission and clearances for its departure from the port, and the ship should be well imprisoned by surrounding batteries; then, what is to be done? what course is to be pursued? Shall those, who ought to be the guides and guardians of the city, admit these pernicious compositions within their walls; patiently behold them displayed in the shops, hawked about the streets, and dispersed throughout the country, with every art of invitation to those inclined to purchase?

Is the city to be deluged with these impieties, and its manners, morals, and liberties undermined, rather than *an united company of merchants trading in mischief* should lose their property? a property not only detrimental in itself, but in this case made a venture, with the direct intention of betraying a brave and generous nation into obedience to a despotic ordinance, containing in it the seeds of a more complete tyranny, and used as the most tempting bait to lure the silly multitude into the political mousetrap; and therefore, on the principles of self-preservation, and agreeable to the spirit of the law of nature and nations, subject to be destroyed, *if not removed upon fair warning*. Are the city guardians, I say, to observe all this, and content themselves all the while with a patriotic resolve, not to buy or to read a single paper, and with preaching to the unlistening people to follow their example? If this, in the enlightened and virtuous city of Dublin, would be an experiment, that even a driveller would hardly dream of making; how much less safe would it have been for the American patriots to have hazarded their all, on the universal good sense, on the piety and public spirit of the people, in the *stupid*, the *hypocritical*, the *impious*, the *ungrateful*, and *rebellious* town of Boston!

What then, I once more ask, ought the patriots of Dublin or of Boston to have done? What! but with indignation to have cast the hated instrument of tyranny into the sea! whither its proprietors deserved also to have followed it headlong. Is it for this wise, brave, and generous action, that not only the actors of it, but the whole people of Boston, are now smarting under the heaviest vengeance of Great-Britain! of a people who have hitherto justly prided themselves in being the undaunted resisters of tyrants! Fie, boasters, fie! Britannia blushes for your degeneracy; she disowns ye for her sons. When a pawnbroker knowingly puts arms into the hands of a highwayman or ruffian, does any law insure to him payment for the same, at the hands of anyone who being assaulted, seized and destroyed them? Are not all deadly weapons, all snares, traps, and poisons, made use of in violation to the laws of civil society, for injuring any man in life, limb, or property, a *lawful spoil* to the injured party? When the miscreant, pick-pocket Jew, in the service of iniquity, was once driving a trade amongst the Westminster school-boys, with a parcel of TEA, out of the *green cannister* of the celebrated Mrs. *Phillips*, who, that had a spark of virtuous indignation, but applauded the *illegal proceedings* of the spirited master, when, disregarding the *laws of property*, he threw into the fire all of this *tea* he could lay his hands on; and, as little considering the penalties for an assault, horsed the vile factor, and scourged him to the quick?

I must therefore repeat, that the destroyers of the tea at Boston were, in my opinion, a band of virtuous patriots, whose names, when once made public, will doubtless be held in eternal veneration by their countrymen; and that the glorious *illegality* (if every statute, *whether just or unjust,* be properly comprehended in the word law) they achieved, was an act of absolute moral and political *necessity,* and therefore exempt from even good laws; of singular wisdom, of strict justice, and remarkable temper and forbearance, considering their provocations since it was done in *self-defence,* with the greatest good order and decency, and unaccompanied with incivility to any one, or the smallest damage to any thing in the ships besides the treacherous tea. I must likewise repeat, that this tea, for the reasons I have given, and agreeable to the spirit of the law of nature and nations, was justly forfeited to the injured Americans; and that the East-India Company are not entitled to any satisfaction or payment for the same.

† The Boston Port Bill.

‡ Notwithstanding the act for the better regulating the government of the Massachusett's Bay, and notwithstanding the Quebec Act, I will not yet part with my hope, that the eyes of the legislature will soon be opened; and that these acts, as well as the other, will only prove temporary acts of violence. They have all been passed before the minds of the ministers have had time to cool.

LETTER X.

April 14, 1774.

NOTHING now remains to be spoken of but the act of parliament necessary to that separation, proposed by the reverend author of the tracts, and seconded in these letters; and that General treaty between Great-Britain and the states of America, which will be the necessary, and doubtless the immediate consequence of it. When Parliament shall have duly weighed this great, this important matter,—the greatest by far that ever came before any national council whatever!— with the attention it merits, and in the temper recommended in my first letter, we may hope to see a *nemine contradicente* act, whose preamble shall run in some such form as the following viz.

'Whereas, at the time of the original planting and settling of colonies on the continent of North-America by the people and the crown of these kingdoms; and afterwards, during the infancy of the said colonies, the future ill consequences of their submission to, and acquiescence under the authority of parliament were not, by reason of their then infant and dependent state, and the general inexperience in matters of that kind, either foreseen or duly attended to; and whereas, through the growing of these once small and helpless colonies to maturity, and their becoming populous, opulent and respectable states, having each within itself the natural rights and proper powers of legislation, the exercise of parliamentary authority hath been found to clash in the most essential points with their respective internal legislatures, and hath tended for a considerable time past, but more particularly of late years, to create dissatisfactions between the said internal legislatures and parliament, and between the people of the said colonies and the people of these kingdoms; and whereas these matters having been taken into consideration, and it appearing upon the principles of natural justice, and agreeable to the established maxims of civil government, that it is inconsistent with the welfare of the people of the said colonies or states, and prejudicial to their natural inherent rights as men, to be governed by the parliament of Great-Britain, or any other power foreign to themselves respectively: be it therefore enacted, &c.' In the enumeration of their names, none of them (fifteen, I think, lying between the Gulph of St. Lawrence and the mouth of the Mississippi) will, I hope, be omitted, but those obtained partly by war and treaty inserted as well as the rest; and that in the clause, it shall be fully expressed, that 'they are all held and declared to be free and independent states, each to be subject to such law and government only as now subsists, or shall hereafter be enacted and constituted within itself by its own proper legislature; and that of each and every of the said independent states, his Majesty is, and shall be held to be the sovereign head, in like manner as he is of the legislature of Great-Britain.' In another clause, I could wish it might likewise be expressed, that 'the parliament of Great-Britain doth farther declare itself to be the guardian and protector of the whole, and of every of the said states or colonies, collectively and individually, against every foreign power whatsoever, as well as the guarantee of the independence of the said several colonies or states, one of another respectively and reciprocally, as well also of the rights and independencies of the several tribes or nations of Indians in amity with, or under the protection of the crown of these kingdoms, until these points shall be more particularly adjusted by treaty.' Another clause would probably provide, that 'commissioners on the part of the parliament of Great-Britain, shall be empowered to enter into treaty with deputies of the legislatures of each of the said colonies or states, in order that a firm, brotherly, and perpetual league may be concluded between Great-Britain and them for their mutual commercial benefit, and their joint security against all other kingdoms and states, as well as for the preservation of that warm affection and harmony which ought ever to subsist between a mother country and her offspring, or kindred states, equally acknowledging one perfect constitution and one perfect religion, as their rule of life in temporals and in spirituals.' The commissioners will be nominated of course. Other declarations and provisions may be contained in this act, as parliament shall see good; but we should hope, as an indispensible requisite towards the security of the general liberties, that it be enacted, that 'no part of the revenue of any one of the said American states shall, by his Majesty, his viceroy, or ministers, be removed out of, or received into, any other of the said states, or into Great-Britain for his Majesty's use; and that in like manner, no part of the revenue of these kingdoms, shall be remitted to America on that account; but that the revenue of Great-Britain, and of each respective state in America, shall be wholly and solely applied to defray the expences of government, and maintain the regal dignity in that country in which it shall be raised, and no other.'

Although, by those unhappy persons, who have no just ideas of right and wrong, and who have not intellects for perceiving, that the original power of Great-Britain over her colonies, is on the point of expiring beyond all help and remedy, parliament may be supposed to be a loser by the proposed separation; yet all must confess that his Majesty will be a gainer, inasmuch as he will thereby receive fifteen independent kingdoms in exchange for as many dependent, and *hardly dependent* provinces, and become the father of three millions of free and happy subjects, instead of reigning joint tyrant over so many discontented slaves, or losing by revolt so many of his people. What a divine glow of satisfaction must expand the royal bosom on an event so full of bliss, so consonant to humanity and to virtue!—an event more full of real lustre—more aggrandizing by many degrees than ever before was experienced by any earthly monarch. How poor, how contemptible, how hateful the triumphs of butchering conquerors compared to this solid glory! May such a transcendant glory, be the glory of George the third.

We must not be surprized if shallow and designing men, some with real, some with affected ignorance, should cry out, 'What! enter into treaty with fifteen independent states, and expect them unanimously to join with you in one general league for mutual advantage and security! How chimerical and visionary the project!'* And I do not doubt, but that the swarm of hireling and prostitute scribblers, whose food is confusion, and whose very existence, like the vermin in an ulcer, is supported by the diseases of the state, will pour forth all their malignity, in order to discredit, and to damn if possible, a plan so wise and salutary. But their baneful influence will not, I trust, extend itself farther than to disturb, for a short time, the confused minds of our coffee-house politicians.

It will still be obvious to all sensible men, especially to those who compose the national council, that when Great-Britain shall have done the noblest act of justice towards the Americans, that the annals of mankind can produce, they will, as one man, fly to her for protection, court her friendship, submit themselves to her advice, and be ready to put into her hands a chart blanche; and so long as she continues to act upon the same principles, she may undoubtedly influence each separate state, and dictate the terms of general accommodation without any fear of even *future* dissatisfactions. To deny these conclusions, would be to deny that effects follow their causes.

The author of the tracts has already proved, that it is not our power, but the superior advantage of our trade, which secures to us the commerce of the Americans, or that can secure it to us. We shall still have the same power to awe America into a faithful observance of her treaties, that we now have, to enforce a disputed and odious sovereignty, and with this manifest advantage, that treating with each state separately, we shall only have one at a time to contend with; whereas we have experienced by our stamp and tea projects, that while we pretend to govern the whole, the whole will unite to resist us.

That bond of union once dissolved, and the natural and necessary jealousy of each other taking place, Great-Britain, as the common umpire, will become in effect the general sovereign, so long as she interposes her good offices for maintaining the common independence; and this her own interest will always dictate. Great Britain, will of course take care, in the first place, to recover all her debts in America, which, instead of bad debts, as they are now too justly esteemed to be, will, in the transports of their gratitude for a declared and guaranteed independence, be punctually paid, though with their last shilling. Not to mention that fear of offending, (for Great-Britain will then become truly formidable to each separate state) would effectually produce this effect, we shall, by the league secure on the most lasting foundation, every advantage of trade with America we now enjoy, and by the separation relieve ourselves from many heavy expences it now costs us; for a proof of which, I again refer to the Dean's work: we may then disband so much of our expensive and unconstitutional standing army, as we now keep up on account of America; and instead of being execrated, as we now are, for that fleet which blocks up their ports, and is commissioned to humble Boston to the dust, and through her sides, to gall every province on the continent, they will readily consent to its presence for seeing to the exact fulfilling of their treaties, and they will then look upon it with a friendly, an affectionate and respectful eye, while they consider it as their sure protector against invasion, their refuge in distress, and the avenger of their wrongs. Not being able to pay Great-Britain in subsidies of ready money for her protection and friendship, they will grant her an equivalent in *exclusive trade*; and they will enter into some general stipulation for the mode and the measure of payment for any such extraordinary assistance of ships as they may at any time solicit, or we, penetrating the designs of our common enemies, may send to their assistance.

As for troops, a country containing millions of inhabitants, never can want any: let them rely upon the natural, the best resource—a national militia; but, for heaven's sake! never more let the face of a British soldier be seen in North-America.

A Flanders or a Germany, on the other side of the globe would be a grave wide enough to swallow the whole strength and treasure of this kingdom. The Americans are in no condition to set themselves up as a maritime power, or to support a navy fit to guard their own coasts, but must rely upon Great-Britain for their safety by sea, as indeed it will ever be their interest so to do, knowing by experience, that with regard to them, *she is not a conquering*, but a commercial state; and having reason to conclude, that a confederacy of their maritime states would probably terminate, like that of Greece, in wars upon one another, and be perverted to answer the ends of ambition to some one, instead of protection to all. After what has been said, I need not point out (but for the sake of my timid and uninformed reader) that it will be totally unnecessary, and unbecoming the dignity of parliament, to hesitate a moment in passing the act of declaration, for fear the Americans should not afterwards consent to the league. 'Tis absurd to imagine they will act in contradiction to the principles of *self-interest and self-preservation,* merely because they shall be free from controul; nor is it more possible to conceive, how they should object to a treaty with Great-Britain, merely because she had just done them an act of magnanimity and generosity unparallelled in history, and given them an undeniable proof, that she was intitled to their unbounded confidence, particularly in its not being possible she should have *any design upon their liberties.* Besides Great-Britain, until she have resigned her assumed sovereignty as the mother country, cannot, on the principles of equity, as before illustrated, give any validity to a contract with her children, while held in subjection to her authority. No! the generous spirit that shall set them free, will disdain the meanness of a proceeding so little and so distrustful; and that wisdom which could form so comprehensive a plan, will despise the crookedness and folly of such a narrow policy.

Thus have I given a faint sketch of the many and great benefits of an American league—the reader's imagination and judgment will finish the picture. If then he can think, that they do not infinitely preponderate against the advantages to be hoped for from persisting to assert our odious sovereignty, and plundering the colonies by arbitrary tax-gathers, I have only to say, that he and I can scarcely be made of the same common materials of humanity; but I shall begin to listen to those profound sages, whose acute penetration, assisted by a certain microscopic species of philosophy, hath discovered, that the Mosaic revelation is a fable, and that, instead of one, there are indeed many different races of men. On the one hand, the most we can expect is a forced and reluctant submission, with some advantages in trade; but these even for a very, *very short period.* Mean while, discontent and detestation, brooding in the bosoms of the colonists, will naturally generate a rancorous hate and abhorrence; which, aided by our restless enemies the French, will shortly terminate in defiance and revenge. On the other hand—but repetition is needless. In short, the multiplying millions of America, must either be our deadly foes, or our steadfast friends. Great-Britain, take thy choice!

What remains, but that we renew our appeal to the manly sense and magnanimity of the great council of this kingdom; a kingdom, great and happy above all the kingdoms of the earth; a council the most august in the whole world, as nursed in the bosom of freedom, and trained in the true principles of just government and pure religion, of which they are the guardians! If men, thus favoured of heaven, thus enlightened, thus elevated, shall not set examples of sterling virtue, where, alas! shall we find it? Consult then your own hearts, ye legislators of Great-Britain! Be true to your own feelings, and let the moral sense prevail. If ye are conscious of a love of power, know that 'tis the genuine offspring of the love of liberty. This the root, that the branch. If your hearts be held in the curling branch's close embrace, think how, in the hearts of all men, the tenacious root strikes to the bottom, and twines its clasping fibres around the very springs of life, never to lose their hold!

Remember that ye are now to decide on the fate of nations—perhaps your own. Remember the great legislator beholds your doings. Be your doings like unto his doings. Be tender to humanity; be firm to freedom; be inflexible to justice. Emancipate in one god-like act, a long roll of nations, whose names it is tedious to recount. In one act, lift up the well-pleasing name of Great-Britain to Heaven, and spread her matchless fame to the ends of the wondering earth. The depth of her wisdom, the transcendency of her virtue, shall be unexampled, and this act remain a monument of her great felicity, an everlasting model of justice, and a theme of praise to all nations, and to all ages. Potentates have, unto dethroned Princes restored their ravished dominions; renowned monarchs, sated with ambition, and the abuse of authority, have, in the plenitude of their power, abdicated thrones; heroes and patriots have given freedom to their native countries; but for the present legislators of Great-Britain was reserved the superior, the supreme glory of bestowing in a foreign soil, liberty on millions!

NOTE, &c. to LETTER X.

* In order to obviate some objections, which, I foresee, both well-meaning and ill-designing persons may be ready to offer to this part of my proposal, let me observe to them, that this negociation will not be attended with those difficulties and embarrassments, which their imaginations or their artifice may possibly suggest. We may presume, that our commissioners would have the outlines of the proposed league ready sketched out, from the most approved general regulations of the acts of trade and navigation, which now relate to the colonies collectively, and taking in such other conditions as should be evidently calculated for the mutual benefit of Great-Britain and North-America; one as the planting, the other as the manufacturing country; one as the client, the other as the patron. This general league might be very concise, compared with national treaties in common; it might be extremely perspicuous, and so clearly established on principles of equity and common advantage, as to leave the American deputies without a pretence, or a desire to propose any but slight alterations, and without a possibility of not acceding to it with the ut-most readiness and satisfaction; and it is still less likely, there should be any insuperable difficulties started by them, when they should come to enter into their respective separate treaties.

How the trade of a colony can be limited, and its manufactures restricted by the mother-country, on the principles of justice, *except with its own free consent,* I confess I have not eyes to discover. If it can be made appear, that the British Parliament hath a right to say to an American, '*you shall not* make a hat to cover your head, nor a shoe to defend your foot; *you shall not* manu-facture a piece of cloth to keep out the cold, nor a knife wherewithal to cut your victuals;' why, I pray, may it not likewise say, 'give us the money out of your pocket?' To obtain a little money may be thought, and by Mr. Grenville and his disciples was thought, as *convenient* to the state, as the employment of our manufacturers.

Observing, that not only the unreasoning multitude, but the members in both houses of Parliament, minority as well as majority, not even excepting the honest opposers of American taxation, all seemed to agree, that Great-Britain hath a right to bind the colonies by her regulations and restrictions in and upon their trade, navigation and manufactures; I, for a long time, suf-fered my own reason to be borne down, and my feelings suppressed by the weight of such respectable, though not infallible authority; but, the self-evi-dent fallaciousness of this proposition for ever recurring upon me, and striking my mind with redoubled force every time I considered it, I was at last obliged to yield to the force of an irresistible internal conviction, and to reject that doctrine as erroneous, and as a national prejudice, arising from *precedents,* established by the mother country, when her children were helpless new-born babes, and carefully instilled into their minds while growing up, as among the sacred precepts of filial piety; from the self-flattering and self-interested suggestions of British minds; and from the general acknowledgement of the Americans themselves. One of their judicious and truly patriotic writers (be-fore referred to in a note to the first letter) on this head, expresses himself thus: Great-Britain has prohibited the manufacturing iron and steel in these colonies, without any objection to her *right* of doing it. The like right she must have to prohibit any other manufacture among us. Thus she is possessed of an undisputed *precedent* on that point. This authority, she will say, is founded on the *original intention* of settling these colonies; that is, that she should manufacture for them, and that they should supply her with materials. The *equity* of this policy, she will also say, has been universally acknowledged by the colonies, who never have made the least objection to statutes for that purpose; and will further appear, by the mutual benefits flowing from this usage, ever since the settlement of these colonies.

"Our great advocate, Mr. Pitt, in his speeches on the debate, concerning the repeal of the *stamp-act,* acknowledged, that Great Britain could restrain our manufactures. His words are these: This kingdom, as the supreme governing and legislative power, [even this great man hath not got over the little idea of nations remaining in perpetual subjection to nations from which they sprang] has ALWAYS bound the colonies by her regulations and RESTRICTIONS in trade, in navigation, in MANUFACTURES, in every thing, *except that of taking the money out of their pockets, WITHOUT THEIR* CONSENT. Again, he says, we may bind their trade, CONFINE THEIR MANUFACTURES, and exercise every power whatever, *except that of taking their money out of their pockets,* WITHOUT THEIR CONSENT. [These are pretty large concessions to the pride and ambition of Great Britain, and yet she is not satisfied with them.] Here then, my dear countrymen, ROUSE yourselves, and behold the ruin hanging over your heads. If you ONCE admit, that Great Britain may lay duties upon her exportations to us, *for the purpose of levying money on us only,* she will then have nothing to do, but to lay those duties on the articles which she prohibits us to manufacture,—and the tragedy of American liberty is finished. We have been prohibited from procuring manufactures, in all cases any where, but from *Great Britain,* (except linens, which we are permitted to import directly from Ireland.) We have been prohibited, in some cases, from manufacturing for ourselves, and may be prohibited in others. We are, therefore, exactly in the situation of a city besieged, which is surrounded by the works of the besiegers in every part *but one.* If that is closed up, no step can be taken, *but to surrender at discretion.* If Great Britain can order us to come to her for necessaries we want, and can order us to pay what taxes she pleases before we take them away, or when we land them here, we are as abject slaves as France or Poland can shew in wooden shoes and with uncombed hair.

"Perhaps the nature of the necessities of dependent states, caused by the policy of a governing one, for her own benefit, may be elucidated by a fact mentioned in history. When the Carthaginians were possessed of the island of Sardinia, they made a decree, that the Sardinians should not raise *corn,* nor get it any other way *than from the Carthaginians.* Then, by imposing any taxes they would upon it, they drained from the miserable Sardinians any sums they pleased; and whenever that oppressed people made the least movement to assert their liberty, their tyrants starved them to death, or submission."

But why, I want to know, are the colonies to be held for ever in the situation of *cities besieged?* Why is the mother-country to be the *sole judge* of such restrictions as may be consistent with the *original intention* of settling colonies; seeing that this original intention was not, in some cases, the intention of the *legislature,* but the intention of *the immigrants themselves,* when they fled from persecution, misery, and want, to take shelter in the more friendly wilds of America? Why are the selfish and arbitrary terms prescribed by *one party,* to be implicitly received by the *other,* in a commercial affair of *mutual concern,* and professed by the dictating party, to be for their *mutual advantage? Voluntary consent* and *agreement, independent bargain* and *contract,* are in the very essence of all *equitable* dealings in trade. I presume the Americans may be as good judges, as the people who ridiculously *assume the right* of judging for them, what it is *their* advantage to restrict themselves to in manufactures and trade; and will be ready to take care to confine themselves to such branches, as will be most consistent with that first political

[190]

maxim, of securing at all events, *the protection of Great-Britain*, and her *valuable trade*, from which they have benefits to expect, that no other European market can yield them. To acknowledge their independency, and to form with them a friendly league, is therefore the only method, *on the principles of equity*, of laying them under restrictions in trade and manufactures, for the exclusive advantage of their protectors; but continuing to impose these restrictions by *our own authority* and by *force*, as it deeply affects them in their property, by *preventing money coming into their pockets*, (which is very nearly allied, when done unjustly, to *taking it out of their pockets without their consent*) is undoubtedly tyrannical.

When our legislators, and others, divesting themselves of every selfish and arbitrary bias, (the characteristics of little and uncultivated minds) and guarding against all suggestions, but those of truth, justice, and benevolence, shall have duly reflected on this very important question, I flatter myself they will perceive the wisdom of our *anticipating* the Americans in a candid discussion of it, and will agree with me, in sentiment, that America cannot, according to any ideas of justice or freedom, be laid under restrictions of any kind, for the purpose of strengthening and aggrandizing the state or legislature of Great Britain, *except with her free-will and consent*, independently and voluntarily given by express stipulation and contract; and consequently, that they will see the moral as well as the political necessity, for the proposed DECLARATION and LEAGUE; and that, in fact, it remains for Great Britain to choose, whether by acting the deaf and haughty tyrant, she shall sink herself into poverty and contempt, or, by a conduct worthy herself and her boasted knowledge, and love of freedom, she shall render herself, not only the all-powerful guarantee of the independence, and monopolizer of the trade of America, but at the same time the dreaded, the dictatorial arbiter of Europe.[4]

F I N I S

N O T E S

[1] Cartwright's sweeping defense of the "band of virtuous patriots" who destroyed the tea at Boston is in his first note to Letter IX, p. 179–182.

[2] The reference is to the work of Josiah Tucker (1712-99), Dean of Gloucester, *Four Tracts, Together With Two Sermons, on Political and Commercial Subjects* (Gloucester, 1774). Cartwright's main interest is in Tucker's fourth tract, "The True Interest of Great-Britain, Set Forth in Regard to the Colonies; And the Only Means of Living in Peace and Harmony with Them," an early formulation of the argument that it was in the best interest of Britain to grant the American Colonies their independence.

[3] Sir Michael Foster (1689-1763), Judge of the King's Bench, 1745-63.

⁴ A five-page extract from the London *Monthly Review* is appended to Cart-wright's work, together with an appeal to readers for aid in locating a copy of the second edition:

IF any GENTLEMAN, possessed of the English second Edition of this Pamphlet, will be so obliging, as to favour the Printer ROBERT BELL with it, for a few days only, he will thereby render an essential service to the cause of LIBERTY and LITERATURE in America.

Willoughby Bertie

EARL OF ABINGDON

ALTHOUGH usually overlooked by students of the American Revolution, the Earl of Abingdon was known to American Revolutionary leaders as one of their most outspoken defenders in Parliament. In fact, his speeches and writings were used to bolster sagging morale during the dark days of Valley Forge. Abingdon had been a relatively obscure figure in America in comparison with men such as Pitt and Wilkes. In September 1777 he achieved sudden fame in England with a vigorous attack on Edmund Burke's published defense of unlimited parliamentary supremacy, however, and within a few months an American edition of his pamphlet and copies of several of his speeches in Parliament were in circulation in the States.[1] In England the pamphlet went through seven editions and sparked a vigorous debate which included several published rejoinders. For the sixth edition, Abingdon added an 89-page preface that constituted his response to English critics, as well as other new material in the form of footnotes.

Born Willoughby Bertie in 1740, educated at Westminster School and Oxford, he became the fourth Earl of Abingdon upon his father's death in 1760. The democratic principles for which he became known were apparently a product of his residence in Geneva as a young man and were confirmed by his activities in support of Wilkes during the late 1760's. After the outbreak of the American war he became more active in politics, frequently taking the floor in the House of Lords to denounce the North Ministry. Abingdon was a personal friend of the Marquis of Rockingham and generally voted with Rockingham's Whig followers. His attack on Burke, however, clearly revealed his independence and pained many of his friends among the Rockinghamites. In later years, Abingdon advanced far beyond most of his contemporaries in defense of liberal causes. He devoted considerable energy to various Irish reform proposals and, during the 1790's, was one of the most ardent English defenders of the French Revolution.[2]

The unusual attention which Abingdon attracted in America in 1778 derived in part from the timeliness of the appearance of his attack on Burke's public espousal of parliamentary supremacy. During the winter of 1777-78, when the British occupied Philadelphia and Congress was in exile at York, the North Ministry attempted to open negotiations with Congress in order to head off a Franco-American alliance. Washington's army was undergoing a severe test in winter quarters because of the breakdown of the supply system, and a clique of disgruntled officers and disenchanted Congressmen was considering a move to replace the Commander in Chief. During these dismal days Abingdon's pamphlet found its way into the hands of Robert Morris, who circulated it among a group of his friends that included Thomas Wharton, the President of Pennsylvania. Praising the work, Wharton obtained an endorsement from the Pennsylvania Council, showed it to the Philadelphia printer John Dunlap, who had set up his press in Lancaster, and returned to Morris to secure his backing for an American edition. "It is a Treasure worth preserving," he explained, "and therefore should be reprinted that every American may have an opportunity of reading it with attention." [3]

At first glance the American interest in Abingdon's pamphlet may evoke surprise, for it was an attack on none other than Edmund Burke, previously known as a staunch American supporter. A member of Parliament for Bristol, Burke had gained a reputation for defending the Colonies before the Commons and in so doing had alienated a large portion of his constituency. As part of a controversial opposition political maneuver that included a boycott of Parliament, he had done nothing to oppose legislation for the suspension of the writ of habeas corpus in Britain. At the suggestion of friends, Burke had adopted the device of an open letter to the Sheriffs of Bristol to explain his conduct and answer charges that he had advocated surrender of British rights to the Americans. In his letter he declared candidly that "if ever one man lived more zealous than another for the supremacy of Parliament and the rights of this imperial crown, it was myself." When he had entered the House of Commons, he had found Parliament "in possession of an unlimited legislative power over the colonies," and he had always labored to preserve that authority "perfect and entire." [4]

Although Abingdon devoted several pages to criticizing Burke's failure to oppose the bill for suspension of habeas corpus, the focus of his attack was clearly on Burke's extreme claim of parliamentary supremacy. "Supremacy of Parliament," Abingdon explained, "is a combination of terms unknown to the English polity." Similarly, *"allegiance to the State,* . . . is allegiance 'run mad.' " In brief, Abingdon denied all arguments in favor of unlimited legislative power. And since such power had never existed in Britain in any form, he concluded, it was apparent that it could never have been legally extended over the Colonies. Burke's claims, he pointedly noted, "are not only new and different from every other writer, but new and different from himself too." Burke's friends and foes alike conceded the force of the Earl's criticism.[5] Abingdon was of course arguing that the Declaratory Act, which had been passed in 1766 by the Rockingham administration, was indefensible. In so doing he was taking a position which most opposition Members of Parliament, save Burke, were now prepared to accept. To the Americans the matter was more clear cut: the political theory embodied in the Declaratory Act had been the stumbling block to peace from the beginning, and the public assertion of this fact by "a noble Lord" provided welcome support for their position.

Few other issues discussed in the pamphlet require separate comment. There could be no doubt, to judge from Abingdon's analysis, that England and not America had been the aggressor in the dispute between the two countries. Because the Americans' claims had often been misunderstood in Britain, they had been wronged on many other counts. They had always acknowledged allegiance to the King of England, but "they were never the subjects of their fellow subjects the Parliament of England, and therefore neither owed nor professed allegiance to Parliament." To surrender the power of taxation to a Parliament in which they were not represented would have been "a surrender of their property . . . and a forging of chains for themselves." In 1777 Americans had no need to be reminded of the point.

It was not to Americans, however, but to Englishmen themselves that Abingdon directed his final admonition. In the light of the many ominous changes that he had witnessed in recent years it was time for all citizens to be vigilant, for "if the liberties of our fellow-subjects in America are to be taken from them, it is for the ideot [*sic*] only to suppose that we can preserve our own. The dagger uplifted against the breast of America, is meant for the heart of Old England."

[195]

NOTES

[1] For evidence of the use that was made of Abingdon's works, see *Letters of Members of the Continental Congress*, edited by Edmund C. Burnett (Washington, 1926), vol. 3, p. 94, 150, 283n, 286n.

[2] For the response of the English Whigs to the American issue after 1774, see George H. Guttridge's *English Whiggism and the American Revolution* (Berkeley, 1942, 1966), p. 72-102. Abingdon's relations with the Rockingham Whigs and Burke can be traced through portions of Burke's published correspondence: Thomas W. Copeland, ed., *The Correspondence of Edmund Burke* (Cambridge, Chicago, 1961), vol. 3, p. 34, 37, 234-235, 368-370, 378-379, 394, 398. Burke's concern over Abingdon's attack is registered in his letters to Abingdon, vol. 3, p. 368-370, and to Rockingham, vol. 3, p. 378-379. General information on Abingdon's life can be found in the *Dictionary of National Biography*.

[3] Thomas Wharton to Robert Morris, February 4, 1778, Robert Morris Papers, Manuscript Division, Library of Congress. The remarkable attention Abingdon received in America during this period can be traced in Dunlap's *General Advertiser* from February 18 to June 10, 1778. See especially the issues for February 18 and 25, March 4 and 9, May 13 and 20, and June 3 and 10.

[4] Edmund Burke, *Letter to the Sheriffs of Bristol* (London, 1777), p. 46-47.

[5] Horace Walpole wrote of Abingdon: "His pamphlet was bold, spirited, and severe, and much above what was expected from him, the arguments being shrewd and clear, and destructive of Burke's sophistry, which was always tinged with monarchic and high ecclesiastic principles. . . . Lord Abingdon was destitute of art and did not aim at eloquence, but his plain dealing and severe truths were far more detrimental to the Court than the laboured subterfuges and inconsistent Jesuitism of Burke." A. Francis Steuart, ed., *The Last Journals of Horace Walpole During the Reign of George III From 1771-1783* (London, 1910), vol. 2, p. 43. The Duke of Richmond, in a letter to the Marquis of Rockingham, called Abingdon's arguments "as unanswerable as his personal attack on Burke is unpardonable," lamenting the rift the Earl's attack had caused in the opposition ranks. But in simultaneously urging Rockingham to propose repeal of the Declaratory Act, which was passed while the Rockingham Whigs had been in power in 1766, he conceded the very point that Abingdon argued so passionately. Richard W. Van Alstyne, "Europe, the Rockingham Whigs, and the War for American Independence: Some Documents," *The Huntington Library Quarterly*, 25:20–21 (November 1961).

THOUGHTS

ON THE

LETTER,

OF

EDMUND BURKE, Esq;

TO THE

SHERIFFS OF BRISTOL,

ON THE

AFFAIRS OF AMERICA.

Willoughby Bertie, 4th
BY THE EARL OF ABINGDON.

OXFORD, PRINTED;
LANCASTER, RE-PRINTED,
And Sold by JOHN DUNLAP,
In QUEEN-STREET.

M,DCC,LXXVIII.

THOUGHTS

ON THE

LETTER of EDMUND BURKE, Esq;

HAVING seen Mr. Burke's late publication on the Affairs of America, I was led to read it with all the attention which every performance of his must necessarily deserve. I sympathise most cordially with him in those feelings of humanity, which mark, in language so expressive, the abhorrence of his nature to the effusion of human blood. I agree with him in idea, that the war with America is "fruitless, hopeless, and unnatural;" and I will add, on the part of Great-Britain, cruel and unjust. I join hand in hand with him in all his propositions for peace; and I look with longing eyes for the event. I participate with him in the happiness of those friendships and connexions, which are the subjects, so deservedly, of his panegyric. The name of Rockingham is a sacred deposit in my bosom. I have found him disinterested, I know him to be honest. Before I quit him therefore, I will first abandon human nature.

So far then are Mr. Burke and I agreed. I am sorry that we should disagree in any thing. But finding that we have differed, on a late occasion in our parliamentary conduct; and that I cannot concur with him in opinion on a matter, as I think, of very great national importance: it is therefore not in the zeal of party, but in the spirit of patriotism, not to confute, but to be convinced, not to point out error, but to arrive at truth, that I now venture to submit my thoughts to the Public. I feel the weight of the undertaking, and I wish it in abler hands. I am not insensible to my own incapacity, and I know how much I stand in need of excuse: but as public good is my object, public candour, I trust, will be my best apologist.

Mr. Burke commences his letter with the mention of "the two last Acts which have been passed with regard to the troubles in America." The first is, "for the Letter of Marque," the second, "for a partial suspension of the *Habeas Corpus*." Of the former, he says little, as

[199]

not worthy of much notice. Of the latter, his distinctions are nice, his strictures many, his objections unanswerable; and yet, although so well apprised of the dangers and mischiefs of this Act, he says, "I have not debated against this Bill in its progress through the House, because it would have been vain to oppose, and impossible to correct it." But this is matter of inquiry. As I thought differently, I acted differently. Being in the country, this Bill was in its way through the House of Lords before I knew any thing of it. Upon my coming accidentally to town, and hearing of its malignity, I went down to the House, I opposed it, and entered my solemn protest on the Journals against it. It is true, I stood single and alone in this business; but I do not therefore take shame to myself. Rectitude of intention will even sanctify error. But Mr. Burke says, "During its progress through the House of Commons, it has been *amended*, so as to express more distinctly than at first it did, the avowed sentiments of those who framed it." Now if the Bill was *amended* in its progress through the House of Commons, Mr. Burke's reason "for not debating against the Bill" cannot be well founded; for his reason is, "that it would have been vain to oppose, and *impossible to correct* it:" but to *amend* a thing is to *correct* it; and therefore if the Bill was *amended*, it was *not impossible to correct it*.

The case was this. This Bill was brought into the House of Commons under the black coverture of designing malice. Some of the honourable Members of that House, seeing it in this dark disguise, endeavoured to unrobe it of its darkness. Their endeavours succeeded, and "it was *amended*, so as to express more distinctly than it at first did, the avowed sentiments of those who framed it." In this shape it came to the House of Lords: bad enough in all conscience: but I use Mr. Burke's own words when I say, "there is a difference between bad and the worst of all." I thought it bad, and therefore I put my negative upon it: had it been worse, *a fortiori*, I should have done the same. But here it would seem as if Mr. Burke and I were not agreed in our notions of *bad* and *worse*: for what he holds *bad*, I esteem *worse*, and what he calls *worse*, I think *bad*. To explain myself. He considers a *partial* Suspension of the *Habeas Corpus* a greater evil than an *universal* suspension of it. I conceive the contrary: though if Mr. Burke's premises were right, I should approve his reasoning, and admit his consequences. He says, "whenever an Act is made for a cessation of law and justice, the whole people should be universally subjected to the same suspension of their franchises." Be it so: but

[200]

then the whole people should fall under the reason and occasion of the Act. If England was under the same predicament with America, that is to say, if Englishmen were looked upon to be Rebels, as the Americans are, in such a case, a *partial* suspension of the *Habeas Corpus* would be invidious, and consequently more unjust than a *general* suspension of it; for why should one Rebel be distinguished from another? but Englishmen are not accounted rebels, and the Americans are; and therefore in the same degree that a *partial* suspension, on the one hand, *might* be just, an *universal* suspension, on the other, *would* be unjust. Where the offence is local, the punishment too must be local. It would have been unjust if the lands in America had been forfeited to the Crown in the year 1745 because Scotland was then in rebellion. I do not use these arguments in favour of the Bill. The principle was *bad* with respect to America: it was *worse* with regard to this country. And herein consisted the very malignity of the Bill: for whilst the *Habeas Corpus* was taken away from the *imputed guilty* Americans, the *innocent* English were at the same time deprived of its benefit; suspicion, without oath, being made the two-edged sword that was to cut both ways.

But, says Mr. Burke, "The alarm of such a proceeding," (that is of an universal suspension of the people's franchises) "would then be universal. It would operate as a sort of *call of the nation.*" As to my part I have heard so many *calls of the nation* of late, without any *answer* being made to them; that I fear the *nation* has either lost its *hearing* or its *voice:* but supposing otherwise, of what avail can a *call of the nation* be against the supremacy of an act of parliament? And who shall dare to resist the authority of a statute that can alter the established religion of the land, nay even bind *in all cases what-soever?* But more of this by and by.

Mr. Burke goes on to say, "As things *now* stand, every man in the West-Indies, every one inhabitant of three unoffending Provinces on the Continent, every person coming from the East-Indies, every gentleman who has travelled for his health or education, every mariner who has navigated the seas, is, for no other offence, under a temporary proscription." But how did things stand *before the amendment* of the bill? Not only every man as described above, but *every individual* in this kingdom was under the same temporary proscription. The writing of a letter to, or receiving a letter from, America, in this country, though the contents were ever so harmless, was ground of suspicion sufficient to immure a man in the castle of Dumfries, or

Pendennis, or wheresoever else persecution should think fit to send him*. We have been saved from this hell-governed proscription. Opposition removed it from us. It had been well to have done so from every subject of the realm: but it did what it could, and the liberty of many unoffending persons has been preserved thereby.

This being the state of the bill, *amended*, as Mr. Burke himself confesses, one might have thought that, though *bad*, it was *better* than it had been; but the very reverse of this is the opinion of Mr. Burke: For in one place, he says, "the limiting qualification, instead of taking out the sting, does, in my humble opinion sharpen and envenom it to a greater degree." And, in another, he adds, "that far from softening the features of such a principle, and thereby removing any part of the popular odium or natural terrors attending it, I should be sorry that any thing framed in contradiction to the spirit of our constitution did not instantly produce, in fact, the grossest of the evils, with which it was pregnant in its nature." So that *amendment*, by softening the features, and removing the popular odium, without producing the grossest of evils with which it was pregnant in its nature, has, if I may use such terms of contrariety, made the bill *worse*. Such is the doctrine of Mr. Burke, and just it may be: but if it be, I can only say that he and I see objects through different mediums; and that if he thinks it right to do evil that good may come of it, I wish to do good, by averting the evil. The physician that stops the progress of a disease, may, at one time or another, hope for its cure; but he that leaves the disease to the efforts of nature alone, trusts to a cause that is very unsure in the effect. Mr. Burke, however, in aid of his opinion, says that "on the next unconstitutional act, all the fashionable world will be ready to say—Your prophecies are ridiculous, your fears are vain, you see how little of the mischiefs which you formerly foreboded are come to pass. Thus by degrees that artful softening of all arbitrary power, the alledged infrequency or narrow extent of its operation, will be received as a sort of aphorism: And Mr. Hume will not be singular in telling us, that the felicity of

---

* *It is said that the number of persons who died in different prisons during the despotic government of the Marquis de Pombal, late minister of Portugal, without having been convicted of any crime, is computed at 3970 persons; and those who were languishing in irons at the time of his disgrace amounted to 800. If this act had passed, as it was first framed, and if we may measure our punishments by those meted out to our brethren in America; what reason is there to suppose that our situation had not been the very counterpart of this?*

[202]

mankind is no more disturbed by it, than by earthquakes, or thunder, or the other more unusual accidents of nature." Now as to the fashionable world, living as they do under the tyranny of that greatest of all tyrants, *fashion*, upon such an occasion, I should hardly look up to them as a fit court of appeal. And as to Mr. Hume, let those remember who adopt his aphorisms—that that great philanthropist and friend of liberty, Doctor Franklin, has not, in the depths of his wisdom thought, "alledged infrequency or narrow extent of opera-tion," any argument to prevent the protection of mankind even "against the more unusual accidents of nature;" and let them in the remembring of this, regret, that his politics, like his philosophy, have not been the subjects of our experiment. Happy, thrice happy, had it been for this country, if, instead of besetting this able man with foulmouthed language, and indecent mockery, (indecent doubly so, because of the venerable council before whom he stood) his advice, like his *conductors*, had been made use of to draw the forked light-ning from that portentous cloud, which, with overspreading ruin, has now burst upon our heads.

Another argument made use of by Mr. Burke for not debating against the Bill, is this. "It is," says he, "some time since I have been clearly convinced, that in the present state of things, all opposition to any measures proposed by ministers, where the name of America appears, is vain and frivolous." I think so too: But then it does not therefore follow that opposition is to be laid aside. The question, how far a member of either house can give over his attendance in parlia-ment because he is out-voted, is a nice question; and worthy the examination of those who have leisure and abilities for the purpose. My own private opinion is, that no member, *individually,* can do this, consistently with his duty. *Collectively* he may: as the precedent of secession, during the administration of Sir Robert Walpole, shews, and as reason proves: For it is not to be presumed that a combination to this end can be obtained, without a sufficient foundation for it; and therefore when it does take place, it is intended, as Mr. Burke elsewhere says, "as a sort of call of the nation." But even here, I must not think it justifiable, unless supported on the following grounds. In the first place, the secession must be general, that is to say, it must not consist of this or that party only in opposition, but must include the whole minority against the measures that have provoked secession. In the next place it must be a secession not *sub silentio*, but proclaimed either by Remonstrance on the Journals, or public address to the people; and when both these circumstances attend the act, then secession is not only justifiable, but is the most faithful pledge of duty that can be given. I have therefore exceedingly to lament that a secession, such as this is, has not been carried into execution; and not only on account of the proof that would have been given thereby to the nation of the sincerity of opposition; but because I do verily believe from my soul, that if it had, daring as Ministers are and have been, they would not have presumed to have gone the lengths they have done in the open violation of the Constitution; though upheld, as they say they are, by Parliament, by the country-gentlemen, and by their long tribe of obsequious addressers.

But to return more directly to the argument of Mr. Burke, and admitting, that "all opposition where the name of America appears is vain and frivolous," and therefore that Mr. Burke was right in not debating against the bill, the same reason must hold good in every case of opposition where the same circumstances exist: For not to debate in this instance, and to debate in another, "where the name of America appears," must be wrong. Both cannot be right. And therefore Mr. Burke's repeated propositions, so ably made, and so well supported, for peace, might have been dispensed with. Objections to taxes, in aid of this destructive war, were unnecessary. In short all debate was

"Time mispent, and language misapplied:"

for "all opposition is vain and frivolous, where the name of America appears."

Having thus stated the reasons, and examined the motives that occasioned *a difference in conduct* between Mr. Burke and me; I shall now, turning over those many leaves of his letter, of which, were I to take any notice, it must be in admiration and in praise, proceed to that part of it wherein our *difference in opinion* prevails. And here, in page 46, Mr. Burke says, "But I do assure you, (and they who know me publicly and privately will bear witness to me) that if ever one man lived, more zealous than another, for the supremacy of Parliament, and the rights of this imperial Crown, it was myself." Now if I cannot join with Mr. Burke in this solemn declaration of his, I trust, it will not be therefore imputed to me, that I am less zealous than he is for the rights of the British Legislature; nor if I object to the terms of his proposition shall I be condemned as catious; for to cavil does not belong to me, and more especially about words. But when I see, and know, and am persuaded, that these very modes of speech, *supremacy of Parliament, rights of this imperial Crown,* with their kindred others, *unity of Empire, allegiance to the State,* and suchlike high-sounding *sesquipedalia verba,* by becoming, in defiance of their impropriety, the deities of modern invocation, and by operating as incantations to mislead mankind, have done more mischief to the State even than the sword itself of Civil War: be their authority ever so great, I can never subscribe to their use. *Supremacy of Parliament* is a combination of terms unknown to the English polity; and as to *allegiance to the State,* though it be the sanctified phraseology of an Archbishop, it is, like the "Whiggism" he censures, allegiance "run mad."* Supremacy is an appendant of the Crown, and so is allegiance. The former is the right of the King, (as heretofore it was of the Pope) in his *ecclesiastical* capacity, the latter in his *temporal*; and there cannot be two rights, in one State, to the same thing. Who ever heard of the oaths of supremacy and of allegiance to the Parliament? And why are they not taken to the Parliament? Because they are due to the King, and not to the Parliament; and it is not fit that the Parliament should invade "the rights of this imperial Crown." Let each possess its own, and so the constitution will be preserved. That the Parliament is *supreme,* I admit. It is the *supreme court,* or *curia magna* of the Constitution; as the House of Lords is the *supreme* court of Justice, or *dernier resort* of the Law. Both are *supreme,* and yet *supremacy* was never attributed to the House of Lords, but ever, in the language of the constitution, belonged to the King, as the *supreme* Head of the Church. In like manner I admit, that the people are bound in obedience to the laws of Parliament; but this does not therefore infer "allegiance to the State." Allegiance is one thing, obedience another. Allegiance is due to the King, so long as, in his *executive* capacity, he shall protect the rights of the People. Obedience is due to the laws, when founded on the constitution: but when they are *subversive* of the constitution, then disobedience instead of obedience is due; and resistance becomes the law of the land.

---

* *Vide the Archbishop of York's Sermon, p. 22.*[1] *It had been well if this, or any thing else that the Primate said, could have set aside the criminal charges to which his Sermon was exposed: but as it was indefensible, so is it matter of great national concern to find such doctrines propagated by the once Tutor of the Heir-apparent to the Crown; though it prove of some consolation, as the Earl of Shelburne remarked, that his Majesty, perceiving the evil tendency of such principles, had, in his wisdom, removed him from the tuition of the Prince.*

These were my reflections, consequent on Mr. Burke's declaration; but my hope was, that although we differed in *words*, in *things* we might yet be agreed. How great then was my disappointment, when instead of seeing this subject unrobed of its gorgeous apparel, and like truth made to appear naked and unadorned, when instead of discussion, which such a declaration seemed necessarily to call for, when instead of reasoning, and of argument, as if afraid of their consequences, I found assertions without the shadow of proof, and precedents importing no authority, but upholding error, substituted in their room. "Many others, indeed," says Mr. Burke, "might be more knowing in the extent, or in the foundation of these rights. I do not pretend to be an antiquary, or a lawyer, or qualified for the chair of professor in metaphysics. I never ventured to put your solid interests upon speculative grounds. My having constantly declined to do so has been attributed to my incapacity for such disquisitions; and I am inclined to believe it is partly the cause. I never shall be ashamed to confess, that where I am ignorant, I am diffident. I am indeed not very solicitous to clear myself of this imputed incapacity; because men, even less conversant than I am, in this kind of subtlties, and placed in stations to which I ought not to aspire, have, by the mere force of civil discretion, often conducted the affairs of great nations with distinguished felicity and glory." This may be very true, but surely it is not very satisfactory. To be *more* zealous than any one man living "for the supremacy of parliament; and the rights of this imperial crown," and *less* knowing than others "in the extent and foundation of these rights," is to profess more of implicit faith and enthusiasm, than, I confess, I expected to have met with, at least now adays, in *civil* concerns. Of fanatics in the church I knew there were still many to be found, but a state fanatic, I thought, was a *phœnomenon* in politics not of modern appearance. If indeed our parliaments were, as our Scottish race of Kings held themselves to be, God's viceregents, and governed the state *de jure divino;* then such a degree of belief had been only correspondent to the occasion of it: but Parliaments have ever been the works of men's hands, as, thank God, we now know that our kings are; or otherwise we had not had our present most gracious Majesty on this throne, nor yet that additional solemn contract between King and People, I mean *the act of settlement,* for the eternal security, as I trust, of those rights of the subject which are intrusted to the executive power. Again: Why should a man be either antiquarian, lawyer, or metaphysician, or what need is there of speculation, to know "the extent and foundation of these rights?" The rights of Englishmen want no such professional authority for their support: neither are they mere abstract terms, the *entia rationis,* or creatures of the understanding; but are, for our knowledge, written in our hearts, with the blood of our ancestors. But "the affairs of great nations are often conducted with distinguished felicity and glory by the mere force of civil discretion." What! are the rights of Englishmen to be held at the *discretion* of Ministers? Is *civil discretion* the rule of our government? Wherein does *civil discretion* differ from *will,* the law of tyrants? And will any minister of this country say, "I am not conversant in this kind of subtlties, the extent and foundation of these rights," and therefore will govern by this unconditional power, the mere force of *civil discretion?* This can never be: but I have said that I found assertions without the shadow of proof, and precedents importing no authority, but upholding error; and this obliges me to be more circumstantial. The subject is a deep one; and the consideration of it the most interesting of any that ever fell under political contemplation. It is no less than to know whether our *civil* existence has any *real* foundation; or whether, as it is said of the sea, it be without a bottom. Perhaps I may be lost in the depths of research: but if I am, I carry this consolation with me, that I sink in the cause of truth. I have this hope, however, of preservation about me, that I shall not dive into mysteries, nor yet venture among the quicksands [of] metaphysical abstractions. The constitution of my country is the ground on which I wish to stand, and if I gain this shore, my safety present will reward the dangers past.

Mr. Burke having given us his creed in the supremacy of parliament, next applies its *unlimited* power to and over the American Colonies; and then tells us what the supremacy of Parliament is in England. I shall consider the last first, namely the supremacy of Parliament in England, as a major proposition in which the minor is contained. He says (in order to shew "the compleatness of the legislative authority of parliament *over this kingdom*") that "if any thing can be supposed out of the power of human legislature, it is religion: I admit, however, that the established religion of this country has been three or four times altered by Act of Parliament; and therefore that a statute binds even in that case." This is conclusive as to Mr. Burke's idea both with respect to the *unlimited right* as well as the *unlimited power* of Parliament: but whilst he is sharp even to a point for the *general unlimited right* of Parliament, he adduces some cases to blunt the edge of its power *over this kingdom*. He says, "But we may safely affirm, that notwithstanding this apparent omnipotence, it would be *now* found as impossible for King and Parliament to change the established religion of this country, as it was to King James alone, when he attempted to make such an alteration without a Parliament." Further: "I see no abstract reason, which can be given, why the same power that made and repealed the high-commission court and the star chamber might not revive them again: but the madness would be as unquestionable as the competence* of that Parliament which should make such attempts." Furthermore: "The king's negative to bills is one of the most indisputed of the royal prerogatives, and it extends to all cases whatsoever; but the exercise is wisely forborne." Moreover: "We know that the convocation of the clergy had formerly been called, and sat with nearly as much regularity to business as parliament itself. It is now called for form only." These then are what I call precedents without authority, but upholding error: for distinguishing, as must be done, between *right* and *power*, Parliament cannot exercise a *power* without a *right* to that *power*; or if it does, it is an *usurpation of power*, which sooner or later never fails of redress. Precedents therefore of Acts of Parliament, repugnant to the fundamental principles of the constitution, are no proofs of the supremacy or omnipotency of Parliament, but instances only of the abuse of Parliament; "and as no government," says Machiavel, "can be of long duration, which, by the original formation of its constitution, is not frequently renewed or drawn back to its first principles," so whenever this happens to us as it often has done, and, I trust, is again not afar off from us, these precedents, like so many clouds dispersed, only serve to shew, that although they may darken the face of the constitution, they can never extinguish its light.

But a word or two more particularly of these precedents. Much stress has been laid on the alterations that have been made in the established religion, in order to shew the right of Parliament to omnipotency: it is the doctrine of Sir William Blackstone†: but as the most able chymist cannot extract *that* from any given thing, *which* does not exist in its nature, so is this precedent, for this reason, by no means a case in point. In the first place, religion has nothing to do

---

* *It is presumed that* incompetence *is here meant, and that* competence *is an error of the press.*

† *Vide his Commentaries, vol. i. p. 161.*

with the *civil* rights of the State. It is set apart from them, and belongs to the Church‡. The *civil* rights of the State are of a *temporal* nature: they are *positive*, they are *general*, affecting every member of the community equal and alike. Religion is of a *spiritual* nature: it is a *negative* duty, and not a *positive* right: it is *not general*, but varies according to mens consciences: it is the subject of *toleration*, for no laws can have power over mens minds. What Act of Parliament can make me believe that *three* is *one*, or *one* is *three,* if I do not chuse to believe it? Or that my salvation in the next world is to be obtained by the belief of 39 articles in this? The *established* religion, therefore, is no more than that *dress* which the *State taylors* have provided for Religion to go to *court* in; and the same *taylors* that made this *dress,* can *alter* it, as we have seen, and as the fashion of the times changes.

But if this was not the case with the established religion, how, in the next place, does its alteration shew the right of Parliament to omnipotency? What effect has it had on the constitution? Are we *less* free now, either in Church or State, than we were before the Reformation? I should imagine that we are *more* free in both, and if so, freedom being the first principle of the constitution, the *power* of Parliament to alter the *established* religion has been but correspondent to its *right;* and therefore, whilst it is no proof of the supremacy of Parliament, I should not be sorry to see a little more alteration of it. I think it may still be *amended,* without offence to the people, or injury to the constitution; nay even with satisfaction to some of the clergy themselves. The second precedent is that of the High Commission Court, and the Star Chamber; which is in direct proof of my argument: for they, being usurpations of *power,* and abuses of the *right* of Parliament, have been dissolved; and therefore I agree with Mr. Burke that it would be madness to revive them, and for the reason he gives too, to wit, "the incompetence of Parliament:" though if the power of Parliament be *unlimited,* is not the *incompetency* of Parliament a position somewhat paradoxical? The third precedent is,

---

‡ *I am aware how much I here differ from the very able Prelate, who is for harnessing Church and State together, like coach and horses, that He as one of the drivers may enjoy the smack of the whip; a smack which he cannot forget, and which he gave me reason to remember when I was at Westminster school: but as I am now out of his clutches so I hope I am out of his books too, at least such as are akin to his political sermons. Vide Archibishop of York's sermon, p. 10.*

"the King's negative to bills, which is wisely forborne." This is the forbearance of a *known right* to a *power* vested by the constitution in the Crown, and not the exercise of a power *unknown* to the constitution. As it therefore shews, that, even where there is a manifest *power*, that *power* is limited, so it proves, of course, that where there is no manifest *power*, there can be no *right* to *unlimited power*. The last precedent is that concerning the Convocation of the Clergy; and to this, what I have said on the head of the *established* religion, inasmuch as *ecclesiastical* matters have nothing to do with *civil* concerns, may here be applied. But I do not recollect that, in bringing the Convocation of the Clergy to its present *formal* state only, there was any exertion of power of any kind to this end. If I remember aright it was a bargain. It was agreed that, on their Convocations becoming merely passive, the beneficed Clergy should pay no further subsidies to the government, as they used to do in Convocation; and that they should be *represented* in Parliament, by being allowed to vote at the elections for Knights of the Shire: for before this they were not *represented* in Parliament, but in their own Convocations; and therefore Parliament had no *right* to tax them, nor were they taxed by Parliament, notwithstanding its *unlimited power*, and "the compleatness of its legislative authority over this kingdom."

If this then be the result of these precedents, and the state of what has been offered by Mr. Burke *for* this *arbitrary right* in Parliament, extending even to religion itself, and whose *power* is limited *only* by "the mere force of civil discretion;" is there nothing further that may be said *against* this *right?* I shall consider. There is nothing so much talked of, and yet nothing so little understood, as the *English Constitution*. Every man quotes it, and upon every occasion too: But few know where to find it. If one enquire after it, an Act of Parliament is produced. If you ask what it is, you are told it is the *Law*. Strange mistake! The *Constitution* and the *Law* are not the same. They differ, and in what manner I will endeavour to point out. In the great *machine* of State there are found three *principal powers*, with a variety of others subordinate to them; particularly the prerogative of the Crown; which is a *power* there vested not to counteract the *higher powers*, but, if at any time there should be occasion, to supply their deficiencies. The first of these *principal powers*, is the *power* of the *people*; the second, the *power* of the *Constitution*; the third, the *power* of the *Law*. Now the *power* of the *people* is first, because, without people, there could be neither *Constitution* nor *Law*. The *power* of the *Constitution* is second, for it is the immediate effect of this first cause; and if the *people* and the *Constitution* make the first and the second *power*, there is no need to prove that the *Law* is the third *power* of the State. It follows in the order I have laid down. As from the *People* then is derived the *Constitution*, so from the *Constitution* is derived the *Law*; the *Constitution* and the *Law* being, in a due course of lineal consanguinity, the descendants of the *people*.

But now I shall be asked, what is this *Constitution*, and what is this *Law?* I answer, that by pointing out their relations, their differences too are marked. But this is not enough: Definition is necessary, and therefore, as a definition *of the name* I would say, that *Constitution* signified *Compact*, and was the same with *public or political Law;* and that *Law*, as here meant, was the *municipal or civil Law* of the State: But as a definition *of the thing*, perhaps *both* may best appear as derived one from the other. I define *Constitution* then to be, those *agreements* entered into, those *rights* determined upon, and those *forms* prescribed, by and between the members of any society in the first settlement of their union, and in the frame and mode of their government; and is the *genus* whereof the *municipal or civil Law* of such established Community is the *species*: The *former*, ascertaining the reciprocal duties, or several relations subsisting betwixt the *governors and governed*; the *latter*, maintaining the rights and adjusting the differences arising betwixt individuals, as parts of the same whole. And this I take to be the true distinction and real difference between the *Constitution* and the *Law* of England. But this is matter of *theory* only. It is the *passive* state of government, and government must be *active*. *Practice* therefore is to be superadded to this *theory*; and hence the origin of *Parliaments*. What then are *Parliaments?* *Parliaments* make the *formal*, as *rights* do the *substantial*, part of the Constitution; and are the deputies, the agents, or appointees of the people, entrusted by them with the Powers of *legislation*, for the purpose of preserving (and not of destroying) the established rights of the Constitution. But what are the established rights of the Constitution? In detail, they are multifarious and many: But reduced to their first principles, they are these, *"Security of life, liberty, property, and freedom in trade."* Such are the great outlines of the *English Constitution*, the short history, or abstract of that *original compact*, which is the bond or cement of our civil union, and which forms, in particular, the relations that exist betwixt the *legislative power* of the State, and the *people*. But there is still another relation to be considered. The *legislaive power* of the State must receive its force from an *executive power*. This *executive power* is lodged in the *Crown*, from whence a relation arises betwixt the *Crown* and *People*, and is called "the Contract between King and People." As *compact* then is that *agreement* of the people with the *legislative power*, or among themselves, concerning their *same* rights; so *contract* is that *bargain* of the people with the *executive power* concerning their *different* rights*. But here it will be said, How is this known, and where is this to be found? I reply, As well in the reason of the things themselves, and our own experience, as in the letter and spirit of our Charters: For instance, in *Magna Charta*, which is not only declaratory of the *original compact*, or fundamental rights of the people, but is *itself* that *solemn contract* which was had between King and people, for the protection of those rights; and therefore, as such, proves *quod erat demonstrandum*.

But now I may be told, that although I have made a distinction between the *Constitution* and the *Law* of England, I have cited *Magna Charta*, which is an Act of Parliament, and consequently the

---

* *Writers upon this subject have confounded the two terms, Compact and Contract together; making them to signify one and the same thing, though really different. Compact is an agreement entered into without any other consideration, than that of the plighted faith of the parties to the articles agreed upon: for the articles being general, it is equally the interest of every individual to observe them without any additional obligation; and such is the original Compact, or Constitution of this country. But Contract is a Bargain, with a condition annexed thereto, that demands a quid pro quo; and such is the "Contract between King and People:" for the executive Power being lodged in the Crown, the King may suffer the Laws to sleep, or pervert them "from their right use to their worst abuse," which, making the articles of this Contract not general, calls for different covenants; and therefore the King, at his coronation, takes an oath to protect the Rights of the People; and the People, in return, owe, and may be called upon to swear, Allegiance to the King. It may be further observed, that as it was not to be supposed that Parliaments, whose rights were precisely the same with those of the People, could possibly enact Laws subversive of those Rights, so the original Compact seeming to require no other sanction, no other agreement between the Legislative Power and the People was ever thought of: but now corruption, that self devouring monster of the State, making fresh covenants necessary, it is to be hoped, that the same explicit, unevasive, express Contract, which exists between the King and People, will soon, very soon, be made to subsist between the Parliament and People. It was the doctrine of unlimited power in the Crown that obtained the former; it is the now new and more dangerous doctrine of unlimited power in Parliament that must procure the latter.*

Law of England, as for the *Constitution* of England. The objection is specious only, for it is groundless. In the first place, it is not true that *Magna Charta* is an Act of Parliament; and for this reason; that it was obtained in the field of battle, with sword in hand, in Runing-Mead, between Windsor and Staines, where the *People* had pitched their tents, and where, as history further informs us "King John and his adherents appeared to be an inconsiderable number, but the Lords and Commons filled the country."

It is therefore true, that *Magna Charta* was the Act of the People *at large*, and not of the Legislature *alone*. Besides: It is proved by Acts of Parliament, that it is not an Act of Parliament; and that Parliament (*unlimited* as its power is now said to be) has no power over it [at] all; for it is declared by the statute of the 25th of Edward I. that *Magna Charta* was obtained by the *common assent of all the realm*, and that it was to be received as the *Folcright*, or common Law of the land. And by the 43d of Edward III. all statutes made against *Magna Charta* are declared to be void: So that whilst *Magna Charta* proves the *Constitution* to be anterior to the Law, Acts of Parliament shew that it is not subject to the Law, nor under the power of Parliament. But, in the next place, admitting *Magna Charta* to be an Act of Parliament, still the objection remains without foundation. For *Magna Charta*, being not *enactive* of new rights, but, as I have said before, *declaratory* only of those old rights of the people, some of which are of Saxon ancestry, others coeval with the first form of British government, is a Law only in proof of the Constitution; and therefore supports my position, that the *Constitution* and the *Law* are not the same.

But there is still another objection, which I must anticipate in order to remove. It may be objected, that if (as I have shewn) *the People be made the source of all power in the State*, in what manner is such an idea to be reconciled with the doctrine, that "Government certainly is an institution of divine Authority?"* for these (upon another occasion) are the words of Mr. Burke; though, he adds, that its *Forms* and the *Persons* who administer it, all originate from the People. What a pity that an "Institution of divine Authority" should ever be found in the hands of *Devils*, as our Government sometimes unhappily is! But I do not mean to enter into the merits of this doctrine. Indeed I am bound not to do so: for I have said, that I will

---

* *Vid. Thoughts on the cause of the present discontents, fifth edit. p. 67.*

not dive into mysteries, lest I be drowned; and I will keep my word. But as this said mode of attributing to *natural* effects *supernatural* causes, or mixing Church and State together, has already done a great deal of mischief to the community; as I perceive that the *divine Right* of Parliaments, like the *divine Right* of Kings, to do what is *wrong*, with its concomitant train, *passive-obedience* and *nonresistance*, is now from the

"Pulpit, drum ecclesiastic,
That's beat with fist, instead of a stick,"

sounding forth in the ears of the* people; as I am content to judge of things *past* by the *present*, leaving to others all better rules of judging; and inasmuch as example goes before precept; so the present state of America affording not only much notable information on this head, but serving to illustrate the whole of what has been here said on the subject of government, I shall, with some advantage I trust, and in as few words as I can, make use of the instance.

America, having declared itself independent of Great-Britain, returned to that state of nature, or state of society, where government was to be instituted; and being so circumstanced, whilst it proceeded to form itself into separate commonwealths, or states, each common-

---

* *See a Sermon preached before the University of Oxford, on Friday, December 13, 1776, being the day appointed by proclamation for a general Fast. By Myles Cooper, LL.D. President of King's College, New-York, and Fellow of Queen's College, Oxford. Published at the request of the Vice-Chancellor and Heads of Houses, and printed at the Clarendon press.[2] This Doctor says, p. 12. "It is difficult indeed to assign any reasons that will justify the rebellion of subjects against the sovereign authority." "Submission to the higher powers is enjoined at least upon Christians, under the severest penalty. But were Christianity altogether out of the question, yet the insurrection of subjects against their rightful governors, is condemned by those laws which are fundamental to society." He says too, p. 22. "When men's principles are wrong, their practices will seldom be right. When they suppose those powers to be derived solely from the people, which are ordained of God, and their heads are filled with ideas of original compacts which never existed, and which are always explained so as to answer their present occasions; no wonder that they confound the duties of rulers and subjects, and are perpetually prompted to dictate where it is their business to obey. When once they conceive the governed to be superior to the governors, and that they may set up their pretended natural Rights in opposition to the positive laws of the State; they will naturally proceed to 'despise dominion and speak evil of dignities,' and to open a door for anarchy, confusion, and every evil work, to enter." What more did Sacheverel say? And yet Sacheverel was impeached, whilst Doctor Cooper may expect preferment.*

wealth or state provided a Constitution or Form of Government of its own; which, although differing in mode and manner, agreed in substance and effect. The precedent therefore of one Constitution answering for every other, I shall here avail myself of such extracts from the Constitution of *the state of Massachusetts,* as are necessary to my purpose. This Constitution then, or form of civil government, consists of forty-three articles, and is entitled, "An Act of the *General Convention* of the Commonwealth, or State of Massachusetts, declaring the same to be a free state, and independent of Great-Britain, and establishing a new Constitution and form of civil government; which *General* Convention was elected by *the whole People* for this *sole purpose, &c.*" It next recites those (but too much to be lamented) arbitrary and despotic measures of this country, which occasioned the Declaration of Independency; and after this proceeds to say, "The ancient government of this Colony being thus *totally dissolved,* and the People driven into *a state of nature,* it becomes their indispensible duty, and what self-preservation requires, to declare themselves independent of Great-Britain, and to establish such a Constitution and form of civil government, as to them appears best calculated to promote their greatest possible happiness:" "And Whereas it is absolutely necessary for the welfare and safety of the inhabitants of this commonwealth, that a just and permanent Constitution and form of civil government should be established as soon as possible, *derived from and founded on the authority of the people only, in whom is the origin of all governmental power,* and who have at all times a right, *by common consent,* (whenever the great end of government, the general good, is not obtained) to alter and change their Constitution and form of government, in such manner as may best promote the safety and happiness of the whole."

"We, therefore, the Representatives of the freemen of Massachusetts, in *General Convention* met, for the *express purpose* of framing such a Constitution and form of government, gratefully acknowledging the goodness of the Supreme Governor of all, in permitting us peaceably, and *by common consent,* deliberately to form such rules as we shall judge best adapted for governing this commonwealth in justice and righteousness; and being fully convinced that it is our indispensible duty to establish, to the utmost of our power, such *original principles* of civil government, as will best promote the general happiness of the People, do, by virtue of the authority vested in us by our constituents, declare, enact and establish the following

[215]

Constitution and form of civil government, for this commonwealth, to be and remain in full force therein, from and after the second Wednesday in ————, and *forever thereafter to remain unaltered*, except in such articles as shall hereafter, on new circumstances arising, or on experience, be found to require alteration; and which shall, *by the like authority of the People, convened for that sole purpose,* be altered, for the more effectual obtaining and securing the great end and design of all good government, *the good of the People.*"

"Be it therefore declared and enacted by the *General Convention* of this commonwealth, assembled *for the sole purpose* of declaring and enacting Independency, and establishing a new Constitution and form of civil government, and by the authority of the same, it is hereby declared and enacted, as in the following general articles, viz.

1. "That this colony is, and of right ought to be, and forever hereafter shall, by the favour of all-gracious Heaven, be a free state, and absolutely independent of the Crown and Government of Great-Britain; and shall be styled, THE COMMONWEALTH OR STATE OF MASSACHUSETTS."

5. "That this declaration of the general, fundamental, and essential rights of the people of this commonwealth, shall, *forever hereafter,* be considered as the general fundamental of the said new Constitution and form of government; *and every order, law, and statute, that shall hereafter be made by the General Court of this commonwealth, shall conform to the spirit, and plain simple meaning and intention of these general fundamentals; and all and every order, law, and statute, that may hereafter happen to be made, and shall be found contrary thereto, shall be null and void, and have no effect, and be immediately repealed: And no alteration in these general fundamentals shall hereafter be made, but only by the immediate consent of the good People of this commonwealth at large, or their Deputies, chosen for that special purpose.*"

6. "That all men are born equally free and independent, and *their Maker has left them free liberty to set up such governments as best please themselves.*" "That Magistrates were set up for the good of nations, not nations for the honor and glory of Magistrates." "That the right and power of Magistrates in every country, was that which the laws of that country made it to be." And "That usurpation gives no right to govern."

7. "That all men have a natural and unalienable right to worship God according to the dictates of their own consciences, and to enjoy a full and free liberty therein; provided that they, under pretence of religion, do not attempt to subvert the Constitution and Form of Government of this State, &c."

Here then is that in *esse*, what Dr. Cooper tells us "never existed," *an original Compact*. A Compact too, with *powers* (which, according to him, "are ordained of God") *solely* derived from the People; and, the *governed* being superior to the *governors*, with natural rights, "pretended," as he says they are, "set up in opposition to the positive law of the state." Such is this Compact, and such, I presume, being all other *original* Compacts in their first institution, it is no wonder that their existence should be denied; inasmuch as they are the sovereign antidotes of those political poisons, *Priest-Craft*, and *State-Craft*, whose objects are dominion over "the Beasts of the People."*

Here too is an "institution of government," but where "the divine authority" of it is, who can discover? Indeed, in a century more, for we are already giving up *things* for *words, sense* for *sound*, and from the *golden* falling back into the *iron* age again, such notions of government may be well received. Tradition will inform posterity that the governments of America were instituted *de jure divino*, and not without some reason on their side; inasmuch as the more *natural* any government is, in my opinion the more *divine* it is: But now that we are witnesses to their *institution* we know, we see, and we find that they are instituted *de jure humano*.

The next observation to be made, is the affinity of these governments to that of our own country. They are founded on original Compact, and so is ours. The lines of distinction betwixt the People, the Constitution, and the Law, are marked there as they are drawn here. The Constitution is derived from the People, and the Law

---

* *Such is Doctor Cooper's humane appellation of those persons in America, who plundered, as he says, the members of the Church of England, Him, I suppose, among the rest, and others, of their property; adding, "without any means of present redress, though it is to be hoped, not without a prospect of future retribution." Methinks the Doctor, having received a slap on one cheek, in the true spirit of a Christian, should have turned the other, and not have looked forward to a prospect of plundering the Americans of their property, because they had plundered him of his. However, when the Americans shall come to this country to deprive us of our Liberties, I will readily join the Doctor in his idea of retribution.*

from the Constitution. The Law cannot alter the Constitution; for all and every law and statute that are, by the *General Courts*, (equal to our Parliaments) made contrary thereto, are null and void: neither is the Constitution *alterable*, but by General Conventions of the People *at large*, held *expressly* and *solely* for that purpose.

If now then I should profess to believe that there is no more of *divine authority* in the government of England, than in the governments of America, a sample of which has been produced; and that the former is derived from the same powers, by the same means, and to the same end, namely, the *good of the whole*, as the latter: I hope I shall not be therefore accounted an *Infidel* by the *Church*, nor an *unworthy member of society* by the *State*. I must hope too, that if our *Parliaments*, who are the *trustees* of the People, and the *guardians* of their rights, (for they are no more, and I am one of its members) should ever attempt to destroy those rights, that, as they will well deserve the fate, so may they feel all that vengeance which the offended *Majesty* of an injured People can bring down on their heads. Parliaments who will support the Constitution, will be supported by the People, and have nothing to fear; but those who will subvert the Constitution, let them tremble, as one man, even as Charles the First did, who lost his head in such an attempt; and which, as Lord Chesterfield tells us, "if he had not lost, we had certainly lost our Liberties."

Having thus gone over the constitutional ground of this country, and taken a comparative view of the foundation upon which its Government is superstructed, the inference to be drawn from thence is this; that if the Government be as I have stated it to be, and as I shall hold it to be, till the contrary be proved, the *right to unlimited power* contended for in Parliament, cannot, in common apprehension, there exist. For although Mr. Burke asserts (and I mention this, because I wish to state, and not to mistate his meaning, and if I do, I trust he will impute it to the want of comprehension, and not to any inattention in me) "that Legislators ought to do what Lawyers cannot; for they have *no other* rules to bind them but the great principles of reason and equity, and the general sense of mankind," and although in arbitrary countries this is true, for there the People being *divested* of all power, and both the legislative and executive authority *vested solely* in the Prince, he may have no other rules than these to bind *him*; yet in free countries the case is different. In England, "the legislative," says Lord Bolingbroke, "is a *supreme*, and may be called, in one sense, an *absolute,* but in none an *arbitrary* power." "It is *limited,*" says Mr. Locke, "to the public good of the Society." I say, it is bound by the rules of the Constitution, for the rules of the Constitution are to the Parliament what the Law is to the Judges. The People make the Constitution, the Parliaments make the Law; and as the Judges are bound to determine according to the Law of the land, so are Parliaments bound to enact Laws according to the rules of the Constitution; and not according to *their own* principles of reason and equity, and *what they call* the general sense of mankind: For these *may* differ with the principles of the Constitution, as we know they *have* done; and therefore arises the necessity of asserting the controul of the Constitution over the Law and the Parliament.

But of the power of the Constitution over the legislative authority, Mr. Burke has himself given the most pointed case. He says, "Before this Act (that is before the Act for the partial suspension of the Habeas Corpus) every man putting his foot on English ground, every stranger owing only a local and temporary allegiance, even a Negro slave, who had been sold in the Colonies, *and under an Act of Parliament,* became as free as every other man who breathed the same air with him." What is it then that, setting this Act of Parliament at defiance, manumits the Negro slave so soon as he puts his foot on English ground? Let it not be said that it is *the pure air* of this foggy island, that can work these wonderful wonders, for these are the half-witted sayings of lawyers, that would be orators, and fit only for the *lullabies* of nurses, of the *sing-songs* of children. Let it not be said that the Act is local, for it is not local. The Act alluded to is the 5th of G. II. ch. 27. (but there are many other Acts to the same effect) and it vests a clear and unconditional property, confined no where, but absolute every where, in the owner to his purchased slave; and yet when the owner shall bring his slave to this country, he shall lose his ownership in him; though he hold him under an Act of Parliament. No: It is neither the one, nor the other, that gives occasion to this manumission. It is the Constitution of England, which maintaining *liberty* and annihilating *slavery,* renders this Act of Parliament a *tabula rasa,* a blank parchment, without operation, without force, without effect. *It is that Constitution, which is now resisting the rebellion of Acts of Parliament against it.* In short, my idea of this government, to speak as a lawyer would do, is, that *Parliaments,* as I have said before, are the trustees of the People, the *Constitution* the deed of trust, wherein they stand seized to *uses* only;

and these *uses* being named, they cannot depart from them: But for their due performance are accountable to those by whose conveyance the trust was made. The *right* is therefore *fiduciary*, the *power limited*. Or as a mathematician would say, more in the road of demonstration; the *Constitution* is a *circle*, the *laws* the *radii* of that *circle*, drawn on its surface with the pen of Parliament, and it is the known quality of a circle, that its *radii* cannot exceed its *circumference*, whilst the People, like the *compasses*, are fixed in the center, and describe the *circle*. These, I say, are my ideas of this government, that is, of the whole political system of this country, for this is what I would mean by government, and I hope that they are just and true; or otherwise, dreadful indeed is the prospect before us! For if Parliaments have the right to alter the "established religion of the land," and "if any thing can be supposed out of the power of human legislature, it is religion;" if they are bound by no other rules than "the great principles of reason and equity, and the general sense of mankind," and not by the more determined principles of the Constitution, nor subject to the controul of the People; if, by the influence of corruption, they are become "the Masters, instead of the Servants," of their constituents, looking *down* on the People, and *up* to the Court for honours and preferments, and granting money that they may receive it themselves: I say, if these things be so, and are they not said to be so? where is the difference betwixt a *free* and an *arbitrary* country? where the difference between the despotism of the King of France, and the despotism of the Parliament of England? And what is this but to erect an *Aristocratic* tyranny in the State, a many-headed *Leviathan*, deplorable and to be deplored, dangerous and destructive, in proportion to the numbers of which its consists.

Hitherto I have considered the *supremacy* of Parliament, or its *right to unlimited power*, in and over *this kingdom*; and if I have shewn, that no such Power can exist in Parliament from the very nature of its institution, for it is a solecism in politics, and an absurdity in terms, to say, that in a *limited* government, there can be *unlimited* power, the application of this power over the Colonies must consequently fall to the ground; and with it the occasion of any further reasoning upon the subject. But as Mr. Burke has made some assertions respecting this "unlimited legislative Power over the Colonies," that are not only new and different from every other writer, but new and different from himself too, I hope, I shall be excused the trespass of a page or two more in the further consideration of this matter.

Mr. Burke says, "When I first came into a public trust, I found your Parliament in possession of an *unlimited legislative power* over the Colonies. I could not open the Statute-book without seeing the actual exercise of it, more or less, *in all cases whatsoever.*" These then are what I have called assertions without the shadow of proof, or more properly assertions with the most convincing proofs of their being without foundation; for the proofs are taken from Mr. Burke himself. Here Mr. Burke says, "I could not open the Statute-book without seeing the actual exercise of this *unlimited power* over the Colonies *in all cases whatsoever.*" But attend to what Mr. Burke says in his speech on American Taxation, April the 19th, 1774, p. 40, 3d edit. printed for J. Dodsley, in Pallmall. There he says, "This is *certainly* true; that no Act avowedly for the purpose of revenue, and with the ordinary title and recital taken together, is found in the Statute-book until the year 1764. All before this period stood on *commercial* regulation and restraint;" and to prove this, that is, that a "Parliamentary inland taxation" was not to be found in the *Statute-book* before the year 1764, is the business of this entire page: But as the extract would be too tedious for this place, so whilst I refer the reader to the page itself, I will take the liberty of recommending to his perusal also the whole speech, as a most excellent oration. If then America was not "taxed *internally* for the purpose of revenue before the year 1764, but all before this period stood on *commercial* regulation," here is a case of Mr. Burke's own former shewing, that contradicts the case he now puts, of an "actual exercise of unlimited legislative authority over the Colonies *in all cases whatsoever:*" for if Mr. Burke could not find the exercise of this Power, that is, of internal taxation over the Colonies for the purpose of revenue, in the *Statute-book,* before the year 1764, no such Power having been ever exercised, he could not find the exercise of *unlimited power* over the Colonies *in all cases whatsoever,* before the year 1764; and if he did not *then* find it, he could not find it *after* the year 1764: for the first instance of the exercise of this power after the year 1764, was that of the Stamp-Act; and this Act, as soon as it was passed, was resisted, and being resisted, it was repealed, and being repealed, it could afford no proof of the possession of the power. And yet Mr. Burke adds, "this possession passed with me for a title." But if, as has been said, Parliament was not possessed of the power of internal taxation over the Colonies before the year 1764, no title to unlimited legislative power *in all cases whatsoever,* before this time, could be founded on possession; for here is a manifest exception to this possession in the

[221]

case of an *inland* taxation; and from the year 1764, no title can be derived from possession; for the title has been always disputed, and possession never obtained. So far then Mr. Burke is new and different from himself. In what follows, he is new and different from others.

No one has ever before contended, as I know of, for the right of Parliament to tax America, without the annexed idea of America being represented in Parliament. The idle phantom, the Cock-lane Ghost, of *virtual* representation, has been ever conjured up, as the *ego sum ille*, of this vile deception. But Mr. Burke has asserted, has maintained, and has proved, that America is not represented in Parliament, and yet insists for the unlimited right in Parliament to bind America in all cases whatsoever. He says, "If any thing can be drawn from such examples by a parity of the case, it is to shew, how deep their crime, and how heavy their punishment will be, who shall at any time dare to resist a distant power, actually disposing of their property, *without their voice or consent to the disposition;* and over-turning their Franchises without charge or hearing*."

Here then is his assertion, that America is not represented in Parliament; and his assertion that Parliament has an *unlimited* legislative power over America *in all cases whatsoever*, has been already stated; which is a position as unaccountable to me, as it is new. But let me see if such a position is defensible, and whether a question or two may not serve as an answer thereto. The first question I shall propose is, whether representation in order to taxation be not an *hereditary* indispensible privilege of the British subject? The next question is, whether the Americans are British subjects or not? for if they are not British subjects, Great Britain has nothing to do with them, no more than France or Spain, or any other country has: And again, if they are British subjects, and representation in order to taxation is the *hereditary* indispensible privilege of a British subject, representation in order to taxation must be the *hereditary* indispensible privilege of the Americans, as British subjects. From whence then can the right to Parliament be derived of unlimited legislative power over the subjects of Great-Britain *in all cases whatsoever* without representation in Parliament, which the Americans do not possess, as Mr. Burke has shewn; and which, in order to taxation, is the *hereditary* indispensible privilege of British subjects? I presume it cannot be

---

* *See also Mr. Burke's Conciliatory Propositions* [The Speech of Edmund Burke, Esq; On Moving His Resolutions For Conciliation with the Colonies, March 22, 1775 (*London*, 1775).]

derived from the Constitution; for no man will assert that the Constitution gives a right to Parliament to levy taxes upon British subjects without representation; and if the Constitution does not give this right, the claim of it in Parliament must be *unconstitutional:* which naturally brings me to the consideration of the *declaratory Act,* as falling under this point of view. Mr. Burke has proved that America is not represented; every wise man says the same; and it is only *folly the last* that would assert the contrary. The declaratory Act declares, and Mr. Burke supports the declaration, that this country has a right to bind America *in all cases whatsoever;* and of course to tax America, though not represented. Upon these principles is it possible to maintain this Act? It has no foundation. It rests not upon the Constitution. It is subversive of the Constitution. It has not the fundamental requisites of a declaratory Law. No Law declaratory of rights was ever before made, or ought to have been made, whose recital did not express the sources from whence those rights are derived; whether *direct* from the Constitution, or *indirect* from other Acts of Parliament founded on the Constitution, or from general customs, or particular customs, which make the common law of the land. Look from *Magna Charta,* through every declaratory law, down to the *Act of settlement,* and it will be found that they are, every one of them, *in perpetuum rei testimonium,* or testimonials only of what had *before* existed: But this law is declaratory not only of what never existed *before,* but of a right, against which *common usage,* which is the *common law of the land,* has been in direct opposition. I say in direct opposition, for America, from beyond the memory of man, nay, even from the very first date of its civil existence to the era of this reign, has been uninterruptedly used to the internal taxation of itself.

This law therefore must be repealed. As it was enacted for the dignity of this country, so for justice sake, which is the true dignity of this country, let it now be repealed. It is against right, and usurped power cannot uphold it. It is true the motives that brought it into being were intentionally upright, but with the patronage of the author of those motives, the motives themselves ceased; and of the Act since, the *double Cabinet,* as Mr. Burke calls them, has made an infamous use. They knew not where to look for the right of taxation. They found it in this Act, and have so tyrannized under it, that America has now stamped its foot upon it, and will never stir a step until "this tyranny be overpast." Every island in the West-Indies look upon it with terror. All Ireland see it with a jealous eye: For who is the casuist that can discriminate between a British Parliamentary right to tax America, and a British parliamentary right to tax Ireland? The case is the same. The right has been avowed in Parliament, and add to the 6. Geo. 1. ch. 5. or Irish declaratory Act, the words only, *"in all cases whatsoever,"* and the matter is at issue: but *Inexpediency* prevents the exercise. *Inexpediency!* curse on the term! What may be *inexpedient* to-day, may be *expedient* to-morrow. *Inexpediency* is as the tyrant's sword, that hangs over the head, suspended by a thread; and which *discretion* only is to keep from falling. But are Englishmen to be thus *worded* out of their rights? Forbid it, Common-Sense! Or rather let the fixed principles of the English Constitution, and the eternal rights of humanity, be the sister fates to cut this thread of danger, by establishing in its room—*Themselves.*

One word more. It may be further asked, What! are the Americans to enjoy all the rights appertaining to this government, and not contribute to its support? I answer, by no means: it is not fitting they should. The fundamental rights of the English constitution I have shewn to be, *the security of life, liberty, property, and freedom in trade*; and to these rights all British subjects *within the realm,* are without exception, entitled, and should enjoy: but it is not so with British subjects *out of the realm,* for *of them* something more is required, and of them something more has been received. They, (I mean the Colonists) surrendered from the first, one of the fundamental rights of the Constitution, to wit, *freedom in trade.* This they gave up, and this they put into the monopolizing hands of their brethren here, as the gift of contribution, for the price of protection. Excellent, and how valuable the exchange! when the very gift of contribution did itself enhance the price of protection! inestimable jewel! than which a nobler did not grace the royal crown; and yet noble as it is, it was not enough to satisfy the appetite of despotism. More must be had. All was required. With *freedom in trade, life, liberty, and property* were to be parted with; or, in the alternative, the revenge of *Herod* was to be taken in the blood of innocents. Revenge has been pursued: but *Herod-like,* and I will use the language of the immortal Shakespear;

When you shall these unhappy deeds relate,
                    then must you speak,
    Of one, whose hand

Like the *base Judean** threw a pearl away
Richer than all his tribe.

I have now done with the Thoughts, which the perusal of Mr. Burke's Letter had awakened in my mind; and find myself arrived at that period where I had designed to stop: but as I am upon the important subject of America, as there are one or two matters more that resting on my mind, I could wish to remove, and as I shall not again trouble the public with any further sentiments of mine upon this occasion (for truth being my only object herein, I shall as readily look for it in others, as seek it in myself) so, if I should advance one or two paces beyond my journey's end, I hope I shall be excused.

Having attended my duty in the House of Lords upon every important debate respecting America, it was there that I derived much useful information to myself; but yet, however instructed, as I truly have been, by the wisdom of those who opposed the measure of a destructive civil war, I must confess, my mind has been more made up on this subject, by what has *not* been said by the advocates for it, than by what has been advanced against it. The *first*, the *chief*, and the *great champion* of all, for this calamity to a country, has been the *now* Earl of Mansfield: but his being so, was to me, at the very first fight, an argument against the war; for his Lordship is no *warrior*, and therefore I supposed that if he had been more competent to the events of such an undertaking, he had been less *sanguine* in his recommendations of it. Let us see, however, what his arguments were. The first point to be settled was, which of the two countries was the *aggressor*; and of course which was to blame: but this would not bear a dispute, for in the year 1764, when all was peace and harmony between both countries, this country, by its Stamp-Act, flung the first *stone* at America, and so (the year 1766 excepted) Great Britain continued this *stoning* of America, like as Stephen was *stoned*, to the year 1775; when, by Negroes and Indians, the Americans were to be *scalped* and *flayed* alive, even as Bartholomew was; and, in both instances, perhaps for the same reason: for Stephen and Bartholomew were *Saints*, and the Americans are called Dissenters, and Dissenters are cursed by some Church-of-England-Men, as *Saints*. To get rid then of this stumbling-block, of *aggressorship*, something was to be devised; and this something was, that America meant to become

---

* *This was Herod, who slew his wife Mariamne.*

independent of this country: But how was this to be supported? The learned Lord proved it by *inuendoes,* by *sayings* and *doings, á priori,* out of the American Assemblies; from Montcalm's Letters, which have been found to be forgeries; and from Kalm's Travels, who made a voyage to America in the year 1749, and who says, that he was there told, that "the English Colonies in America, in the space of thirty or fifty years, would be able to form a state by themselves, independent of Old England." But here I must beg leave to make an observation or two. Supposing Mr. Kalm, instead of going to North America in the year 1749, had come into England and on his arrival had been told, that there were men in this country who *on their bare knees had drank the Pretender's health*; would not the inference have been just as fair to say, that this country meant to put the Pretender on the throne of this kingdom, in exclusion of the present family, as to say, what Mr. Kalm does say, that America meant independency? I think it would: for the question is not what individuals say, but what is the sense of the nation. And it is plain it was not the sense of this country to put the Pretender on the throne, and I hope it never will, notwithstanding his health has been so drank, &c. &c. &c. &c. and what the sense of America was, appeared by the unanimous declaration of the people themselves in the most solemn and authentic manner. They say, through their Congress, (and if ever the sense of any people were taken, it was here found, for so free and general an election of Representatives was never before known in the annals of the world) "We *chearfully* consent to the operation of such Acts of the British Parliament, as are, *bona fide,* restrained to the regulation of our external Commerce, for the purpose of securing the commercial advantages of the whole empire to the Mother Country," &c. &c.* it may be indeed said, that America has declared herself independent of this country, and therefore the prophecy of Mr. Kalm was true; but this does not follow; for this country, by putting America out of the protection of its laws, forced it, for self-preservation sake, into that state of Independency. Admitting, however, that America did mean Independency, I will now ask, Were the measures pursued the means to prevent their becoming so? I apprehend not: For although the force of this country be sufficient for conquest, ten times its force would be insufficient to hold the country in subjection. Three

---

* *Vid. Votes of the Congress, reprinted for J. Almon, opposite Burlington-house, Piccadilly, and also the last Petition of the Congress to the King.*

millions of people, not only with their affections lost, but their inveterate hatred gained, at three thousand miles over the Atlantic, distant from the arm of power, are not so easily held prostrate at the feet of Parliament, as Lord North was directed to say could be done. No: One hour of justice and moderation would have done more, than all the German Blood-hounds hired from all the German Traffickers in blood, in all the petty Principalities of Germany can achieve in twenty years to come.

But to return to the learned Lord. Having set up Independency, and upon what grounds I have shewn, as the object of America; his Lordship argued, that the Rubicon was passed, that we should kill the Americans, or the Americans would kill us, and that we could not look back, but must go forward, though our destruction be certain and inevitable. In short he drove us on, until we are all now driven, like so many asses, into a *Pound*; and are so *impounded*, that Fourteen Shillings Land-Tax in the *Pound*, nay, all the *Pounds*, Shillings, and Pence in the Nation, will not *unpound* us. Such is our disgraceful, and truly to be lamented, situation. The contempt of ourselves, and the mockery of all Europe besides. Bullied by Frenchmen, insulted by Spaniards, memorialized by Dutchmen; and yet, happy would it be for us, if these were the only calamities we are to suffer.

Another argument for our entering into this savage war was, that the Americans were Cowards; an argument as full of indignity to this country, as it was of reproach to him that made it. Of Indignity, for are We to go to war with our enemies because they are cowards? Does English valour want such motives of inducement for its exertion? Shameful Reflection! Of reproach, for it was the argument of the first Lord of the Admiralty, the Earl of Sandwich, that high Officer of the State, placed at the Head of the British Navy. And is this the language of the gallant Navy of England? No: the brave love the brave, and had rather meet bravery in the wounds of themselves, than cowardice in the disgrace of others. To fight with Cowards is the loss of Honour, and "Honour is the Sailor's, as the Soldier's care." But the Americans are not Cowards, and this I say for the honour of this country. If they were, such an Army and such a Navy doing no more than has been done in America, would well warrant the propriety of those incitements to action, which the Earl of Sandwich thought necessary to hold out in the cowardice of America. When the Americans, therefore, are called Cowards by us, let us remember that it is not them, but ourselves, that we accuse of Cowardice.

The last argument I shall take notice of, (for it is endless to recount the absurdities that have been urged in support of this iniquitous warfare) and which I mention for that it seems to contain a secret that should be known, is the argument of Lord Cardiff, son of the Earl of Bute. His Lordship said, as a reason for carrying on this war of Parliament, that the Americans had offered to lay kingdoms at the feet of the Crown, but which his Majesty disdained to accept.* This is an heavy charge, and, as I am as much an enemy to *arbitrary* power in the Crown, as I am to *arbitrary* power in Parliament, if true, I must confess, except so far as the justice of this nation is concerned in such a war, I should feel little concern else for America: But as it seems very unnatural that men should be surrendering their liberties, at the very time that they are fighting for them, so I have reason to believe that this argument has been formed upon grounds that will not support it. It is true, the Americans acknowledge the authority of the King, and will not acknowledge the authority of Parliament. It is from hence, therefore, I presume, inferred, that the Americans are laying kingdoms at the feet of His Majesty; and if so, to explain this matter, is to remove the charge. The Americans were the subjects of the Crown of England, and of course owed allegiance to the King of England. They were never the *Subjects* of their *fellow subjects* The Parliament of England, and therefore neither owed nor professed allegiance to Parliament. Besides, the King of England, by the Constitution of England, cannot levy taxes on his subjects; and therefore, for the Americans to acknowledge the authority of the King, is no surrender of their property to the King: Whereas if they acknowledged the authority of Parliament, who do exercise the right of taxation over the People when represented, it would be, without their being represented, a surrender of their property to Parliament; and a forging of chains for themselves. Under the acknowledged authority, then of the crown, the Americans still preserve their constitutional rights: Under the *required* acknowledged authority of Parliament, they would lose them, and this is the reason that the Americans acknowledge the one, and will *never* acknowledge the other. But it is feared, that some future King, not his present Majesty, for he has not a wish to govern but through his Parliaments, may, upon requisition to his faithful American subjects, procure such large grants of money,

---

* *The Archbishop of York has adopted the same assertion. See his Sermon,* p. *22 and 23.*

[228]

as shall enable him to govern without Parliaments. Indeed, if we are to judge of what America may do, by what it has done, upon such-like occasions, this argument is not without its force; and therefore, to prevent such generosity from being hereafter hurtful to this country, (and there cannot be a better time for it, as it is the object of his present Majesty to maintain the *supremacy* of Parliament) let an Act be passed, (if it be not too late) declaring that all money obtained from the Colonies by requisition from the Crown, shall be carried into the Exchequer, and accounted for in Parliament. This will remove the danger apprehended, and prevent those *lovers of slavery*, the Americans, from making, at any future period, the Crown of England arbitrary.

Upon the whole, when I perceive a war, and such a war too, so weakly supported, and yet so violently pursued: When I find the most elevated of the Church, preaching and publishing to the world passive obedience and non-resistance to the supremacy of Law*, whether that Law be right or wrong, whether it be good or bad, whether it be to establish Popery or Protestantism, whether it be enacted by an honest, or by a corrupt and abandoned Parliament: When I see men that were pillored in the reign of good old George II. pensioned in this, and for the same reasons: When I hear of others hired to root

---

* *The Archbishop of York says, "the foundation of legal freedom is the su-*premacy of law." *This I suppose is an apology for his Grace's* allegiance *to the Quebec Act, and for his making this act a pattern for cramming Bishop-ricks down the throats of the Americans, by the help of the civil power, that is, on the points of bayonets. See his Sermon, page 19 and page 24.*

His Lordship says too, "As there are in the nature of things, but two sorts of government; that of Law, and that of Force; it wants no argument to prove that under the last Freedom cannot subsist." This is a distinction without a difference; for when Law *is contrary to the natural or civil rights of mankind, it is* force, *and the worst of all force: For it is as "a wolf in sheep's cloathing," and cometh unawares, "like a thief in the night." See p. 19 of the above Sermon.*

Again, his Lordship says, "These indeed" (that is "Despotism and An-archy) have usually gone together, for no anarchy ever prevailed, which did not end in despotism." This is a bull, but an Irish one; and not a Popish bull. If where anarchy prevails despotism ends, anarchy and despotism cannot usually go together. See p. 20.

His Grace will excuse the attention I have paid him in the course of my observations: But as I am unfortunately one of those parties who have (according to him) "no principle belonging to them," and are "in the last stage of political depravity," I was willing to examine, a little, his Lordship's principles; that if I approved them, I might adopt them.

out the very idea of *public virtue* from the minds, and tear *benevolence* from the hearts of Englishmen: When I reflect, but why add more to the black catalogue of public dangers? It is time to look at home: It is time, even with *stentorian* voice, to call for union among the friends of the Constitution: It is time that private opinion should yield to public safety: It is time that we keep both "watch and ward"; for if the liberties of our fellow-subjects in America are to be taken from them, it is for the ideot only to suppose that we can preserve our own. The dagger uplifted against the breast of America, is meant for the heart of Old England. *Non agitur de vectigalibus, libertas in dubio est.*[3]

In fine: These are my sentiments, and these my principles. They are the principles of the Constitution; and under this persuasion, whilst I have signed them with my name, I will, if necessary, as readily, seal them with my blood.

FINIS

NOTES

[1] Abingdon's note refers to the Archbishop's *Sermon Preached Before the Incorporated Society for the Propogation of the Gospel in Foreign Parts* (London, 1777), which had already been attacked in the House of Lords by Grafton, Shelburne, and Chatham. Abingdon's criticism of the Archbishop (William Markham, 1719-1807) was apparently fueled by his personal as well as intellectual distaste for Markham, who had been headmaster of Westminster School when Abingdon was a student there.

[2] Cooper's sermon was published under the title *National Humiliation and Repentance Recommended, and the Causes of the Present Rebellion in America Assigned, in a Sermon Preached Before the University of Oxford* (Oxford, 1777).

[3] It is not a question of taxes, liberty is in doubt.

Advisory Committee on the Library of Congress American Revolution Bicentennial Program

John R. Alden, James B. Duke Professor of History, Duke University
Whitfield J. Bell, Jr., Librarian, American Philosophical Society
Julian P. Boyd, Editor, *The Papers of Thomas Jefferson*
Lyman H. Butterfield, Editor, *The Adams Papers*
Jack P. Greene, Professor of History, Johns Hopkins University
Merrill Jensen, Vilas Research Professor of History, University of Wisconsin
Adrienne Koch, Professor of American Intellectual History, University of Maryland (died on August 21, 1971)
Aubrey C. Land, Research Professor of History, University of Georgia
Edmund S. Morgan, Sterling Professor of History, Yale University
Richard B. Morris, Gouverneur Morris Professor of History, Columbia University

Library of Congress Publications for the Bicentennial of the American Revolution

The American Revolution: A Selected Reading List. 1968. 38 p. 50 cents. For sale by the Superintendent of Documents, U.S. Government Printing Office, Washington, D.C. 20402.

The Boston Massacre, 1770, engraved by Paul Revere. Facsim. $1.50. For sale by the Information Office, Library of Congress, Washington, D.C. 20540.

Periodical Literature on the American Revolution: Historical Research and Changing Interpretations, 1895-1970. 1971. 93 p. $1. For sale by the Superintendent of Documents, U.S. Government Printing Office, Washington, D.C. 20402.

☆ U.S. GOVERNMENT PRINTING OFFICE: 1975 O—592-517